Earth Federation Now!

Earth Federation Now!

Tomorrow Is Too Late

2nd Edition

Errol E. Harris

The Institute for Economic Democracy

ISBN: 978-1-933567-49-5

The Institute for Economic Democracy
PO Box 309, Appomattox VA 24522, USA.

And he shall judge among many people, and rebuke strong nations afar off; and they shall beat their swords into ploughshares, and their spears into pruning hooks: nation shall not lift up a sword against nation, neither shall they learn war any more. But they shall sit every man under his vine and under his fig tree; and none shall make them afraid.

Micah 4.3–4

Contents

About the Author

Errol E. Harris (1908–2009) was John Evans Professor of Moral and Intellectual Philosophy at Northwestern University, and Honorary Research Fellow at the Center for the Philosophy and History of Science, Boston University. He held named chairs at four universities and taught worldwide.

Professor Harris was author or editor of 30 books in political philosophy, theory of knowledge and mind, metaphysics in relation to science, logic and the dialectical method, and the implications of holism. For many years he specialized in the revolutionary implications of contemporary science and its social and political implications for human life.

Professor Harris was also President of the Hegel Society of North America and a Vice-President of the World Constitution and Parliament Association. Among his many honors and awards was the Global Peace Award, presented to Professor Harris by the Provisional World Parliament at its Sixth Session in Bangkok Thailand, March 2003.

Professor Harris exemplified the ideal of the engaged philosopher and intellectual; a person who devotes his considerable talent and energy to creating a decent future for human beings.

Introduction: Revolutionary Holism

Science, Ethics, and Political Philosophy in the Thought of Errol E. Harris

The impact of the work of Errol E. Harris continues to mount as the state of our planet falls ever more deeply into the deplorable condition that he understood was the consequence of our fragmented institutions and ways of thinking. During his long lifetime (1908–2009), he rose to prominence as a highly respected rationalist philosopher and scientific cosmologist. In many of his more than 30 books and approximately 100 articles, Harris illuminated the profound implications of the new scientific paradigm emerging from the revolutions of 20th century science and related these implications to the great thinkers and fundamental issues of the Western philosophical tradition.

He was born in South Africa to parents who had emigrated from England, and received advanced degrees in philosophy from universities there. His dissertation studied the thought of Samuel Alexander and Alfred North Whitehead, evidencing his lifelong interest in scientific cosmology and theories of emergent evolution. He served on the South African Race Relations Board and, during the Second World War, was Chief Instructor at a military college in Palestine and a Major in the Education Corps of the British Army. His first important book, *Nature, Mind, and Modern Science*, was published in 1954, and in 1956 Harris became a guest lecturer at Yale University and was soon appointed Professor of

Philosophy at Connecticut College.

From that time on, Harris' reputation as a first rate thinker continued to spread. He spent a year as Acting Professor of Logic and Metaphysics at Edinburgh University in Scotland, then served as Roy Roberts Distinguished Professor of Philosophy at the University of Kansas, and by 1966 joined Northwestern University where he later became John Evans Professor of Moral and Intellectual Philosophy. After retiring from Northwestern in 1976, he became President of the Metaphysical Society of North America and later President of the Hegel Society of North America. He was an honorary research fellow at the Center for Philosophy and History of Science at Boston University, and his considerable philosophical reputation led to subsequent opportunities to teach as visiting professor at Marquette, Villanova, and Emory Universities. After retiring from active teaching to his home in rural England, he continued to produce one major philosophical work after another, the last of which, *Twenty-first Century Democratic Renaissance: From Plato to Neoliberalism to Planetary Democracy*, came out in 2008, one year before his death at age 101.

The very first sentence of the Preface to *Nature, Mind, and Modern Science* expresses the spirit of Harris' lifetime work: "When philosophical speculation has taken a wrong turning and followed an old and long-abandoned track, which has led it into a *cul-de-sac*, the only proper course is for us to retrace our steps and return to the high road, there to take our bearings again and redetermine the direction of progress for the future." Harris understood the deep connections between the philosophical assumptions we make about ourselves and the world and the terrible consequences of wrong assumptions in the form of wars, weapons of mass destruction, injustice, human rights violations, terrorism, and destruction of our planetary environment. Overviews of the work of Errol Harris often overlook the fact that he was an intellectual activist deeply concerned about the fate of human beings and the Earth and actively committed to fomenting a revolution in human thought that embraced ethics, politics, economics, fundamental institutions, and our ways of living on the Earth.

Among his published books, Harris' theoretical works, such as *The Foundations of Metaphysics in Science* (1965), *The Reality of Time* (1988), or *Cosmos and Anthropos: A Philosophical Interpretation of the Anthropic Cosmological Principle* (1991) always contained reflections on the ethical and political implications of the revolution in thinking (the fundamental "paradigm-shift" in our ways of thinking about human life and the world) that his writings elucidated and promoted. In his last major theoretical work that came out in the year 2000, entitled *The Restitution of Metaphysics*, Harris synthesizes this lifetime of work regarding the paradigm-shift of the 20th century and its philosophical implications. Nevertheless, in addition to this considerable theoretical philosophical achievement, he wrote six books entirely devoted to spelling out the transformations that are necessary if we are to survive much longer on this planet: *The Survival of Political Man* (1950), *Annihilation and Utopia* (1966), *One World or None* (1993), *Apocalypse and Paradigm* (2000), *Earth Federation Now! Tomorrow is Too Late* (2005), and *Twenty-first Century Democratic Renaissance: From Plato to Neoliberalism to Planetary Democracy* (2008).

The present book, of course, is one of these six. As a prophet of our impending doom and a visionary of our possible redemption toward a decent world order, Harris' basic arguments have not substantially changed since his 1950 work, *The Survival of Political Man*. Like Albert Camus' famous 1946 essay *Neither Victims Nor Executioners* and Emery Reves 1946 classic *The Anatomy of Peace*, Harris immediately understood the implications of the development and use of nuclear weapons in Hiroshima and Nagasaki in August of 1945—in each case an entire city was wiped out with a single bomb. What kind of world civilization would continue to develop, build, and threaten to use these horrific super-weapons? Few people understood the significance of that moment as a turning point in human history—human beings had acquired the weaponry that had the potential for entirely wiping out the human race itself. There was obviously something very wrong with human civilization. As Christian theologian Jürgen Moltmann writes in *The Ethics of Hope*:

> When the atomic bomb was invented and dropped on Hiroshima and Nagasaki in August 1945, it was not just the Second World War that was ended. The whole human race entered its end-time as well. That is meant in an entirely non-religious sense. The end-time as an age in which the end of humanity is possible at any time. Through the potentialities for a global nuclear war, the human race as a whole became mortal. No human being could survive the nuclear winter that would follow a major nuclear war. (2012: 46–47)

What kind of paradigm or model of human life is assumed by a world divided into some 193 militarized nation-states, each living in fear, suspicion, and hatred of some of the others, and in which these nuclear weapons are proliferating? What are the basic patterns of thought in a world that fails to respect human rights and human dignity, and instead tolerates massive injustice, humiliation, torture, and terrorism? What kind of morality informs the lives of people who are willing to let extreme wealth accumulate in the hands of a very few people while the majority of humanity lives in poverty, misery, and hunger? What are the basic presuppositions of a global civilization that relentlessly continues to destroy its planetary environment in full awareness that it is doing so? What unspoken assumptions about the world and human beings have led to such terrible consequences?

These are the questions that occupied Harris' philosophical journey. He understood that philosophy is not just an insignificant theoretical speculation on abstract issues. Philosophy, rather, is about the most fundamental issues of living. Indeed, it is about the very possibility of human beings living well—with justice, freedom, integrity, sustainability, and peace. Harris was also a lifelong practicing Christian. Yet he was not a Christian of the "faith-only" persuasion, like the famous 19th century Danish philosopher, Søren Kierkegaard, who believed that faith was necessarily blind and irrational. Rather, Harris argued in several of his books, such as *Revelation through Reason* (1958) and *Cosmos and Theos* (1992), that reason could prove the existence of God and that reason (including science) and religion were in perfect harmony with one another. The emerging contemporary scientific paradigm made the compatibility of religion and science very clear.

I first met Errol Harris in London in 1998, at a meeting of the World Coordinating Council of the Global Ratification and Elections Network (GREN). Harris was there as a member of the Council, as a Vice President of the World Constitution and Parliament Association (WCPA), and as an Honorary Sponsor of the *Earth Constitution*. Before I became aware of this movement on behalf of the *Earth Constitution* in 1995, I had also known of Harris as a member of International Philosophers for Peace (IPPNO), an activist peace organization of philosophers of which I was an officer. I met him a second time at the fifth session of the Provisional World Parliament (PWP) on the island of Malta in 2001. The Parliament meets under the authority of the *Earth Constitution* to enable and foster the development of a democratic world government, and Harris, like myself, was there as a voting delegate to the Parliament. From that point on, I corresponded with him regularly (first by surface mail and later by email), both on philosophical and practical issues, and I was privileged to write the Foreword for his 2008 book *Twenty-first Century Democratic Renaissance.* He was an active participant in our work for a just and democratic world order.

In the background of this present volume, therefore, is a lifetime of profound philosophical work by a first rate thinker concerning the fundamental issues at the heart of the human situation and the fundamental assumptions or paradigms by which we operate as human beings within our planetary civilization. In this introduction, I want to elucidate some of this philosophical thinking that lies behind Harris' affirmation of the *Earth Constitution* and the concept of democratic world government. This can be done through examining his thought in terms of each of the traditional broad areas of Western philosophical concern—epistemology, metaphysics, ethics, and political philosophy: What are the foundations of knowledge? What is reality and the nature of the world? What are the requirements of moral reasoning and living? And what are the philosophical foundations of government and political life? Through examining his thought pertaining to the worldview of the early-modern paradigm in contrast to the contemporary scientific paradigm with its recognition of universal holism, we will begin to understand the rich background behind Harris' advocacy of enforceable, democratically legislated laws for the world.

The Early-modern Newtonian Paradigm.
Harris argues in a number of places that the early-modern paradigm results in both skepticism concerning human knowledge and relativism concerning ethical and political values. Skepticism has a long history going back to some of the ancient Greek philosophers. But systematic doubt concerning human knowledge is a difficult position to maintain as the ancient Greeks themselves realized: for to argue that everything is relative and that there is "no truth" (as the 19th century German thinker, Frederick Nietzsche, for example, maintained) is to be caught in a contradiction. To make an argument of any sort, presupposes that one is using valid reasoning and that the conclusion logically follows from the premises. To make an argument that there is no truth, therefore, presupposes the claim that "it is true that there is no truth," an explicit contradiction. The skeptic, in making his or her argument, is already in self-contradiction. The implications of this are profound, since the very structure of argumentation appears to confirm that knowledge is possible and presupposed in the operations of human thought.

Harris understood these principles very well, having written an entire book on logic (1987). Yet, even though this so-called "paradox of skepticism" is well known, he asked the question why so many thinkers of modern philosophy since the Renaissance have been skeptics concerning knowledge, a list which includes well-known philosophers like David Hume in the 18th century and Richard Rorty in the 20th century. The answer to this question, Harris understood, has to do with the dominant paradigm within which modern philosophical thinking has taken place. In book after book, Harris undertook an analysis of this dominant paradigm in order to expose its limitations and its implications for the crisis of modern civilization and to contrast this with the profound implications of the new holism of the universe discovered by 20th century science.

In 1543, Nicholas Copernicus published his book, *On the Revolution of Heavenly Bodies,* which became one of the founding documents for the development of the early-modern scientific paradigm. The ancient Aristotelian paradigm for explaining the world, the heavens, and human life was entirely replaced within the next two centuries. With the publication of Sir Isaac Newton's *Principia Mathematica* in 1687, early-modern science appeared to triumph. The new paradigm synthesized by Newton appear to explain matter and motion in both the heavens and the natural world around on the Earth. It understood the universe as a vast machine made up of bodies in motion, governed by the law of universal gravitation, within a framework of absolute space and time. The Enlightenment of the 18th century applied the implications of this paradigm not only to science but to social theory, morality, politics, and human institutions in general. It is this paradigm that still operates in the thinking of most people in the early 21st century and in the dominant institutions under which human civilization is organized. Harris writes:

> The idea of the natural world characteristic of Newtonian science was that of a vast machine, in which the mind of the observer found no place. Consequently, mind became unbridgeably separated from matter and the subjective from the objectively real. This alienation of the external world from the observing and manipulating activity of the scientist generated the notion that nature was at the disposal of human beings and could be exploited at will as the discov-

ery of laws governing natural processes enabled men and women to control and utilize natural products. ...

Atomism dominated the thinking of the period in every field. ... All these currents of thought have continued to the present day. ... Morality has declined due to the insidious belief in relativism resulting on the one hand from the Newtonian subjectivization of value judgments and the demand for value-free science. ... From this a political liberalism has developed that is radically individualistic and issues in a tension between individual rights and government action with consequent resistance to all government as such and the pursuit of factional demands. The same individualism has spawned the capitalist self-interested pursuit of profit in economics, to which all else has been subordinated, creating an ever-widening gulf between the rich and the poor. In international relations, the nation-state, in keeping with the prevailing separatism, insists on its independence and gives precedence to its own national interests at the expense of the common interests of humanity. (2000a: xi–xii)

The implications of the great 20th century paradigm-shift in the sciences spanned all the branches of philosophy: metaphysics, epistemology, ethics, and political philosophy. In philosophical book after book, Harris systematically articulates the new breakthroughs in the sciences that overcome the assumptions of Newtonian science. His work carefully elucidates the philosophical implications of contemporary science and shows the dangerous errors and consequences of Newtonian science. The titles of several of his books reveal the scope of this project: *The Foundations of Metaphysics in Science* (1965), *Nature, Mind, and Modern Science* (1968), *Cosmos and Anthropos: A Philosophical Interpretation of the Anthropic Cosmological Principle* (1991), *Cosmos and Theos: Ethical and Theological Implications of the Anthropic Cosmological Principle* (1992), and *The Restitution of Metaphysics* (2000).

The amazing success of early-modern science, from Copernicus to Newton, in applying mathematics systematically to nature appeared to explain the entire world, from the Earth to the planets and the stars as a giant mechanism of bodies in motion linked together by the law of universal gravitation. These bodies were in turn, it was thought, reducible to building blocks called atoms, and the human body, of course, was matter in motion governed according to the same laws of physics as any other. This entire mechanistic world process took place, it was believed, within the framework of absolute space and time. That is, space was conceived of on the model of an empty container for the bodies of the universe and time was conceived of as sheer temporality, another framework that, like space, simply went on and on.

Early modern philosophers attempted to understand the patterns of knowing and observation behind these successes of science. Rationalists, such as Descartes, Spinoza, and Leibniz, emphasized the idea that there are invariable elements in the construction of knowledge that came directly from "pure reason." Empiricists, such as Hobbes, Locke, Berkeley, and Hume emphasized careful sensory observation and constructed a theory of knowledge in which the mind merely linked together the discrete sensory observations. Immanuel Kant in the 18th century made a monumental attempt to salvage what was valuable from both the Rationalist and the Empiricist traditions. However, ultimately, his *Critique of Pure Reason* of 1783 affirmed the worldview behind the Newtonian paradigm insofar as this applied to the natural world studied by science.

During the early-modern period, empiricism substantially won out in terms of influence, and many theories were constructed about how careful, objective observation under experimental conditions was the key to progress in human knowledge. During the 19th century, beginning with August Comte, the doctrine of "positivism" developed, which argued that all human knowledge was reducible to collections of discrete "facts" about the world. Each factual claim could be determined to be true or false by careful empirical observation. "Metaphysics," any claim about the reality of the world that was not confirmable by empirical observation, was dismissed as nonsense. Religion, the worship of God as ultimate reality and the ground of all being, was also often dismissed as nonsense. In the late 19th century, German philosopher Friedrich Nietzsche attempted to sum up the developments of early-modern science by declaring that "God is dead, and we have killed him." All human values, he claimed, have now been called into question.

Throughout this entire process of development of early-modern science and its epistemology of empiricism, no credible theory about the nature of the human mind or its relation to the world was developed. The world-machine envisioned by Newton could not explain the nature of mind or the relation of the mind to the world. Science, it was thought, required "objective" observation, setting aside all emotions, feelings, and personal attitudes, and simply acting as an observer standing apart from what was observed. Theories were developed reducing the mind to the bio-chemical processes in the brain. Other religious thinkers followed Descartes in concluding that the mind or soul was made of a different kind of substance than matter. Assuming the mind was identical with brain-processes made it seem as though human beings were determined by the same universal causality that appeared to operate throughout nature. Universal causality in nature appeared to deny human freedom. Morality was often conceived as simply emotional reactions stimulated in a person's mind due to childhood training or social conditioning. Freedom and responsibility appeared to be an illusion. Human subjectivity with its persistent feeling that we are making free choices was, for much empiricism and positivism, merely an illusion.

In *Apocalypse and Paradigm*, Harris sums up the assumptions of the early-modern Newtonian paradigm with the following list. This paradigm included the following assumptions:

1. An absolute frame of space and time.

2. Materialism and mechanism.

3. Atomism.

4. Reductionism.

5. The assumption that all relations are external.

6. The demand for unbiased observation and value-free science.

7. Rejection of teleological explanation.

8. Complete matter-mind dichotomy. (2000b: 21–22)

Harris was not alone, of course, in making the argument that there is something very wrong with this early-modern model of the universe and its view of human beings. Serious thinkers such as Max Weber, Martin Heidegger, Herbert Marcuse, and Karl Jaspers also presented major critiques of the early-modern set of assumptions. Nevertheless, civilization as a whole did not listen, but continued blindly clinging to the institutions and patterns of thought developed in the early-modern era. Few of these critics, however, understood as deeply as Harris the implications of the revolutions taking place in our scientific understanding of the world throughout the 20th century, and few understood as clearly as Harris the devastating implications of the early-modern paradigm. Contemporary science has either disproved or transformed all these assumptions made by the early-modern paradigm.

The New Paradigm of 20th Century Science.
Beginning in 1905 with Einstein's theory of special relativity, the entire worldview of early modern science began to collapse. Newtonian science was encompassed by a much larger and more fundamental framework that profoundly altered its implications. Einstein's theory, overwhelmingly corroborated since then, reveals the holism of the universe: space, time, matter, and energy are not four different kinds of things but are merely aspects of one holistic field that we call the universe. Since then scientists have discovered that the pattern of holism operates at all levels in the universe from the micro level of quantum physics, to the

mid-level of biological processes and ecological systems, to the human level of psychological, social, and civilizational development, to the macro level of the universe as a whole. In *Apocalypse and Paradigm*, Harris quotes a number of great scientists who have drawn these conclusions. Here are just a few of them:

> Modern physics has taught us that the nature of any system cannot be discovered by dividing it into its component parts and studying each part by itself, since such a method often implies the loss of important properties of the system. We must keep our attention fixed on the whole and on the interconnection between the parts. (Max Planck)

> The world thus appears as a complicated tissue of events, in which connections of different kinds alternate or overlap or combine and thereby determine the texture of the whole. (Werner Heisenberg)

> A centrally relevant change in descriptive order required in the quantum theory is thus the dropping of the notion of analysis of the world into relatively autonomous parts, separately existent but in interaction. Rather, the primary emphasis is now on *undivided wholeness*, in which the observing instrument is not separable from what is observed. (David Bohm)

> The basic oneness of the universe is...one of the most important revelations of modern physics. It becomes apparent at the atomic level and manifests itself more and more as one penetrates deeper into matter, down to the realm of subatomic particles.... As we study the various models of subatomic physics we shall see that they express again and again, in different ways, the same insight—that the constituents of matter and the basic phenomena involving them are all interconnected, interrelated, and interdependent; that they cannot be understood as isolated entities, but only as integrated parts of the whole. (Fritjof Capra) (2000b: 85–86)

Harris delved deeply into the work of these thinkers and other scientists, in quantum physics, biology, and cosmology, mastering their theories and using his extensive philosophical background to interpret the implications. In this Introduction, of course, we can only summarize his substantial work that systematically contrasts the fundamental ideas of the early-modern paradigm with the implications of the contemporary scientific paradigm. We can briefly contrast these new implications with the eight features of the early modern paradigm quoted above:

1. Instead of matter in motion within an absolute space-time framework, since Einstein's theory of relativity we have understood that the universe is a finite, unbounded whole in which space, time, matter, and energy are all aspects of the same holistic cosmic field (1965: 488).

2. Instead of materialism and mechanism, the universe is now understood as being much more like an organic whole than like a machine (2000b: 93–94). And, as we will see, the materialist exclusion of mind from nature is no longer tenable (2000a: Chaps 12 and 13).

3. Instead of being reducible to atoms as building-blocks, the universe is now understood as exhibiting the structure of multiple fields. It is more like a web of relations than a machine made of parts (2000b: 77–79).

4. In a holistic world system, reductionism is no longer possible, as Planck and others quoted above point out. For thought to understand the world, we need not only analysis but also synthesis and dialectical patterns of thinking embracing the whole and discerning the relationships of wholes to parts (1992: Chap. 4).

5. In a universe understood in terms of holistic field structures, relations within the fields and the relations of parts to wholes become "internal relations," not merely external

relations. Under the mechanistic model a change in one part does not affect the other parts. However, for internal relations, a change in one part affects the rest of the field or the whole of which it is a part. Things do not exist independently of the fields or wholes within which they are embedded (1965: 456).

6. Quantum physics has shown that scientists cannot be independent observers apart from the phenomena they are investigating. Rather, they are now better understood as "participants" in the experiments: the very act of experimenting influencing the outcome of events (2000b: 80).

7. In a holistic world, causality can no longer be understood as a "push from behind" so to speak, like one billiard ball causing the one it impacts to move. Traditionally this was known as "efficient causality." Rather causality must now also be understood in terms of the relations of parts to whole in which the whole "teleologically" directs the development, movement, and nature of the parts. The nature and movement of the parts are now understood in terms of their ends or purposes within the whole (2000a: Chaps. 10 and 11). We can now again ask the question of value: what are the ends or purposes of human life? Why have human beings evolved out of the world process?

8. The new holism understands mind as integral to the universe, as an emergent natural phenomenon of the universe. The universe is not just "physical," but naturally produces sensation, perception, consciousness, and mind. Whereas under the early-modern paradigm there appeared to be no way to account for mind within that set of assumptions (2000a Chaps. 12 and 13).

Physicists themselves have proposed the "anthropic cosmological principle," which Harris studied at length in his 1991 book by that name. This principle argues that human life is not merely an accidental product of evolution on the Earth but rather that there are scientific reasons for believing that the emergence of human beings and human thought was built into the structure of the universe from its very beginnings some 14 billion years ago. The principle remains controversial among scientists, but Harris makes a strong argument for its validity. One thing many are agreed upon, however, is that the contemporary scientific world view does not exclude mind from the evolving natural world, nor does it make mind some mysterious "mental substance" intrinsically different from natural processes, as Descartes proposed in the 17th century. Rather, the whole of the universe brings forth mind: the capacity of the universe to self-consciously understand itself, to produce perception, self-consciousness, reason, knowledge, morality, religion, art, and all of civilization.

Harris argues that mind is now easily understood as an aspect of all matter and energy that slowly emerges into self-consciousness as the evolutionary process creates evermore complex structures, culminating in the human brain (which is the most complex structure found anywhere in nature to date). Mind, therefore, emerging with the complexity of the human brain, is a natural evolutionary development. Its capacity to use self-conscious thought and reason to understand the basic principles of order in the universe itself shows that the mind reflects that order, and is itself a product of that order.

In the human mind, as the 19th century philosopher Hegel had already observed, the universe is becoming conscious of itself in us. "The important point," Harris writes, "is that reflective intelligence and reason are seen as intrinsic and essential to the universe as a whole" (2000a: 280). The holism of the universe and the holism reflected in the human mind are two aspects of the same phenomenon. Both are present in reason and intelligence, as well as in all the overlapping "field structures" found everywhere in nature. In *Apocalypse and Paradigm* he declares: "If the implications of this scientific revolution and the new paradigm it introduces are taken seriously, holism should be the dominating concept in all our thinking.... Such holistic thinking would make an incisive and far reaching difference to both theory and practice in every field of human interest and activity" (2000b: 90).

As far back as *Nature, Mind and Modern Science* (1954), Harris had understood the philosophical principles that are implied by the paradigm-shift of contemporary science. The immanence of mind in the natural world must now be recognized and "value" is once again a fundamental principle for interpreting the world and for guiding human life:

> The philosophical theory demanded by the modern outlook must, accordingly, maintain five main theses: (i) that mind is immanent in all things; (ii) that reality is a whole, self-sufficient and self-maintaining, and that coherence is the test of truth in any theory about it; (iii) that the subject and object of knowledge are ultimately one—the same thing viewed from opposite (and mutually complementary) standpoints; (iv) that events and phenomena can adequately be explained only teleologically, and (v) that the ultimate principle of interpretation is, in consequence, the principle of value. (1954: 206)

The early-modern separation of fact from value has been overcome. We can look for a telos or goal implicit in the evolutionary processes of the universe, and we can look for a telos or goal implicit in the progressive development of human civilization. We can also look for a telos or goal implicit in the moral development of our individual lives. It is the "coherent order and unity" of knowledge, values, and the resultant social order that reunites the false empiricist split between fact and value:

> Once the unity of the universe and the biosphere has been fully grasped, and the consequent dialectical structure of the universal system appreciated, morality will be seen as the practical exercise of reason, which is itself the conscious operation of the organizing principle active throughout nature. The new metaphysic abolishes the opposition of fact to value, for the criterion of truth and value is the same: coherent order and unity. No fallacy is involved in deducing

what ought to be, and to be done, from the general nature of the world and its organizing principle, which, when it becomes self-conscious, characterizes and defines human nature. For what ought to be done is what promotes health, unity, and harmony, as well in the biosphere, as in human society. (2000a: 261–262)

Ethics

From this understanding that the human mind, manifesting its own holism, with its structures of reasoning and reflective intelligence reflecting the structure of the universe, it is clear that we have overcome the skepticism and relativism concerning values and can restore morality and ethics to objective validity within human life. Harris writes:

> The world, to be intelligibly conceived at all, must be conceived as a coherent whole, and, if so conceived, it will be such that, without contradicting its intrinsic nature, physical reality can produce life and mind. The emergence of consciousness must bring with it a perception of the world that is necessarily related to its object, and a nisus to self-fulfillment that will actualize the totality immanent within it. Values will then indeed be the fulfillment of human need, and that must include the need to find intellectual satisfaction in harmony with moral and aesthetic, so as to become a unified and freely self-determining personality. That, again, will prove possible only in social harmony with others, and finally it will point to the development of a common consciousness of belonging to a reality that transcends the merely finite. (2000a: 230)

The tradition of virtue ethics, going back to Plato and Aristotle, argued that there was a goal inherent in the proper development of our human potential—the goal is to develop human intellectual and moral excellence. Virtue means the excellent development of our human potential. Aristotle argued that our need and desire for happiness or well-being was only satisfied by this harmonious development of both moral and intellectual virtues.

On the basis of the holism pervasive in the universe, and present within us to be actualized in each of our lives, and on the basis of the holism within human civilization, Harris argues that the holistic perfection of ourselves and society is indeed the fulfillment of fundamental human needs. And one aspect of human need is the religious dimension. Like philosopher of law and ethics, John Finnis, who identifies "religion" as one of the fundamental human needs and basic goods that contributes to a "flourishing" human life (*Fundamentals of Ethics*, 1983: 51, 144–152), so Harris recognizes "belonging to a reality that transcends the merely finite" as part of the nisus toward human fulfillment and perfection. He spells out the meaning of religion in a number of works (for which there is not space to pursue in this Introduction).

The alternative tradition of deontological or duty ethics, made famous by Immanuel Kant, separates moral duty, as understood by reason, from human needs, and argues that we should do our moral duty "regardless of our desires and inclinations." Harris also recognizes the sense of duty as a necessary part of the holism of human perfection. However, he asserts that there is no need to reject inclinations such as the desire for happiness, holistic perfection, and human fulfillment as part of the ethical domain. There is a "nisus" or desire in us for the perfection of wholeness. The same principle applies to the planetary society of all human beings, as well as to our local societies. There is a nisus within human history toward wholeness: toward cooperation, friendship, mutual understanding, even love. Morality, treating others with respect, kindness, courtesy, compassion, and love is fundamental to the holism that is both a feature of what is the case (we are all parts of one, holistic human race) and of what should be (we should be striving for peace, harmony, and justice for society at all levels). He writes:

> It is generally recognized that morality consists in the endeavor to realize what is the highest good, and that has been variously defined as pleasure, expedience, or duty (and to these we have added devotion); but in the final issue it

turns out to be all of them, for they are three forms in the scale of overlapping species of the universal (good). The good is the harmonious organization of both society and personality, both of which must necessarily be a whole (because they would otherwise involve internal conflict and, to that extent, be evil). To these forms correspond the levels of morality previously indicated: the morality of self-gratification, the morality of reciprocity (of claims and counter-claims), the morality of conscientiousness, and the morality of love. . ...

How the common good is to be achieved will depend on numerous and diverse factors and conditions, including skills and techniques, economic arrangements, legal regulations, as well as knowledge and beliefs about the world. To none of these is scientific investigation irrelevant. The last especially involves a general conception of the nature of things and of the place of humankind in the world. In short, it involves a worldview, to which scientific theories have direct relevance and on which they exert profound influence. Without some such world-concept, no moral system can be complete. . ... (1992: 30–31)

Human beings, as beings who pursue their own holistic development and perfection, will develop through various overlapping moral stages such as the moralities of self-gratification, of reciprocity, of conscientiousness, and of love. The earlier stages are not left behind has one grows. Self-gratification, for example, will be more mature and sophisticated in an adult than in a teenager. At early stages we affirm the morality of reciprocity of contract, agreement, and mutual benefit: I do this for you and, in return, I can rely on you doing that for me. Again, we do not leave this behind as we grow, since reciprocity needs to be there even at the higher levels of morality. Eventually we develop to the morality of conscientiousness: we learn the value of doing our duty to others or to society regardless of possible reciprocity or rewards. This is the level of Kant's ethics of duty, which is complemented by the striving, characteristic of virtue ethics, for a virtue that molds inclinations in the service of duty. We want to do what is right regardless of whether others approve or reciprocate, and we also want to develop the virtues that make us excellent as human beings.

At the highest level, for Harris, is the morality of love—the kind of compassionate self-giving and willingness to self-sacrifice that was modeled, for example, by Jesus Christ (1966:130–133). Since human beings are the same everywhere, and since our lives express a nisus for holistic development, all these forms of morality can be affirmed as valid. Human beings as a species can make this same kind of "moral progress" that characterizes individual growth (ibid. 133). What is not valid are skepticism, relativism, and actions that harm people, society, or the natural world that sustains us, in other words, immoral actions are those that destroy the development or maintenance of harmony between people, within society (at any level from the local to the global), or that destroy the natural world.

Harris has contrasted the world view implicit in early-modern science with the worldview implicit in the 20th century scientific revolutions that have discerned holism everywhere in nature and human life. A moral system is an aspect of one's world view: what one takes as reality is closely related to how one lives one's life. If reality seems fragmented, competitive, conflicted, and entirely relative, as in the early-modern paradigm, then this has consequences for one's moral views and actions. But 20th century science has opened up dimensions of reality unrecognized by early-modern science. In addition, he points out that science is a collective endeavor of many people working together to understand the world. It cannot be accomplished by even the most extraordinary individuals. Harris is pointing out that the same is true of society in general. Our education, our moral principles, the languages we speak, the technical inventions that we use—all are collective social products (1966: 243–44).

Morality therefore, will involve the concept of the common good. How do we achieve holistic harmony in society and in world civilization? How do we end hatred, discrimination, violence, war, and injustice? The common good of morality is planetary, for all these collective social products are planetary. Harris very much affirms universal human dignity as recognized, for example, in the UN Universal Declaration of Human Rights, or as recognized by Kant in his categorical imperative: "always treat every person as an end in themselves, never merely as a means." Human dignity derives from the astonishing fact that human reason and the human mind mirror the rational structures of the universe itself. In traditional religious language, our dignity derives from the fact that we are made in the image of God. The holism that should be the guiding principle in all our thoughts and actions, for Harris, dictates that this principle of dignity be universal and planetary, just as it was when Jesus gave the great commandment in Matthew 22 to love God with all one's heart and mind and, like unto it, to love our neighbor as ourselves. Harris calls this "rational love":

> There is a sense in which love pervades the entire universe as that universal tendency towards unity and coherent harmony previously stressed.... At the biological level it surfaces as sexual attraction, parental tenderness, and filial dependence, as well as in the gregariousness of many species. But these are only the precursors of human life, in which they become transformed by self-reflection into something more than mere sentiment. While the emotive and conative aspects are not lost, love now becomes rational. It is genuine concern for the welfare of each and every individual, it is the universal respect for persons, that treats each as an end and none merely as a means. And because every individual is a social being, it is a concern for the welfare of the entire community, in which all are integrated and on which all depend. Nor can that welfare, for which this rational love is concerned, be confined to any one local or national community, because the welfare of every community depends, like that of each individual, upon the welfare of all.
>
> Genuine rational love, therefore, must extend to the entire human race.... As human rational activity is socially organized and embodied in political institutions, love com-

prehends and transcends all political and social virtues. It is
the emotional and sentimental counterpart and expression
of the unity of the perfected human community—referred
to as "the Kingdom of God." (1988: 162–63)

The morality of holism is ultimately the morality of universal
rational love. Reason and science reveal the holism of humanity,
of society, of the ecology of our planet, of quantum phenomena,
of the cosmos, and of God (1992: 75–81). The holism that per-
vades the universe could be called love. Here we have the moral
guide for human life, the new, expanded form of the categorical
imperative: create harmony and holism in our own lives and everywhere on the planet; create peace and security for all people;
create a world of justice and well-being where most people are
no longer living in poverty and misery; live in harmony with the
ecology of our planetary biosphere. The common good is now
the universal common good of humanity and should serve as the
moral ideal: the idea of establishing the "Kingdom of God" on
the Earth. How we are to do this as a civilization requires that
we move from ethics to political philosophy: that we examine the
political and economic implications of holism.

Political and Economic Ideas and Institutions.
Most people and societies on our planet continue under the ideas
and institutions derived from the early-modern paradigm. They
continue to think in atomistic, mechanistic, and deterministic categories. Similarly, in ethics and politics, they continue to be skeptics and relativists who believe that values are relative to personal belief, upbringing, and/or culture. But the early-modern
paradigm was not just different. It was wrong about the nature of
the world and human life. It was wrong to the point where our
future on this planet has been placed in danger. Our very survival
is threatened by gigantic errors and institutions deriving from the
early-modern paradigm that continue to dominate human civilization.

Two planetary institutions that were born during from the early-modern paradigm and continue to dominate the world today are global capitalism and the system of sovereign nation-states. Adam Smith's classic, *The Wealth of Nations*, appeared in 1776, and much of it simply described the operation of a system that had been developing for some 200 years since the Renaissance. This system is a clear development of the early-modern paradigm. Harris writes:

> In economics, the prevailing ethical utilitarianism is reflected in a capitalism that has become worldwide and a market economy that prevails universally.... Gain and commercial advantage is the primary consideration, even when the contemplated commerce is in genetically engineered products, the dangers of which to the planetary ecology are still unknown.... The prevailing motive is gain and self-interest, and moral considerations are ignored, or if given lip service, are argued away....The criterion of economic success is growth, and growth is measured by profit rather than welfare; prosperity is judged by the standard of living of the "haves" in disregard of the plight of the "have-nots"....
>
> The attitude to the natural world encouraged by post-Renaissance science was to regard it as a merely mechanical instrument to be exploited for the benefit of human beings. Accordingly, no sense of obligation to conserve the environment was fostered either in the prevailing moral consciousness or by economic practice. Today the effects of this attitude have been to exhaust and destroy the very means that world capital seeks to exploit (human beings and the natural capital of our planet), and, by polluting the environment and disrupting the ecology, threaten the very survival of life itself upon the Earth. (2000b: 48–50)

Capitalism not only views the natural world as a mechanism to be exploited, it is also based on an atomistic view of human beings and human society. According to Adam Smith, every person (or business) operates out of "rational self-interest," calculating the advantage of buying this or that or making this or that business deal. Smith states that the greatest good of the greatest number (what Harris calls "ethical utilitarianism") will result if all these individual self-interests are allowed to compete with one another in a "free market." But the real result of this atomistic view of human relations, Harris points out, has been an ever-growing disparity between the "haves" and the "have-nots" and a destruction of the planetary environment placing all of civilization in danger. On the rare occasion that morality does enter into business practices, it only involves humans and feels little or no obligation toward the natural environment. In the chapters that follow in this book, Harris will give many examples of this ongoing destruction of the planetary ecology.

With the growing awareness of holism, and the development of a globalized economy, Harris states that we are beginning to understand the interdependence of all nations and peoples upon one another, so that the world economy must be viewed as a "single system" and treated as a whole. The concept of profit must be "socialized," rather than individualized. In other words, profit must be seen in terms of the common good that is served by enterprises. "Production and supply have to be as a cooperative enterprise," he writes, "rendering service to the community, rather than a venture undertaken for personal gain" (2000b: 107). Economics must mirror the holism of humanity and the common good. It must serve protection of the environment and the welfare of all human beings, not simply the lucky few who profit from this system. And for this to happen, Harris' books have argued, we must have democratic world government. What, then, about political philosophy?

From the time of *The Survival of Political Man: A Study in the Principles of International Order* (1950), Harris studied theories of democracy, philosophies of law, and theories regarding the system of sovereign nation-states, some of which theories go all the way back to Plato and Aristotle. Most of the thinkers in this tradition saw political life as an extension of morality, and most thought that the "natural law" of morality was binding on the behavior of rulers, kings, political arrangements, and nations. Harris, of course, agrees. The system of sovereign nation-states that now dominates the world system, however, did not develop until the 17th century. Most scholars give the date of 1648 when the Treaty of Westphalia was signed in Europe after the Thirty Years War. Implicit in that treaty were the features that we associate with sovereign nation-states: absolute authority over internal affairs within each one's territorial boundaries and independence of each in its "foreign affairs," that is, in its relations with other nations.

The system of sovereign nation-states was established, therefore, from the very center of the early-modern paradigm, at a time when people were still fighting with swords and did not possess weapons of mass destruction. As the early-modern paradigm dictates, the system is *atomistic*—dividing the world into autonomous, independent regions called sovereign nation-states and structurally denying the holism of humanity and civilization. These autonomous units exist primarily in *external relations* with one another. Each is expected to deal with its "internal affairs" (its economy, well-being, system of law, etc.) largely independently of the others and to relate to the others as "foreigners" whose interests are different from its own, and as possible enemies.

As a consequence of these features, as with the capitalist system that also derives from the early-modern paradigm, the system is competitive, and, when the rivalry turns violent, it results in absolute winners and losers. Ultimately, it is a war-system: war is intrinsic to the system since there is no enforceable rule of law or structural integration that can unite the nations within a peaceful, holistic framework. Harris quotes perceptive thinkers who pointed this out during the early-modern period:

> [Sovereign states] are potentially hostile one to another and perpetually in a posture of antagonism and war, which, as Clausewitz put it in the 19th century, is simply politics conducted by other means. Hobbes maintained that

"in all times, Kings and Persons of Sovereign authority, because of their independency, are in continual jealousies, and in the state and posture of Gladiators; having their weapons pointing, and their eyes fixed upon one another".... Spinoza likewise contended that "two states are enemies by nature. For men in the state of nature are enemies; and so all who retain the right of nature outside the state remain enemies." And Hegel was of the same opinion: "since the sovereignty of a state is the principle of its relation to others.... it follows that if states disagree and their particular wills cannot be harmonized, the matter can only be settled by war." (2000b: 57)

Another consequence of this international system deriving from the early-modern paradigm is that the moral skepticism and relativism implicit in that paradigm have been applied to the relations between the nations. This resulted in the so-called doctrine of "political realism," which declares that the relations between nations are power-relations, not moral relations. This doctrine was explicitly formulated in the 1948 book by Hans Morgenthau, *Politics Among Nations*, and involved an attempt to factually (objectively) describe the relation between nations as relations of power, strategic maneuvering, threat of force, and the use of force, rather than moral, law-abiding, or harmonious. Power relations and war ultimately mean the breakdown of moral relations and the rule of law. Harris writes:

Meanwhile, the effect in the international sphere of the prevalent relations between sovereign states, in which war has been endemic ever since the sixteenth century, has led to increasing and more destructive conflicts. That enmity and war between sovereign states is inevitable has been recognized by political theorists from Hobbes to Hegel, and, as we have seen, by several more contemporary writers. As far as sovereign nations are concerned...Morgenthau also realized that in the international arena "neither science nor ethics nor politics can resolve the conflict between politics and ethics into harmony".... There ensues an ever-accelerating arms race impossible to check, with intermittent international tensions, which lead to progressively increasing crises and to minor wars, tending toward more and more widespread conflict....

This parlous situation is the direct consequence of the claim to sovereignty of the nations of the world, a claim that admits no law superior to its own, and which gives unquestioning priority to national interests, especially those regarded as "vital", namely, first and foremost, security from foreign aggression, and secondly economic prosperity. (2008: 122–23)

Just as the relations between capitalist enterprises is not considered a moral one, but rather one following the amoral laws of the market, so the dominant mode of operations of nation-states has not been considered a moral mode but one following the amoral laws of power relationships and self-interested competition for markets, resources (such as oil), and national ascendancy. The holism and dignity of individuals, of humanity, and of our planetary ecosystem are violated at every turn. The early-modern paradigm is clearly at work here, with its false repudiation of values in favor of the idea of the "objective," mechanistic operations of both capitalism and the nation-state system according to amoral laws of economic competition and power relationships. The result has been the disaster for humanity that is visible all around us today: "Neglect of these considerations in the pursuit of ends inspired by the Newtonian paradigm has plunged humankind into a global crisis from which it can extricate itself only by thinking globally" (2000b: 108).

The on-going collapse of our planetary ecosystem and the destructive, militarized conflicts everywhere in the world (which Harris details in the chapters that follow) cannot be converted to environmental sustainability and peace: "these aims cannot be achieved as long as nations remain sovereign and independent; in fact, it is clear as daylight that no nation is in actuality any longer independent of the others." The idea of the common good, which we saw is fundamental to ethics, that is, the idea that every person on Earth has the right to lead a flourishing, decent life within a framework of peace and environmental integrity, is violated by both capitalism and the system of sovereign nation-states. Therefore, "national sovereignty is no longer competent to serve the common good of the people over whom it rules, and the ethical justification of its power has withered away" (2000b: 108).

When Harris deeply understood the implications of the invention and use of nuclear weapons in 1945, and published his 1950 book *The Survival of Political Man,* the *Constitution for the Federation of Earth* (that he placed as an appendix to the present volume) had not yet been written. But in 1950 Harris advocated world government and understood how important it was to write and ratify such a constitution for the Earth. The *Constitution* was written through a process of collective effort by thousands of world citizens over a 33 year long process from 1958 to 1991. This included four large "constituent assemblies," meeting in different cities of the world in 1968, 1977, 1979, and 1991, in which world citizens and legal experts went over drafts paragraph by paragraph. Harris was naturally very interested and supported this work, both in his writings, financially, and through his presence in meetings. He became a Vice President of the World Constitution and Parliament Association (WCPA), the organization that was responsible for the process of writing the *Constitution.* He received the Global Peace Award for this work at the Sixth Session of the Provisional World Parliament that met in Bangkok, Thailand, in March 2003.

He understood that the holism discovered by contemporary science, with its implications for ethics, political philosophy, our planetary ecology, and human civilization itself mandated a new globalized economics of cooperation and sustainability, a new global legal order ending war and guaranteeing human rights, and these together making possible a dignified human life for every person on the Earth. That is what *Earth Federation Now!* is about. In *Apocalypse and Paradigm,* he writes:

> It follows that a political system must be devised that can effectively legislate for the common good of humanity as a whole. Such a system would have to be democratic and

federal in form.... At the present time, because the customary way of thinking is molded by the Newtonian paradigm, few people give serious consideration to the establishment of world federation; but if, in accordance with the new scientific holism, global thinking were to prevail, that would be our immediate political goal; for it is the only condition under which global measures could be enacted to cope with the global problems which face humanity and threaten the survival of the species. Clearly, such all-embracing actions cannot be accomplished by the individual efforts of private persons and organizations. They must be universally enforced, and that requires global legislation and the global maintenance of the rule of law, which is possible only under a world government. (2000b: 108–109)

Earth Federation Now! Tomorrow is Too Late examines the human condition in which we find ourselves in the early 21st century and the potentially lethal issues and fundamental choices that we face in the here and now, choices that cannot be ignored or avoided any longer. It is a book for everyone, written with a minimum of academic language, and it comes with a special appendix containing the *Earth Constitution*. It is this *Constitution* that should be studied in every high school, college, and university classroom on Earth.

Glen T. Martin
Radford, Virginia
October, 2014

Works by Errol E. Harris cited in this Introduction

The Survival of Political Man: A Study in the Principles of International Order. Johannesburg: Witwatersrand University Press, 1950.

Nature, Mind, and Modern Science. London: George Allen & Unwin, 1954, second impression, 1968.

The Foundations of Metaphysics in Science, London: George Allen and Unwin LTD., 1965.

Annihilation and Utopia. London: George Allen & Unwin, 1966. *Formal, Transcendental & Dialectical Thinking: Logic & Reality: Logic and Reality.* Albany, NY: State University of New York Press, 1987.

The Reality of Time. Albany. Albany: State University of New York Press, 1988.

Cosmos and Anthropos: A Philosophical Interpretation of the Anthropic Cosmological Principle. Atlantic Highlands, NJ: Humanities Press International, 1991.

Cosmos and Theos: Ethical and Theological Implications of the Anthropic Cosmological Principle. Atlantic Highlands, NJ: Humanities Press International, 1992.

One World or None. Atlantic Highlands, NJ: Humanities Press International, 1993.

The Restitution of Metaphysics. Amherst, NY: Humanity Books, 2000a.

Apocalypse and Paradigm: Science and Everyday Thinking. Westport, CT: Praeger Publishers, 2000b.

Earth Federation Now! Tomorrow is Too Late, Appomattox, VA: Institute for Economic Democracy Press, 2005, Second Edition, 2014.

Twenty-first Century Democratic Renaissance: From Plato to Neoliberalism to Planetary Democracy. Appomattox, VA: Institute for Economic Democracy Press, 2008.

Chapter 1

The State of the Planet

1.1 Threats to Survival

As we enter the twenty-first century C.E., human-kind is threatened with extinction from numerous angles. Scientists have established the fact that the Earth is a single system maintaining itself as a congenial habitat for life in the plenteous energy flow from the Sun; but the activities and the life-style of mankind is now disrupting the environment and destroying the ecology that sustains life, its own along with all other. This insidious depletion of the biosphere results from deliberate, as well as inadvertent, human behaviour.

But, as human beings are intelligent animals, once they have been apprised of the menacing facts, they should be able to seek ways of countering the impending dangers, and, it is to be hoped, to find effective remedies. Until now, however, in spite of authoritative scientific reports, no very reassuring measures have been taken to stem the deterioration, the scale of which, as we shall presently discover, is truly daunting.

Since 1945, the continued existence of human civilization, and more recently of human life itself, has been put in jeopardy by the imminent possibility of war, in which the use of nuclear weapons,

1

would wipe out living beings, not only by their immediate destructive power, but also through the resultant radio-active fallout, and pollution of the upper atmosphere, that would reduce the global temperature and inaugurate a new and severe ice-age (the so-called nuclear winter), which few if any species could survive. If, since the end of the Cold War, that threat has temporarily receded, it has not been eliminated, as we shall later see reason to admit.

But, meanwhile, new menaces have arisen, from destructive causes operating in almost every quarter of the globe, the mitigation and removal of which, if it is possible, presents mankind with the most pressing and the most egregious problems.

The purpose of what follows is to set out what the most urgent of these problems are and to consider what action is essential if they are to be met. Let us begin by reviewing the state of the planet at the present time. Human beings are today surrounded by the most horrific threats from several causes, all the result of their own practices, in a man-made situation that is endangering the very survival of life on Earth. We are undoubtedly intelligent enough to do something to improve matters, yet nobody seems to be doing very much that is either adequate or sufficiently expeditious.

We usually consider ourselves to be the most intelligent animals on Earth, and some would say that we are the only ones. Certainly, no other species is capable of reflective thought, of taking stock of the situation in which its members find themselves and of the way they conduct themselves in it.

Even when we blame ourselves or others for being stupid, it is only because we are intelligent animals that we can do so -we never accuse trees or snails of stupidity, and we only regard higher animals as stupid when we judge them by standards that we apply to ourselves. Being intelligent, then, if we find ourselves in unpleasant or dangerous circumstances, we commonly do something about it, and try to improve conditions, to protect ourselves against dangers, or to extricate ourselves from uncomfortable entanglements -why not now? What the reason for this perilous inertia may be I shall try to determine in what follows, as well as what courses of action can remedy it, and which cannot, and why they cannot.

The planet Earth is uniquely endowed with attributes that support life. No other planet in the solar system is like it in this respect, and the conditions indispensable for the generation, evolution and sustenance of intelligent life are so interlinked and finely adjusted that the probability of their all occurring together anywhere at all is extremely low. Yet the way of life that has become common to the most advanced peoples on Earth in the past century is fast undermining this delicately balanced environmental system.

No other planet known to us is provided so copiously with water[1] a very unusual compound with very special properties all especially favourable to life -in fact, living creatures are mostly composed of water, and for a large proportion of them it is the medium in which alone, they can survive. It was almost certainly in the seas that life originated, and it invaded the land only after millions of years of evolution. Moreover, water is the only liquid that is lighter in the solid than in the liquid state, so ice floats leaving warmer water below in which living things can survive.

No other known planet has an atmosphere consisting of just the right mixture of gases essential for the support of life. The most important of these gases are oxygen and carbon dioxide, and both oxygen and carbon have special properties distinguishing them from the elements most closely related to them chemically. For instance, carbon dioxide (C02) is gaseous at those temperatures suitable for life, whereas the oxide of silicon, an element similar to carbon, is a rock-hard mineral

Only in the gaseous state can C02 be absorbed by plants, and its ready solubility in water makes it easily transferable from the air into living bodies, and from them again back into the air. A

---

[1]One of Jupiter's moons may be an exception, but it is so far from the sun that it is encased in ice.

layer of ozone, a gas akin to oxygen (its molecules are composed of three oxygen atoms), protects the surface of the Earth from ultra-violet radiation from the Sun, which is lethal to living forms.

Moreover, oxygen is produced by plants in the course of photosynthesis, the use of the Sun's light to synthesize substances essential to all life, which animals (unable to photo-synthesize) must obtain by eating plants. But chlorophyll, the chemical indispensable for photosynthesis, can absorb only light of a certain yellow colour, which happens to be the colour of sunlight, peculiar to stars of the mass and age of our Sun.

The Earth revolves around the sun in an almost circular orbit, so that it is always virtually the same distance away from its source of light and heat. Its temperature, therefore, does not vary excessively between summer and winter. It rotates on its axis just at the right speed to prevent one hemisphere from heating up enormously, while the other becomes exceedingly cold, as happens on the Moon. Its atmosphere, containing water vapour, moderates changes of temperature between night and day, as well as between the seasons; so too water vapour contributes to the greenhouse effect (the trapping of heat within the envelope of the atmosphere), produced by the presence of carbon dioxide and some other gases, maintaining an equable temperature throughout the year.

These are just a few examples of the extraordinary combination of conditions existing on this planet conducive to the maintenance of intelligent life such as our own. But today people all over the world are behaving in ways that are rapidly destroying this wonderfully harmonious convergence of physical and chemical characteristics of our planetary environment, threatening climatic catastrophe and profound changes inimical to life on Earth. The facts have been known for over four decades, but what has been, or is being, done to change people's behaviour, or to improve matters is far from sufficient. What is being done, although itself hardly adequate, is confined to single nations; but the problem is global and can be solved only by measures adopted globally.

What separate nations do is easily (and commonly) defeated by what others do or fail to do. This parlous situation must not be allowed to continue. As we are rational beings, we should not behave like the Gadarene swine, rushing headlong, blindly and mindlessly, to our own destruction. That is why I am once again setting out to consider the current condition of mankind, to examine its underlying causes, to discover why they are not being removed, and to advocate what seems obviously to be the one feasible and effective way of devising a remedy.

The arguments I shall present are not new. I have myself urged them before, once as long ago as 1950 and again fifteen years later[2] and other writers more influential than I have done likewise. But they are still widely ignored. The conclusion to which they cogently lead is commonly discounted, or even contemptuously dismissed out of hand. With mankind in so perilous a situation as at present, such obtuseness is not simply frightening, it is intolerable. That is why I am again trying to state and update, what seems to me to be an unanswerable case for the only prudent and practicable course of action, and one urgently, or indeed desperately, necessary.

1.2 Population

THE present population of the world is more than 6.3 billion, double what it was at the beginning of this century, and it is increasing at the rate of approximately one billion every decade (annually, roughly the population of Mexico). If this rate of increase continues world population will reach 8.5 billion by the year 2025 and will grow to about 16 billion by the end of this century. It is quite clear, and is generally agreed by the experts, that this rate of growth cannot be sustained because the resources of

---

[2]This book is a revised and updated version of *One World or None*, which I wrote in the early nineties and was published by Humanities Press in 1993.

the Earth cannot supply the vital needs of so enormous a population.

Whenever the numbers of a species increase so as to exceed the sustenance that the environment can provide, either it tends to die back through lack of provender, or is reduced by predation, or both; or in its search for food it may self-destruct, as the lemmings of Norway are reputed to do, running until they reach the sea-shore and then swimming out to sea until they drown. In one or other of these ways the balance of nature is restored. But when the species is human its members take deliberate steps to overcome the shortage of provisions, their medical science helps them to reduce the ravages of disease, and other conscious efforts to keep the race alive are adopted.

At the present time, however, these deliberate measures are having effects which are contrary to those intended; they are depleting natural resources and disrupting the ecology in ways that endanger the survival of mankind along with the other species on which that survival depends.

More people need more food, the main sources of which for human beings are agriculture and fisheries. They need more housing and shelter, and, as the countryside offers less means of living and insufficient work, they tend to congregate more and more in the cities. They need more clothing, furniture, appliances, and countless other amenities, which swell the demand for manufacture and industry, which require energy, more light and heat, and intensify the need for yet more energy. They seek recreation, which among other effects, increases the appeal of tourism.

All these demands, at the present time, are creating environmental strains, polluting water and air, depleting the soil, destroying the forests, and endangering other species along with our own, and in numerous ways threatening the survival of the very people they are intended to sustain. The effects are not simply additive, but mutually interactive and exacerbating. Let us consider each of the most significant factors in turn, beginning with the supply of food.

1.3 Agriculture

ALREADY in the earlier decades of the last century the means of feeding so rapidly increasing a population had become a world problem of major dimensions; but then, in the 1960s, there occurred what has come to be called the green revolution. The generation by biologists of new varieties of grain giving increased yield, the use of mineral fertilizers and chemical pesticides, and new methods of land management expanded agricultural production to such an extent that, even despite the burgeoning population figures, consumption per capita was increased during the 1970s and later.

But since 1984 the world production of grain has ceased to keep pace with population growth, new ways of repeating the green revolution have not been available, and its more sinister effects have begun to take their toll. Conditions for agricultural production have seriously deteriorated, and we are now faced with global problems of immense proportions, because the natural varieties of cereal have been lost that might have supplied the deficiencies.

Remedies are being sought in genetic modification of crops, but the main danger involved in this is that modified pollens can be spread by the wind over large areas and can contaminate natural varieties, decreasing the means of circumventing future crises that might arise if the modified crops become victim to unforeseen diseases or newly adapted insect pests. This danger is likely to be increased by the growth and industrial exploitation of genetically modified crops, not only directly, but by cross-pollination with native species almost impossible to prevent.

Grain production always tends to concentrate on the growth of a few high-yield species, but the effect of the green revolution has been to confine this concentration to the new varieties that biologists have more or less invented by hybridization and selection, if not by biological engineering.

The result has been and increasingly is the loss of natural

species better adapted to local environments, which would have been more appropriate to local needs, and on which agriculturists might have relied as reserves when conditions deteriorate so as to make those strains in use less satisfactory. As we shall later observe, the loss of species is itself a lamentable feature of current environmental deterioration, with direct and indirect effects on the chances of human survival.

Recent studies have shown that the world has lost one fifth of its arable land in the past decade (an area equal to China and India combined) through causes such as erosion, over-intensive cultivation, poor irrigation practices, deforestation, desertification, and urbanization. New methods of land management encouraged by the need to increase crop production, has enlarged the size of fields and has led to the abandonment of traditional practices, such as the rotation of crops, and alternate crop raising on small allotments. Farmers have been induced not only to omit rotation, but also to cultivate continuously fields formerly left fallow in alternate years.

Where contour ploughing was needed to conserve the topsoil, it has now been discontinued. This, as well as the extension of cultivation to less fertile areas with the help of artificial fertilizers, has exacerbated soil erosion and hastened its exhaustion. The U.S. Department of Agriculture estimated in 1980 that nearly 2.8 billion tons of topsoil (6.8 tons per acre) was lost to wind and water erosion per annum in the United States; estimates for what was formerly the Soviet Union are at least as great; for India they show the situation there to be twice as bad, and even worse in China.[3] Al Gore records that once Iowa had an average of 16 feet of topsoil on its surface, but today only half that depth is left, the rest having been carried away to the Mississippi and the sea.[4]

---

[3]Cf. Jonathan M. Harris, *World Agriculture and the Environment* (Garland Publishing, Inc., New York, London, 1990), pp. 110-111. See also J.M. Harris (Ed.), *Rethinking Sustainability: Power, Knowledge and Institutions* (Ann Arbor, The University of Michigan Press, 2000).

[4]Cf. Albert Gore, *The Earth in the Balance: Ecology and the Human Spirit* (Houghton Mifflin, New York, Boston, London, 1992), p. 3.

The felling of woodland wind-breaks and the grubbing up of hedgerows to enlarge ploughlands for modern farming has increased wind erosion in the drier areas and has further destroyed the habitats of numerous species of birds and small mammals. In Britain the corn-crake and the night-jar are only two of the many species of birds that have become well-nigh extinct as a result of the contemporary revolution in farming methods.

Natural manures and vegetable composts enrich the soil, but mineral fertilizers required by contemporary intensive cultivation tend to impoverish it. Even worse, they are washed out into the rivers and lakes and pollute waters that then become uninhabitable by the fish and aquatic mammals that normally live in them. Many species of water-fowl and waders thus lose their source of food and either migrate or die off; and water needed for human consumption and other uses is poisoned. As we read in *The State of the World, 1992*:

> Chemical run-off and soil erosion from farms on the Belize coast... constitute one of the greatest threats to that nation's barrier reef; aquatic ecosystems in the United States and Europe suffer acutely from pollution from croplands. In the United Kingdom, many bird species have declined over the past 20-30 years, likely due to herbicide use and the elimination of hedgerows and unused lands from agricultural landscapes.[5]

Nitrogen and phosphorus in fertilizers increase the growth of algae in streams, estuaries and lakes, which use up the oxygen supply and choke out vegetable life, starve the fish and decimate the water-fowl.

Another effect of intensive farming is the increased dependency on chemical pesticides, which kill not only the insects against which they are directed but also many others which are beneficial rather than harmful. Often the local extermination of

---

[5]Cf. *The State of the World, 1992*, (W.W. Norton and Co., New York, London, 1992), p. 24.

one species of pest leads to the multiplication of another due to
the incidental elimination of a natural predator. Moreover, birds
are poisoned by the insecticides when they eat fruits that have
been sprayed or the poisoned insects themselves, or else those dependent upon an insect diet die out as they are deprived of their
natural source of food. As long ago as 1962, Rachel Carson's *Silent
Spring* gave evidence of the effects on bird life of DDT and other
insecticides used agriculturally.

Crop-raising, however, is only one branch of agriculture, the
other is livestock farming. In earlier times this was carried on
without undue harm to the environment, but today it is a cause
of major damage. As grain harvests have increased following the
green revolution, so has animal farming, with grain being used as
additional feed.

And in the poorer countries, where grain is not available as
feed, overgrazing and the need in the drier areas to drive cattle
long distances to water, further exacerbate erosion. The consequences have been unexpectedly devastating. Alan Thein Durn-
ing and Holly B. Brough write in *The State of the World, 1992*:

> Rings of barren earth spread out from wells on the
> grasslands of Botswana. Heather wilts in the nature
> preserves of the southern Netherlands. Forests teem-
> ing with rare forms of life explode in flame in Costa
> Rica. Water tables fall in the United States. Each of
> these cases of environmental decline springs from a
> single source: the global livestock industry.[6]

And these are by no means all. Animal waste pollutes rivers
and groundwater; it also generates methane, one of the more virulent greenhouse gases in the atmosphere; nitrogen from manure
combines with atmospheric gases producing ammonia and is a
contributing cause of acid rain. Nitrates from manure also pen-
etrate into ground-water to cause diseases like methemoglobine-
mia (blue baby syndrome) and cancer in humans.

---

[6] Ibid, p. 66

Overgrazing is a main cause of erosion and desertification, while the destruction of forests to make room for more pastures adds to the environmental destruction. Latin America has lost over twenty million hectares of tropical forests to cattle pasture since 1970, with knock on effects of land degradation, because the exposed soil is shallow, acidic and low in nutrients, so that weeds abound and the pasture soon becomes unusable, leading to further ravaging of the forests. The United States Food and Agriculture Organization has reported that Central America alone has lost more than a third of its tropical forests since the early nineteen sixties.[7]

In the United States the consumption of beef is prodigious. In 1991 fast food shops alone sold six billion hamburgers, to say nothing of other diners and restaurants. A United Nations report showed that 85% of cattle ranges in the United States is being steadily destroyed by overgrazing. Jeremy Rifkin, in the New York Times of March 23, 1992, revealed that, nearly half the water used every year in the United States is needed to grow feed for livestock. According to a study by the California Department of Water resources, it requires more than 1200 gallons of water to produce an eight-ounce boneless steak. Cattle, in the United States alone, consume more than 70% of the grain harvest, and in the world as a whole about one third. In this way millions of people, the world over, are deprived of adequate nourishment, as grain is fed to cattle, while people, especially in Africa, starve.

1.4 Fishery

ANOTHER primary source of food is fish, the burgeoning demand for which in recent decades has induced fishermen to adopt modernized methods which have so decimated the fish stocks in many of the fishing grounds that whole species are in danger of extinction. Cod and salmon stocks off the Newfound-

---

[7]Cf. op. cit., p. 74

land coasts have virtually disappeared and illegal overfishing beyond Canadian coastal waters is depleting them even further.

Devastation has been wrought in the North Sea by fishing ves-
sels using nets that scour the sea bed and destroy the breeding
grounds of some species. Overfishing has had drastic effects on
stocks. More damage to the breeding places of certain species,
like salmon, that migrate up rivers to mate, has occurred through
pollution, and damming for reservoirs or hydro-electric energy
production, so that the fish populations are further threatened.
Enormous drift-nets, sometimes thirty miles long, strung out to
catch tuna, along with all and sundry, capture and kill unnecessar-
ily important and valued aquatic mammals, especially dolphins.
And the decimation of whale populations, threatening the extinction of some varieties altogether, has become a matter of grave
concern.

Measures have been taken to counteract some of these excesses, but the legislation enacted by anyone country is ineffective
in others, and solution to the problems can be found only in international cooperation, which is up to the present not forthcoming.
And as we shall later have reason to observe, international agreements are difficult to reach and their observance even more difficult to ensure.

The economies of many maritime countries and the livelihood
of millions of people, quite apart from the demand for sustenance
by millions more, depend on fishing, which draws upon a highly
important part of the food chain that cries out for protection and
conservation.

1.5 Industry

INCREASE of population leads to burgeoning demands for manufactured goods of all kinds, and that again to the growth of
industries which require greater consumption of energy, most of
it derived from fossil fuels. Mechanized industries all over the
world belch out thousands of tons of pollutants into the atmo-

sphere daily, probably the most dangerous of which, in the long run, is C02, the main greenhouse gas. Burning some kinds of coal and oil also emits sulphur compounds and produces acid rain, which destroys forests, damages crops (including the sugar maples of the north-eastern United States), and pollutes rivers and lakes, decimating all kinds of aquatic species. Other gases, such as ozone, nitrogen oxides and carbon monoxide, along with volatile organic compounds are discharged into the atmosphere and combine under the influence of sunlight to form numerous other compounds.

These, with minute suspended particles of ash, soot, dust and liquid droplets of various kinds, together create smog, which has become a serious problem for many large cities, notably Los Angeles, and especially Mexico City, for it causes respiratory ailments, like asthma and lung diseases, as well as cancer, and presents many other hazards to human health. Refineries, chemical plants, dry-cleaning concerns, and other industries required to fulfill the needs of growing urban and rural populations are the source of most of the toxins in the atmosphere. Nor is air pollution confined to cities and the wealthier countries. It is spreading to the countryside and to the poorer nations. Unhealthy levels of ozone have been detected in rural Maine and serious atmospheric pollution has occurred in Eastern Europe and the Third World, in Prague, in Bombay and in Bangkok.[8]

Refrigerators and air-conditioning systems use chlorofluorocarbons (CFCs), which, when they are released into the air as happens especially when old and used out appliances are scrapped, percolate into the upper atmosphere, where they combine with (and so remove) the ozone that shields the earth's surface from ultraviolet rays. Excessive exposure to ultraviolet light is fatal to many plants and crops and causes skin cancer and cataracts in human beings.

Already a large hole in the ozone layer has been detected over the Antarctic and alarming thinning over the northern hemi-

---

[8]Cf. *Environmental Almanac* (Houghton Mifflin, Boston, 1992), pp. 147ff.

sphere has induced some governments to accelerate steps to reduce the production of CFCs. But those now in the atmosphere will last for many years, and doubts remain whether the reduction of the ozone layer is not already irreversible.

People need houses and the construction industry among others consumes large quantities of timber. Citizens nowadays also seek information and read newspapers, which, especially in the United States, grow ever more and more voluminous; and paper is made from wood-pulp. The result is systematic destruction of forests in the temperate zone, in addition to the vast exploitation of the rain forests occasioned by the demand for hard woods, without regard for the environmental impact. Only five percent of the original forests in the United States still remain, and in the Pacific north-west all unprotected old growth forests will be gone by the year 2023. These forests have been described as the lungs of the Earth, because they breathe in the carbon dioxide from the atmosphere and breathe out oxygen.

Furthermore, they are unique, irreplaceable ecosystems, in which the region's soil and water resources are preserved, and the climate stabilized, providing habitat for many rare plants, animals and birds (for instance, the northern spotted owl). As wanton destroyers of rain-forests, some Japanese corporations have been egregious culprits, felling enormous areas in Indonesia and elsewhere; and this devastation is additional to the slashing and burning that has been perpetrated to extend agricultural and pastoral land, all with grave consequences (which we shall presently discuss further) for life on Earth in general and for human beings in particular. Depredation of the forests has been made easier by the development of power tools that enable loggers use to fell whole groves in the time that was once needed to fell a single tree. As a result, new methods of forest management have proved ever more destructive with what are now becoming disastrous consequences.

1.6 Mining

INDUSTRY today is highly mechanized and so requires vast quantities of metal of all kinds for its plants, besides what it converts into articles and appliances for general use. Moreover, to drive machines energy is needed, and this for the most part comes from fossil fuels. For both these reasons mining has become an expanding industry with its own peculiar problems and significantly shattering effects on the environment.

Not long since, there were widespread misgivings about the possible exhaustion of reserves both of ores and of oil needed to serve the growing needs of a proliferating population, but this has given place more recently to even greater concern about the human and ecological damage that is associated with mining activities: devastation of areas of natural beauty, polluted waters, expulsion from their traditional habitation of indigenous peoples, and the disruption of natural fauna and flora that are vital not only to these peoples but to mankind as a whole.

Since the industrial revolution in the eighteenth century, which was the occasion for increased mining, the use of minerals has grown in conjunction with population, but has greatly outstripped it. In the century and a half before 1900 world population doubled while the use of minerals increased by a factor of ten. During the last century that has again multiplied thirteen times more. John E. Young writes:

¡p style="quote_lonepara"¿Annual production of pig iron -the crude metal that is usually converted into steel -now stands at 552 million tons, 22,000 times what it was in 1700. Outputs of copper and zinc are 560 and 7,300 times greater than in 1800. Although aluminium was not available commercially until 1845 and was far too expensive for large-scale production until the modern electrolytic process was invented in 1886, smelters currently turn out 18 million tons of the metal each year[9]

---

[9]*State of the World, 1992*, Ch, 7, p. 101; Cf. also Rex Bosson and Bension Varon, *The Mining Industry and Developing Countries* (Oxford University Press,

Of all industries mining is the most destructive and defaces nature the most. With modern machinery it does so vastly more rapidly and on a scale immeasurably greater than ever before. It is a copious source of hazardous waste, it produces great scars on the face of the landscape, it pollutes rivers and atmosphere, chokes streams, kills vegetation, and poisons animals that live on the plant-life it contaminates.

From many mines arsenic, lead, zinc, cadmium and other poisonous substances seep into rivers and reservoirs to impair the local drinking water, and many extraction processes involve poisonous substances such as mercury and cyanide, which are collected into ponds, spilled into rivers, or, saturated in finely ground waste heaped into piles, from which the substances are blown by wind, to pollute soil and air as well as water. In this manner, mining becomes one of the main sources (indeed, perhaps the worst) of hazardous waste, the disposal of which has nowadays emerged as one of the most urgent, yet most intractable, of problems.

Mining devastates huge areas of countryside. 10,400 hectares round the Sudbury nickel smelter in Ontario, 7000 hectares around Copper Hill in Tennessee, are but two examples of the creation of yawning "dead zones". Japan has sacrificed 6,700 hectares of rice producing land to mining which has made the soil unfit for cultivation; in Great Britain hundreds of thousands of acres of agricultural land have been lost to mining.

Smelting, especially of copper, spews out millions of tons of sulphur dioxide into the air, which produces minute droplets of sulphuric acid and creates acid rain, destructive of forests and crops as well as of aquatic life. In other ways also mining is destructive of forests. John Young tells how wood-fired smelters ate up the local Sussex woods in England, and how, from the same cause, smelting became "the tomb of the forests of the Sierras" in Nevada in the late nineteenth century.

In Brazil, at the present time, mining enterprises at Carajas, will consume 2.4 million tons of charcoal a year, requiring the

---

New York, London, 1977).

felling of 50,000 hectares of forest annually, and this is projected to continue for 250 years. Other Brazilian undertakings, mining seven different kinds of mineral, will involve processing plants, hydro-electric dams, deep-water ports, using up vast quantities of electrical energy and causing untold environmental damage to rivers and forests.

In the course of all this exploitation of the Earth's mineral wealth, the eviction of indigenous people from their traditional homelands and the attendant suffering they experience is largely forgotten. The life-style of these tribes is integrated with the natural processes of the regions in which they live, and they are not destructive of the forests they inhabit, but rather they tend to conserve the local environment. When they lose their traditional heritage, however, not only is their place taken by others who disturb the ecology, but the original inhabitants are not adequately compensated (if at all) for loss of land and possessions, and they become impoverished vagrants, or, like the Yanomami of the Amazon, are dying out, while miners take over their ancestral lands.

Yet minerals are indispensable to most of the industries on which we depend for a civilized life, and their production and export is commonly a vital factor in the economic development of the countries in which they are found. Brazil is a case in point, where so much environmental destruction is threatened by mining, as well as by pastoral expansion, for these developments are urgently needed to keep the nation solvent. The ecological disruption, however, does not affect Brazil and her neighbours alone, but, as we shall emphasize again later, menaces the balance of nature not only in the western and southern hemispheres, but in the world as a whole.

1.7 Energy

CONTEMPORARY civilization differs from earlier civilizations in that it has expanded to encompass the whole world and that it is predominantly scientific and technical. The technical revolution that began in Britain in the 18th. Century has advanced and invaded all other countries and continents, transforming the habits and ways of life of the peoples and now also the landscape.

The immediate prospect is that it will soon transform the climate as well, but of that more anon. Energy is something we cannot do without, but the sources of supply, other than the natural muscular energy of ourselves and domesticated animals, have brought with them disadvantages that are now arousing grave concern.

Industry needs prodigious supplies of energy, while it also supplies energy for industry, household purposes and public amenities. Much of this comes from fossil fuels, which, when burned emit carbon dioxide, and that is a main cause of global warming.

Today the most widely used form of energy is electricity which can be produced only with the help of fossil fuels in power stations, and coal, fuel-oil, petroleum and natural gas are all significant contributors to atmospheric pollution emitting great quantities of greenhouse gases into the atmosphere, and some of these are also sources of other harmful emissions. For this and other reasons (cost being one) many nations have, since 1960, turned to nuclear power, which, as we shall presently observe, brings its own disadvantages.

The top twelve oil producing countries in 1990 pumped out 44.51 million barrels a day. Much of this had to be transported overseas in enormous tankers, which are occasionally wrecked spilling out millions of gallons of oil that pollute the ocean, kill fish and bird-life and threaten the survival of plankton which is the basic food for many species and the base of the food chain for humans. Further oil-spills from pipelines and refineries have, in recent years, been the cause of enormous environmental damage, and those occasioned by the Gulf War, along with the burning of hundreds of Kuwaiti oil wells amounted to a major ecological disaster.

Originally developed for military purposes, nuclear power

has been adapted for ordinary more peaceful employment. Its civilian use grew spectacularly until about 1979, when alarm was spread by the Three Mile Island nuclear melt-down, and concern mounted further in 1986, when the nuclear power plant at Chernobyl exploded. Meanwhile, nuclear power plants have been found to present risks to the health of their employees and to the surrounding population. Greater than average incidence of leukemia, especially in the children of workers at the plants, has been recorded at Sellafield in Britain, and elsewhere.

The whole issue of energy supply today presents mankind with one of its most difficult and complicated problems. The burning of fossil fuels produces greenhouse gases increasing global warming, but nuclear energy poses even greater hazards from accidents spreading deadly radio-active substances that remain toxic for thousands of years, from leakage of such substances, and from the so-far unsolved problem of nuclear waste disposal.

1.8 Hazardous Waste

THE disposal of waste of all kinds has become a headache for administrators from town halls to capitals. The accumulation of rubbish in spreading conurbations has nowadays got to the stage at which no further space can be found safely or healthfully to contain the swelling mountains of refuse. Industrial waste, much of it toxic, cannot be disposed of without widespread pollution of rivers, soil and air. Even waste that is not immediately dangerous, old cars and scrap iron, grows and expands until the dumps become eye-sores and scenes of desolation. To all this must now be added the disposal of mounting quantities of radioactive waste from nuclear installations, both military and civilian.

Radiation, aside from burns and skin ulcers, has been found to cause cancer, leukemia, cataract, mental retardation, and genetic diseases. Exposure to even quite low levels can be dangerous, in fact, some scientist say that there is no safe lower limit and that the available evidence shows any radiation, however small, to be a risk because the effects are cumulative. High level radioactive waste remains dangerous for thousands of years. The half-life (the time it takes for half the original material to decay) of some isotopes, such as plutonium is 24,000 years, of others as much as 710,000.

Wastes from military installations have already contaminated air, water, vegetation and wild-life in many areas. Nobody has yet discovered any really safe way of disposing of the ever mounting quantities. Konrad Krauskopf maintains that "no scientist or engineer can give an absolute guarantee that radioactive waste will not someday leak in dangerous quantities from even the best repositories.[10]

It must be housed in impenetrable containers, which will not corrode or leak for thousands of years, and none have yet been invented that are entirely dependable. It cannot be dumped in the sea, for fear that its housing will corrode and leak, which would make water and fish radioactive and would contaminate an important human food source. The Irish Sea has become so radioactive from leakages intermittently occurring at the Sellafield nuclear plant that bathing beaches can no longer be used with safety.

If nuclear waste is buried deep in the earth, there is the possibility that containers may at some time be fractured by earthquakes. If water collects in contact with heated containers explosions of steam could rival volcanic eruptions. Even less spectacular causes of leakage, always possible at some stage, are liable to affect groundwater and soils and so prove hazardous to human health.

Whatever scheme is devised, and wherever the disposal is contemplated, there are risks, and if the site is, or is near, a populated area, the local people will always strenuously resist its use. Consequently, the problem of waste disposal, both hazardous and other, remains unsolved and intractable.

---

[10]"Disposal of High-Level Nuclear Waste," *Science*, Sept.14, 1990.

1.9 Cities

PEOPLE need shelter and housing, and as populations increase so does migration from the country to the towns. More and more people congregate in cities and all too soon urban sprawl eats into the countryside and industrial sites invade fields. Marcia Lowe, writing in The State of the World, 1992, recorded that at the beginning of the century only one tenth of the world's population lived in cities, but if present trends continued more than half would be city-dwellers by its end:

In industrial and developing countries alike," she continues, "chaotic, uncontrolled urban growth -whether measured in rising numbers or in the amount of space humans spread out upon -draws ever more land, water, and energy from surrounding regions to meet people's needs.[11]

City populations are not only increased by migration but also swelled by internal procreation, and the disconcerting results range from currently irremediable smog affliction (as in Mexico City and Los Angeles), and accumulation of perilous waste (as in Alexandria), to the draining off of underground water, such as is causing Venice, Bangkok, Shanghai and Jakarta to sink and to suffer flooding at high tides. Feeding the city-dwellers requires more agricultural production, while the spread of urban development encroaches continuously on arable land.

Cities consume water and energy in ever increasing volume, and make ever heavier demands on agriculture, fishing and forestry, but perhaps today the most difficult and urgent problem that they face is transportation, with ever growing traffic jams, air-pollution, death-dealing accidents and noise. Especially in America first consideration is given to cars, delivery vans, trucks and their drivers, while pedestrians tend to be overlooked.

The planning of most cities has been seriously at fault for several decades. Urban sprawl has given rise to suburban develop-

---

[11]Cf. op. cit., p. 119; United Nations, World Urbanization Prospects (New York, 1991).

ments extending far out from the cities' centres. In the absence of efficient public transport systems commuters have to rely on private cars, which is good for the motor industry, but creates major traffic problems for inner cities and adds to atmospheric pollution.

The exhaust from automobiles not only contributes to smog, and, where legislation does not compel the use of lead-free petroleum, poisons the air we breathe, it also contains a significant percentage of carbon dioxide. Every day millions of tons of this gas is pumped into the atmosphere by many millions of motor vehicles, adding to the greenhouse effect and contributing to global warming.

At the same time the increasing numbers of vehicles creates a growing demand for new and bigger roads and highways which desecrate the beauties of the landscape, further decrease the area of cultivable land, disturb the habitats of wildlife and birds, and augment the disruption of the ecology.

1.10 Tourism

PEOPLE need recreation and amusement and one very important provision of both comes from tourism. As populations grow the demand for holidays increases and as methods of transport have become more rapid and more available the number who seek holidays abroad in ever more distant localities has risen spectacularly. The result has been a widespread development of the tourist industry, with the construction of phalanxes of hotels along sea-fronts and in mountain resorts, the establishment of recreation facilities in wilderness areas reserved as national parks, and the setting up of lidos and marinas.

Motor cruisers have multiplied by the thousand along scenic coasts, lakes have become crowded with water-skiers, climbers hike in droves over scenic hills and uplands, ski-resorts abound in the higher mountains, orienteers flock to outlying countrysides, and regiments of ramblers range over fields and through woodlands.

What all this does to the environment is distressing. Paths up hillsides become worn broad and deep permitting erosion and increased weathering; plant-life is destroyed; habitats of wild animals, shy of humans, some of them rare and endangered from other causes, are invaded; beauty-spots are ravaged; the wash of speedboats erodes shorelines; ancient remains, like the Parthenon in Athens, are worn down by sightseers' feet, while others, such as Stonehenge are commercialised and thronged with sight-seers.

Wetlands, the home of thousands of species of birds, mammals and amphibians, and the gathering points for many migrants, are drained for "development", or plundered by hunters and fishers (when this has not already occurred for agriculture). More roads for more cars carve up the countryside, and remote haunts, attractive for their peace and tranquil beauty are overrun by ever growing crowds of visitors. In addition the increase of air and road traffic not only creates congestion but also enhances atmospheric pollution.

All these untoward developments follow directly from the egregious growth of population during the last century and the natural and, for the most part, legitimate quest of ordinary people for food, shelter, warmth, comfort and amusement. We read in the first chapter of Genesis that God blessed mankind and bade them "Be fruitful, and multiply, and replenish the earth, and subdue it." This they have done in full measure, but the promised blessing that should go with their proliferation looks very dubious.

Before we contemplate future prospects in more detail, let us consider the broader aspects of the effects flowing from the current conditions we have been reviewing.

Chapter 2

Cautionary Tale

2.1 Interrelation of Problems

THE many interactive and mutually reinforcing menaces now bearing down upon the human race stem from exceeding population growth, and the many attendant problems described in Chapter One. Their overall consequences affect the planet as a whole, not simply one region or one race. It is the global character of the problems facing mankind that is new and unprecedented, and it is with that prominently in mind that they should be addressed. Let us then consider them briefly with the emphasis upon their comprehensive scope.

The population explosion has immediate effects which spring from the spread of urbanization, such as intensification of agricultural production, multiplication of recreational facilities, and accumulation of waste, which in turn lead to deforestation and to loss of topsoil, with the consequent tendency to desertification, the destruction of habitats and endangering of species. But the key factor in environmental deterioration is pollution, brought about by human activities, industry and energy use—pollution of soil, water, and air. This has more widespread effects which intensify those already occurring, so that the process set in train by pollution is further reinforced. As climate scientist James Gustave Speth writes: "Climate change could spark enormous transformations of uncertain probability that would be devastating to human societies. We may not get a good scientific resolution before it is too late. So the burning question is: Why are we running these huge risks when we do not have to do so?"[1]

2.2 The Necessity for Species Diversity

IT has now been scientifically established that the planet is a single ecosystem, with all living species subsisting in symbiosis, each dependent on many others, and in the last resort on all the rest. This applies just as much to mankind as to other species, although we have habitually thought of ourselves as set apart, superior (as in some important ways we are), and independent of surrounding nature, which we think we are at liberty to exploit for our own benefit. No such conception can be entertained any longer. If we are to have any hope for survival we must realize immediately and vividly our unity with and dependence upon nature as a whole, and upon all other species, however remote they may seem, however obscure or apparently insignificant.

Nobody knows how many living species exist on Earth. There may be as many as eighty million, and probably not less than ten million, of which scientists have discovered fewer than 1,500,000. Of these it is estimated that, at the present time, 140 species of invertebrate animals and at least one species of plant, reptile, bird, mammal, or fish are exterminated every day.[2] The causes of this dereliction are first and foremost the destruction of the forests in which about half the living species on the planet find their home, and of which already half the original area has been destroyed.

---

[1]James Gustave Speth, *Red Sky at Morning: America and the Crisis of the Global Environment* (New Haven, Yale University Press, 2004).

[2]Cf. John C. Ray, "Conserving Biological Diversity", *The State of the World*, 1992, Ch.2

The second most important habitat is wetlands, now threatened, or already eliminated, by drainage for agriculture, urban development, industrial demands, and similar pressures. Of these more than 90% in developed, and a rapidly growing proportion in developing, countries have already gone, and human pursuits are encroaching upon what remain. Water pollution is yet another cause of species loss in the wetlands of the world, not to mention aquaculture, and the silting up of estuaries due to soil-erosion. In comparison to these losses, the ravages of hunting and uncontrolled fishing pale almost into insignificance although they are by no means negligible.

It is obvious that human beings depend for food on many of the species now under threat, and these again depend for their survival on others in what is called the continuous food-chain. The preservation of biological diversity is, therefore, of the utmost importance for life on Earth. Nor is it only the food-chain that is vital for survival. In-breeding weakens progeny, while interbreeding between different varieties strengthens the stock. Lack of diversity, therefore, is apt to debilitate the species, as has happened to many kinds of fish on the west coast of America, and of trees where natural forests have been replaced by plantations of a single commercial variety. The reduction of diversity, for instance, in grain, where varieties have been ousted to make room for new high-yield types, has exposed crops to diseases and pests against which the lost varieties were, or could become, resistant, and which now are liable to ravage enormous areas, where at one time they could have been confined within manageable limits.

The original wild varieties of most of the world's important crops are concentrated in only a few places (about twelve), in different parts of the world, all of which are now being threatened environmentally, or have already been largely destroyed by drought, desertification, or some similar deleterious agency, and attempts to counteract this loss of genetic diversity by the development of gene banks has had little official support from governments, is very ill organized, and grossly underfunded.[3]

The use of pesticides, as we have noted, is a virulent cause of species decimation, destroying not only the verminous kinds, but also those that feed on them, as well as others quite innocent that are inadvertently poisoned. Likewise, intensive farming methods deprive wild-life of habitats, and intensive fishing exterminates valuable, beautiful, and much needed species.

It is pollution that causes most of the damage: pollution of earth and soil, causing disease, or immediate poisoning; of water, making wetlands uninhabitable and destroying fish and vegetable life in streams and lakes, depriving ducks and waders of their provender, as well as gulls and ospreys; pollution of the atmosphere, with even more ominous and potentially devastating consequences (to which we shall return), the most far-reaching being climate change, with which many species, already adapted to the zone they now inhabit, are unable to keep pace, and they cannot migrate quickly enough to escape.

Most alarming of all is the report made to a conference of scientists on climate change at Exeter in England that the excessive emissions of carbon dioxide into the atmosphere are increasing solution of the gas by the oceans and transforming the sea-water from alkaline to acid in which thousands of marine organisms cannot live. These include plankton, the basis of the food chain affecting most sea creatures and those that feed on them including some mammals, not least humans.

2.3 Deforestation

PERHAPS the most calamitous of all forms of environmental damage is the execrable loss of the rain forests. We have already observed how prodigious the destruction has been. And the most frightening thought is that the rain forests are the chief source of oxygen in the Earth's atmosphere. It is oxygen that we

---

[3]Cf. Steven C. Witt, *Biotechnology and Genetic Diversity*, CSI, San Francisco, California, 1985

breathe, that supports the combustion of the fuels which give us warmth and energy, and without which most life cannot endure. Moreover, the forests absorb carbon dioxide and maintain the balance of atmospheric gases. It is the excessive increase in CO_2 more than any other gas that creates the greenhouse effect and gives rise to global warming and climate change. Further, the forests transpire vast quantities of water vapour that cools the air and keeps the temperature tolerable, even (or especially) in the tropics.

It replenishes the clouds and maintains rainfall, affecting the climate the world over. Deforestation thus causes widespread drought and contributes to the encroachment of deserts upon arable land and pasturage, which today, especially in Africa, is causing mass under-nourishment and starvation among the inhabitants. Reduction of rainfall in part of the Amazon basin has produced unprecedentedly dry conditions in the forest itself, so that biologists fear a gigantic and uncontrollable conflagration if it should accidentally be set alight.

The forests themselves depend upon rain, and they give back to the atmosphere the water they drink from the soil; but logging, slashing, and burning, by reducing the forest area, leads not only to soil exhaustion and erosion, but reduces the rainfall, and so endangers the forest that remains.

2.4 Desertification

WHAT was once known as the bread-basket of the Roman Empire is now the Sahara Desert. Today over-grazing over-cultivation, soil-exhaustion and denudation of top-soil is creating new deserts and extending old ones in almost every continent. While population grows apace, agricultural and pastoral lands are shrinking, so that more and more people go hungry. As with deforestation, so the creation of deserts is a self-reinforcing process: more desert means less rainfall; reduced rainfall creates more desert. Droughts in Africa are becoming more frequent and more prolonged as the years pass, and much the same is occurring in parts of California, South America, Asia, and Australia; and not even Europe is immune. A major contributing cause, however, with reciprocal enhancing effects is global warming and consequent climate change, another result of pollution, to which we shall now turn our attention.

2.5 Atmospheric Pollution

JAMES LOVELOCK has put forward the hypothesis that the Earth as a whole is a single organism, and Lewis Thomas has compared it to a living cell.[4] The atmosphere functions like the protective membrane of the cell, regulating the Earth's energy intake from the Sun and protecting it from harmful radiation, regulating its temperature and circulating life-supporting substances. The ozone layer in the upper atmosphere filters out ultra-violet radiation and protects living things on the Earth's surface from its deleterious effects. This sensitive membrane is now being seriously damaged by the current practices of human civilized living.

To many plants ultraviolet radiation is lethal, and in humans and other animals it causes blindness, cataract and skin-cancer. CFCs manufactured by man and released into the air, ascend to the ozone layer and destroy it, exposing the creatures below to the dire effects of ultraviolet radiation. The thinning of the ozone layer has by now proceeded far enough to have alarmed the governments of Britain and the United States into decreeing strict limitation of the production of CFCs; but the effects of these gases will continue, even after all production has ceased. Measurements of CFCs in the atmosphere made in 1991 have shown a slight decrease (about 2%), a trend which has continued to the present, but this is only of some and not all the varieties. Those that remain are expected to last for from 50 to 100 years.

---

[4]Cf. J.E. Lovelock, *Gaia: A New Look at Life on Earth* (Oxford University Press, New York, Oxford, 1979,1987); Lewis Thomas, *The Lives of a Cell*, (Viking Press, New York 1974, Penguin Books Harmondsworth, 1987)

Meanwhile some substances used as substitutes are themselves destructive of the ozone layer, and scientists speculate whether the damage may not already have become irreversible. This form of atmospheric pollution, therefore, poses a serious threat to human health, and, as it destroys crops, to human survival.

Emissions that create smog, inhalation of which impairs human health in other ways, are more localized in their impact. But among them are the greenhouse gases that trap the sun's heat and raise the average temperature of the entire planet, with manifold and far-reaching results that augur catastrophe on a world-wide scale. There is now fairly conclusive evidence that global warming has actually occurred and is increasing:

> Some scientists predict an average surface temperature increase of up to 9 Fahrenheit in the next 100 years, which is comparable to the temperature difference between the extreme climate of the last ice age 18,000 years ago and today's climate.

So reports the World Resources Institute.[5] Christopher Flavin records that carbon dioxide concentrations in the atmosphere were 354 parts per million in 1990, while global temperatures have reached the highest levels of the past century.[6] Today, we are approaching 400 parts per million. This level of C02 content is more than 30% higher than in the pre-industrial era. One billion tons of carbon dioxide a year enters the atmosphere from the burning of tropical forests alone, while transportation (motor vehicles and aircraft) and electric power generation together account for more than half the carbon dioxide emissions from fossil fuels.

Other warming gases are methane (constituting 12% to carbon dioxide's 54%, but contributing a disproportionately greater greenhouse effect), nitrous oxide, CFCs, ozone and other trace gases. It is clear that the prospective global warming trend is the

---

[5]The 1992 Environmental Almanac, p. 273

[6]*The State of the World*, 1992, p. 33.

result of human activities, and it is human activity that must be enlisted if it is to be counteracted and, if possible, reversed. This may still be feasible, if appropriate action is taken with sufficient promptitude, but it will require drastic changes in living-styles, methods of production, and economic and political policies.

There is no clear consensus about the probable effects of global warming, other than that, whatever they may be, they will cause quite stupendous climatic changes. Only a relatively small increase in global temperature is sufficient to melt a significant proportion of the polar ice, which already has been found noticeably thinner in the north than a few years ago, and has detached enormous masses of ice from the Antarctic continent. In recent years, for the first time in recorded history, there has been open water at the North Pole during the summer season.

Such melting will raise the level of the oceans, and a rise of only a few feet will be enough to inundate low-lying coastal areas, where half the world's population live. Recent reports maintain that the collapse of the West Antarctic ice sheet will raise sea levels globally in excess of 16 feet; and the melting of the ice-covering of Greenland would raise sea levels by 20 feet; a temperature rise of no more than 1.5 degrees centigrade above pre-industrial levels will bring this about. Already atmospheric levels have increased half that amount.

The eastern United States, Bangladesh, Indonesia, are only a few of the places that would suffer. Many of the world's most populous and historic cities as well as small islands in the Indian and Pacific Oceans would be altogether submerged. The warming effect would, moreover, be intensified by an exceptional thaw in the northern polar region, because some greenhouse gases (methane, in particular) now trapped in the arctic ice would be released.

Yet more alarming are the results of recent oceanographical researches revealing that the largest glacier in the world, in Greenland, is moving and melting faster than ever recorded hitherto and, combined with the discharge into the sea of fresh water from rivers in northern Siberia where the gulf stream sinks to lower levels and reverses its course to flow southwards again to the warmer tropical regions, this is reducing the salinity of the current which, if it continues, will stop its flow altogether. The result will be a dramatic change in the climate of Western Europe engulfing it in temperatures similar to a new ice age.

Sharp differences in pressure and temperature will produce greater atmospheric turbulence, causing increased hurricane and tornado violence in areas where they are already common (and have already increased significantly), and violent storms in places not hitherto subject to extreme weather conditions. This has already occurred in such unwonted places as the south coast of England, where hurricane force winds have swept across the southern counties. In the Caribbean hurricanes and cyclones are increasing in frequency and violence doing even greater damage than heretofore, as tornadoes become more numerous, bigger and more violent in their destructive effects.

If present trends continue at the rate already detected temperate climates will become more tropical, and arctic conditions will become more temperate. Some kinds of flora will succumb to new and uncongenial conditions and others will thrive where they could not before. Many animal and plant species will have to change their habitat, but, because the climate change is now occurring faster than any that has occurred in the past several thousand years, they might fail to do so in time to save themselves from extinction. All this is likely within the next few decades.

It has been suggested that global warming could be an advantage, if arctic tundra, for example, becomes suitable for agriculture. Unfortunately, no such optimism is justified, because the deep permafrost of the tundra would not melt and would prevent the growth of crops. Moreover, it is clear that any possible marginal advantage would be greatly outweighed by the destructive effects of the enormous and relatively rapid climatic changes that would occur world-wide, evidence of which is already being detected.

Many of these predictions are based on computer models, and

not all such models agree. Some, in fact, predict conditions almost opposite to those above described. Higher temperatures, it is presumed, will increase evaporation, and that will generate excessive cloud cover, shutting out sunlight and warmth, so that the ground temperature will actually fall dramatically and initiate a new ice age.

This may sound incredible, but whatever prognostication one accepts the prospect is grim, and the one point on which all agree is that global warming and climate change are actually happening. As 2004 was coming to a close, a United Nations weather agency alerted us that nine of the 10 hottest years on record occurred since 1995, the last four years were among the five hottest, and 1998 was the hottest on record.

Other signs of global warming have multiplied, become more obvious, and more drastic. Summers the world over have become unprecedentedly hot, with uncontrollable forest fires raging in California, Portugal, Spain, Australia and elsewhere, with extreme violent weather conditions in places that have not experienced them before. Melting of the ice-caps, as noted above, has increased; great ice-sheets the size of whole countries have broken away from Antarctica and the average atmospheric temperature has risen to record levels above anything previously recorded. Nobody now seriously questions the fact that climate change is proceeding apace, that it is not just an occasional natural variation but a trend largely the effect of human activities, such as the excessive burning of fossil fuels and unprecedented emissions of greenhouse gases.

One of the most disturbing effects of this process is the drying up of the water supply in many continents. Along with global warming the increased consumption of water by modern industries is reducing the water tables and drying up rivers so that populations, especially in tropical zones, are becoming desperate for fresh water supplies. Water is indispensable to life and fresh water essential for health. It is, therefore, hardly surprising that disputes arise between governments of neighbouring countries dependent upon the same water sources, disputes which could, and probably will, escalate into conflict with unpredictable effects destructive of life and property.[7]

But what should trouble us most of all, especially those in government, is that nothing significant is being done to remedy and counteract these sinister and exceedingly dangerous developments. What (generally inadequate) measures are taken by some (mostly European) administrations are contradicted and nullified by what is done, or left undone, by others (especially the United States and many developing countries). We seem never to recognize the universal reason for this dilatory and negligent inaction—namely, that sovereign governments invariably serve what they see as their own national interests inconsiderate of global requirements.

2.6 Taking Stock

SANDRA POSTEL, in the first chapter of *The State of the World, 1992*, has summarized the world situation as follows (I am not following the order she adopts):

> World population is growing by 92 million people annually. Of this total 88 million are being added in the developing world.
>
> The protective ozone shield in heavily populated latitudes of the northern hemisphere is thinning twice as fast as scientists thought just a few years ago.
>
> A minimum of 140 plant and animal species are condemned to extinction each day.

---

[7]See "Coming Soon: A Thirsty Years' War," in *The Times*, London, 31st. July, 2003: "The Permanent Court of Arbitration in the Hague, which aims to resolve water conflict cases, says that there are 263 river basins shared between countries, and one third of those are shared by three or more. The potential for dispute in the coming five or ten years includes not just the Ganges and Brahmaputra... but La Plata, Limpopo, Mekong, Ob, Okavango, Orange, Senegal and Zambezi... The world is facing its worst human crisis with 'inertia at the leadership level and a world population not fully aware of the scale of the problem.'

> Atmospheric levels of heat-trapping carbon dioxide are now 26 percent higher than in the pre-industrial concentration, and continue to climb.

> The earth's surface was warmer in 1990 than in any year since record keeping began in the mid-nineteenth century; six of the seven warmest years on record have occurred since 1980. [Update: Nine of the ten warmest were since 1995, the warmest being 1998.]

> Forests are vanishing at a rate of some 17 million hectares per year, an area half the size of Finland.

In the 22 years since this was written, all these trends have continued largely unabated. Beset as we are by so many and such complex and interconnected crises the situation is fast becoming hopeless, and its desperate urgency is obvious.

There are, nevertheless, feasible remedies to most of these pressing and multiplying ills, which could save the planet if they were expeditiously and comprehensively applied. First, and most imperative, is the necessary change from fossil fuels to renewable energy sources. This is by no means impracticable.

Natural gas can be substituted for petroleum, and it releases far less damaging exhaust. Although its use would not finally solve our energy problems, the first step in the right direction would seem to be to turn to it as a substitute for other fuels. Transition from natural gas to hydrogen would then be possible by methods already projected by engineers, and hydrogen burns without any detrimental atmospheric emission. Solar and wind energy are harmless and renewable, and already they are contributing in some places to the provision of electricity; and the same is true of energy derived from the tides and from biothermal sources. What is urgently needed is increased funding for more intensive research into the methods of using these resources, so that they can replace coal and oil as energy providers. Christopher Flavin, writing in *The State of the World*, 1992, contends:

> The solar-hydrogen economy is compellingly simple in design, economically practical, and ecologically necessary.

Moreover, it does not require any radical scientific break-throughs or discovery of entirely new resources. This vision of the possible may finally spark an energy revolution. If so, the pace of change could surprise us all.[8]

In *State of the World 2008*,[9] Flavin describes many promising innovations in this area, showing that the necessary changes could be made given the proper institutions and political will globally. Other expedients are called for to stop the destruction of the rainforests and, if possible, to renew their growth. It is also necessary to change agricultural methods, and to reform our dietary habits, to decrease the consumption of meat; and none of these policies are impracticable. The disposal of hazardous waste would be more difficult, but reliance on nuclear energy should be reduced as other renewable sources become available, and that would at least stem the flow of nuclear waste.

In general, it may be said that it should not be beyond the intellectual powers of mankind, nor should it defeat our ingenuity, to overcome these problems. But all nations must act quickly and in concert if we are to succeed. And this is improbable as long as sovereign states give priority to their own national interests.

2.7 Conditions of Success

WHAT should be recognized, but is not widely admitted, is that no remedies are likely to be effective if they are not universally applied. The problems are global and local expedients will not remove them. Using wind power in California and solar power in Arizona may mitigate the accumulation of greenhouse gases, but it cannot altogether prevent global warming and climate change.

Emission of carbon dioxide from fossil fuel burning, wherever it occurs, affects the Earth's atmosphere as a whole. Reducing

---

[8]*The State of the World*, 1992, p. 45.
[9]*State of the World 2008: Innovations for a Sustainable Economy*, 2008, pp.75-90.

it in one region will not help if it is increased or maintained in another. The destruction of the ozone shield exposes not just one, but many, nations to ultra-violet radiation; so the decision by the Europeans, or the Americans to phase out the production of CFCs will not protect them if undeveloped nations (who resent having to make sacrifices to counteract the follies of the richer countries) continue to use them.

The damage done by the Chernobyl explosion was not confined to the Ukraine, nor would the effects of any other nuclear accident that might occur. Increased radiation levels from the Fukushima disaster have already crossed the Pacific Ocean and are being registered in California. Nuclear waste from Sellafield worries the Irish even more than the English; and sulphur emissions from British coal-burning plants plague the forests of Norway with acid rain. The destruction of the rain-forests is a threat to the entire world, not just to Brazil or Indonesia. Global problems demand global solutions.

Further, voluntary action is unlikely to be sufficient to cope with these matters. Corporations are too preoccupied with profits and dividends to give much heed to the environmental effects of their production methods. Legal regulation and enforcement is essential if results are to be ensured.

And when several different states are involved, legislation is unlikely to be universal, or expedients to be widely adopted. Co-operation can be brought about by nothing less than international agreement; but that, we shall find, is not easy to come by, nor is conformity guaranteed, even when agreements are reached. What is indispensable is a new global World Order with authority and power to legislate remedial measures.

2.8   Resistance to Change

FOR centuries we have been encouraged by our religion and by our educators to think of human beings as somehow different from other natural creatures. Religion has taught us to regard ourselves as differing from other animals by having immortal souls. Scientists, operating under the early-modern Newtonian paradigm, have made us believe that nature is a sort of machine put at our disposal to use and exploit in whatever ways we can devise, and the Bible (for instance, the first chapter of Genesis) seems to justify the belief.

Only very recently has science discovered that the universe is a single whole, that nature is one system of interdependent parts with humankind totally dependent upon the maintenance of the balance of nature for its survival. A paradigm-shift to holism is an absolute imperative. But we still tend to think we can get along quite nicely while ignoring the effect that our behaviour has upon the environment, and we are reluctant to give up our habits of exploiting natural resources for our own immediate comfort and convenience, without consideration of the consequences. As a result, we find it hard to realize the nature let alone the acuteness) of the problem that confronts us today, and we resist admitting it in all kinds of devious ways.

The changes demanded of us if the planet is to be saved are so great and so unprecedented that few are ready to accept the need for them. It is now fifty years since disturbances to the balance of nature have been systematically studied by scientists; yet, in spite of valiant work done by Greenpeace, taking vigorous and courageous action from Iceland to the Antarctic, as well as public pronouncements and reports issued by concerned bodies, admirable books written by worried authors, and excellent nature films broadcast on television, many people seem still unaware of the multiple dangers we face.

True, there is now a growing awareness among the public that "green" issues are important, a gradually increasing realization of the fragility of the ecosystem and a more eager search than hitherto for ways of extricating mankind from the predicament in which it is placed. Even so, the majority feel that they can probably carry on more or less as usual, as long as they modify their behavior slightly in one or two respects. Perhaps the very enormity of the problem makes people unwilling to face it and prompts them to seek to deny that it exists, or, at least, to think it is not as bad as it is made out to be.

This kind of denial is quite common and is perhaps the greatest danger of all for, unless swift and resolute action is taken, environmental deterioration may pass the point of no return and become irreversible (if it has not already done so). Our planet is regularly passing what the scientists call "tipping points"—lesser points of no return that are building toward a disastrous cumulative effect. But even when people do realize the threats of impending disaster, they do not always understand their causes, still less do they appreciate the extent and nature of the changes needed to our ways of thinking and conducting our affairs for which the situation calls, especially in the international sphere.

One way of evading the pressing issues is to point to disagreement among scientists about the reported facts, or disputes as to their causes, even when the facts are admitted. Some disagreement there may be between the experts, but the salient facts are generally recognized and the main causes are well known. To appeal to scientific differences of opinion as an excuse for delaying action, therefore, is no more than an evasion of the issue.

A sufficient body of knowledge has been established to make it sheer folly to ignore the dangers and obviously prudent to take the urgently necessary steps to avert them, especially when those steps are practicable, relatively easy, and promise to be salutary.

Then again, there are vested interests that prevent some people from facing up to what may seem rather remote problems. The changes necessary are often costly, and business people are distracted by cost-benefit calculations. Manufacturers fight shy of large changes to plant or the use of materials unless they see a prospect of short term gain. It takes effort and often causes temporary inconvenience to change heating systems and manufacturing processes.

Retailers tend to respond to public demand, rather than to offer to their customers commodities that are environmentally friendly. There are so many factors encouraging such resistance that every means of publicity and advertisement is necessary to educate the population of the world and to impress upon their imaginations the severity and relentlessness of present dangers, so as to arouse and confirm their determination to take appropriate action. For it should by now be apparent that the costs of delay will far outweigh the expense and inconvenience of necessary change, and that the situation calls for immediate action.

At the moment there is little sign that the situation is being given the attention its seriousness warrants. Where today do we see any very reassuring progress in any of the indicated directions? What sign is there as yet of automobile manufacturers contemplating a changeover to natural gas engines? Who has yet seen, or what company has yet seriously engaged in, the production of electric cars, although the idea has been mooted and enthusiastically advocated by environmentalists?

What encouragement do governments give to research on the harnessing of renewable energy, and how many are willing to spend money on it? Where is there any movement towards persuading people to adopt a vegetarian diet, even if there is one to promote cholesterol-free foods. What plans are evident of new environmentally friendly agricultural policies? There is very little evidence of progress in any of these directions, even where they are much discussed.

Certainly, there have been some promising scientific conferences, which have made significant pronouncements about impending dangers and the measures that ought to be taken to meet them; but the response from governments has been half-hearted and grudging.

The British government at first agreed to legislate only to limit C02 emissions to the then current levels by 2005; and although Britain had decided to advance that date, the American Administration was still dragging its feet even more sluggishly. Meanwhile, what was needed was not simply limitation to current levels, but, as far as possible, total elimination of excessive C02 production.

The United Nations convened a World Summit meeting in Rio de Janeiro in June 1992, but the United States refused to commit itself to what relatively little was agreed, in particular to giving aid to developing countries unable to meet the cost of environmental policies. In fact, many environmentalists considered that the Summit was destined to fail, if only because it did not represent the majority of the world's population who live in the poorer countries; they cannot afford to attend, say the critics, and, unless they can speak English, nobody will listen to them.

By April 1992 the delegates seeking to draft an agenda (known as "Agenda 21") had achieved little success; nor did environmentalists expect that they would, because the nations, north and south, with the United States to the fore, were all balking at measures which might prove difficult or costly. Few if any are thinking in terms of radical change, the wealthier states anxious about costs and the poorer ones stressing poverty above conservation of the ecology.

Since 1992 other similar conventions have been held in Tokyo (1997), Johannesburg (2002), and Copenhagen (2009) with virtually no effective result. Such agreements as have been reached have been non-binding and have been for measures that are totally inadequate to meeting the problems, few if any of the targets that have been agreed have been met and nothing spectacular has been done to meet them. The reason is that each country puts its own national interests before the global requirements for a safe environment. In short, there is no sign yet that people in general or their leaders are really aware of the imminence or the magnitude of the threats to human survival, nor is there any evidence of a corresponding feeling of urgency. But if determined action is not taken very soon, our race will court its own extinction, along with so many other endangered species.

2.9 Cautionary Tale

THE story is told of some school children who decided as part of their nature study to try an experiment. They caught a frog and threw it into a beaker of hot water. The frog frantically leapt out of the beaker, scalded but still surviving and able to recover. Then the children placed the frog in a beaker of cold water and heated it gradually over a bunsen burner. Now the frog found its surroundings quite congenial and was lulled into inactivity by the pleasant warmth; but as the temperature rose it became comatose and by the time the water boiled it was dead.

At the present time the human race is in an analogous situation. As a result of our own activities the world we inhabit is heating up. Until now we have been unaware of the fact and even now our attention is not much attracted to it. But if we go on ignoring it, we are in danger of suffering the fate of the frog in the fable. Nobody knows precisely what the temperature of the water in the imagined beaker would be, corresponding to the present deterioration of the global ecosystem. It is surely time for us to find out.

Chapter 3

Twenty-First Century Crisis

3.1 September 11th, 2001

THE second millennium, having been ushered in by diverse celebrations, was promptly overshadowed by an event that horrified the entire world. The twin towers of the World Trade Center in New York were destroyed with thousands of fatalities allegedly by Islamic suicide hijackers, who (though showing scant interest in landing techniques) had been trained as pilots in the United States, reputedly having followed the plans and devices of the Al Qaeda organization under the leadership of Osama bin Laden. The FBI earlier had issued warnings that some such attack was likely to be made, but apparently they went unheeded.

President Bush immediately declared "war" on any state that harboured terrorists and demanded of the Taliban regime in Afghanistan that Osama bin Laden be handed over to justice. On their refusal, Afghanistan was attacked by United States and British troops, the Taliban were driven from power, but bin Laden was not found.

Bush immediately planned a further war on Iraq, on the grounds that Saddam Hussein was hoarding weapons of mass destruction with which he could threaten the West, or which he could hand on to terrorist organizations that could do so. The fact that Hussein was antagonistic to Al Qaeda was generally known but was either denied or disbelieved by the American Administration, as well as by the British Prime Minister, who seemed immediately to commit Britain fully to support the United States in its war against terrorism.

It is generally agreed that the September 11th atrocity changed the international scene. Other almost as destructive terrorist attacks followed in Madrid, Spain, London and elsewhere, causing Western governments to assert that now such atrocities might occur anywhere in the world without warning. New laws were passed in Britain and America empowering them to detain suspects indefinitely and, in other ways to restrain them without charge or trial, violating democratic principles of civil rights.

The United States imprisoned hundreds of war captives from Afghanistan at Guantanamo Bay without charge, without access to civil courts or legal representation, and for an indefinite period. In many ways it began to look as if the terrorists were succeeding in disrupting Western democracy.

The authority of the United Nations, dubious as it ever was, was further damaged when Tony Blair persuaded President Bush to seek a resolution of the Security Council authorising military force against Saddam Hussein before the appointed arms inspectors had completed their work. France, Russia and China recommended giving the inspectors more time, and the French threatened to veto any resolution authorising military action before the arms inspectors had submitted their final report. The British and Americans then withdrew their proposal and proceeded forthwith to attack Iraq.

Officially the Iraqi war was short and, for the Western Coalition, successful. But the attempts to settle the country under a democratically elected Iraqi government was derailed by continuous guerrilla attacks on American and other foreign forces, on humanitarian organizations, and the interim government. Within less than three months before the announced general election for a democratic government in Iraq, senior American officials have estimated that the strength of insurgency against American and Iraqi forces had grown to 20,000, counting foreign fighters and the network of supporters of the Jordanian militant Abu Musab al-Zarqawi, and have said that the core of the insurgency consisted of at least 50 militant cells with access to unlimited finances from underground sources. Since the official US withdrawal, the country remains in chaos. This is the result of a war started on the pretext that Saddam was hoarding weapons of mass destruction which were never uncovered in Iraq, so it seems that the war had been undertaken on what amounts to false pretenses.

Apart from all this, other crises still beset the region. The conflict between the Israelis and the Palestinians has, in one way or another, been ongoing ever since the establishment of the state of Israel. The so-called "road map to peace" proposed by the Americans has been bypassed and is generally believed dead as the result of the continuing feud between the Israelis and Palestinian suicide bombers, each in turn provoking violent response from the other. The Israeli punitive attacks have been and invariably are excessive and the loss of life, deplorable on both sides, is far greater among the Palestinians.

Israel has ignored Security Council resolutions aiming at pacifying the situation and has long been known to possess nuclear weapons in disregard of the Non-Proliferation Treaty. Yet no sanctions have been proposed nor has any pressure been exerted against her, as they have against Iraq; no suggestion has ever been mooted of an attack by NATO (as was made in Kosovo), and the action and influence of such UN peacekeeping forces as have been stationed in Israel have been more or less invisible. This is due to the persistent support of Israel by the United States, in its turn resulting from pressures in that country from the Jewish lobby and their effect on the possible results of American elections. It is more than likely that the Israeli-Palestine situation is the root cause of the current outbreak of world terrorism against America and her western allies.

While the Middle East remains the cockpit of the world crisis in the first decade of the twenty-first century, it is by no means the only source of tension. North Korea's refusal to accept the Non-Proliferation Treaty and its resistance to demands for international inspection of its nuclear facilities is a serious cause for anxiety, not only in Japan and the Far East, but just as much in the West.

Troubles in the Russian federation,Russian Federation particularly with Chechnya and the Ukraine, have provoked the most appalling terrorist activities. Genocide and widespread atrocities in western Sudan causing the flight of millions of refugees into Chad, have resulted in a major humanitarian crisis, and have produced negotiations with the United Nations but with few ameliorative results.

America has come to consider itself the champion and defender of democracy throughout the world. And in this capacity President Bush has revived the American anti-missile strategy which constitutes a renewed threat to world peace, as many believe it to be as much a means of preemptive attack as of defence. The nations, wherever they can, continue to augment their military capabilities, maintaining the trend towards a persistent arms race, and the prospect of world peace seems as distant as ever. Such is the general world situation in the opening decade of the new century

3.2   Weapons of Mass Destruction

THE end of the Cold War relieved mankind of the appalling threat of preemptive nuclear conflict, a strategy advocated by Hermann Kahn and seriously considered at one time in the American Pentagon.[1] But we should be gravely wrong to believe that the danger from nuclear weapons is no longer with us. The nuclear menace is far from having been eliminated.

---

[1]See E.E. Harris, *Annihilation and Utopia* (London, G. Allen and Unwin, 1966), Ch.VII.

At one time it was necessary to argue at some length to persuade most people that a major nuclear war would exterminate humanity, either immediately or in the longer term (as the result of its after-effects). Later, the prediction of a nuclear winter as the consequence of such a war was generally accepted and there was no further need, in order to convince the public that nuclear war is to be avoided at all cost, to expatiate on the widespread and catastrophic destruction from blast and fall-out that would result, or the total disruption of organized (or even disorderly) life, or the reduction and poisoning of food supplies, or the devastation of everything that makes survival feasible.[2]

Now, however, this threat has receded, although it has by no means been altogether removed. It has receded because of the foresight and wisdom of the one great statesman of the age who had the courage to take the necessary practical steps to bring about international *detente:* Mikhail Gorbachev, whose introduction into the Soviet Union of *glaznost* and *perestroika* transformed the face of Europe and put an end to the Cold War.

It was on his initiative that a hectoring American President (who had likened the Soviets to "the Evil Empire") was persuaded to agree to sign the first significant disarmament treaty in history and to set afoot the movement to reduce nuclear arsenals. Presidents Bush Sr. and Yeltsin pledged themselves to reduce the numbers of nuclear warheads yet more drastically, and even suggested the substitution of a cooperative means of security for the American Strategic Defence Initiative.

George W. Bush has done much to reverse this initiative by reviving the project of missile defence but, on the whole, the situation is now very different from what it was in the nineteen eighties. The threat of nuclear holocaust that had come so close is now less imminent, and the doomsday clock, which was already pointing to within five minutes to midnight, has been set back a quarter

---

[2]Cf. E.E.Harris, The Survival of Political Man (Witwatersrand University Press, Johannesburg, 1950), Introduction, and Annihilation and Utopia (G. Allen and Unwin, London, 1966), Ch. I and the Constitution.

of an hour or so.

Nevertheless, the nuclear menace still hangs over us. The United States and the new Commonwealth of Independent Republics retain thousands of warheads, quite sufficient, if used, to produce the deprecated effects. Neither Britain nor France has shown any intention of abandoning or reducing their so-called nuclear deterrent (why "so-called" will presently appear). India and Pakistan have recently acquired nuclear missiles, and Iraq, before the first Gulf War, came perilously near to doing so. Israel has long been known to have them, China also has developed nuclear capability, and there are other countries still aspiring to belong to the nuclear elite.

The problem of proliferation remains and nobody has yet devised any method of prevention. The newly independent republics that constituted the former Soviet Union have not all given firm assurances that they will forego the possession and use of nuclear weapons, and in dire economic predicaments they are quite likely to try to dispose of such expertise and materials as they may have to other nations eager and able to buy them for hard currency. Problems arising from the circumstances surrounding the break-up of the Soviet Union were both numerous and complicated, and the disposal, or use, of nuclear weapons is among them.

Moreover, the danger that nuclear explosives may fall into the hands of terrorists has become more imminent. A nuclear device capable of wiping out a major city can be carried in a suitcase, and suicide bombers are proliferating all too rapidly.

The possibility of accidents of the Three Mile Island, Chernobyl or Fukushima variety is very real. Many nuclear devices belonging to the former Soviet republics are said to be in poor and hazardous condition, with nobody able to prevent their further deterioration, nor any authority with adequate means to render them secure. The effects of any such accidents on the environment and on world ecology is virtually incalculable.

They can certainly not be confined within the borders of anyone country, nor can measures be taken by anyone government to remedy them. Not only nuclear but also chemical and biological weapons are well within the ability of any number of nations to develop, and the possibility of their exploitation by terrorists is exercising the minds of many western politicians.

3.3 The World Trade Center and Global Terrorism

THE atrocities committed on Sept 11th, 2001 by suicide terrorists who, without the use of sophisticated weapons, had hijacked civil aircraft and destroyed the World Trade Center in New York as well as a large section of the Pentagon in Washington, killing thousands of innocent people, was a turning point in the history of world security.

The American administration reacted to it as "an act of war" President Bush declared war on what he called "the evil Axis" of rogue nations. He was immediately joined and supported by the British Prime Minister, *neither of them, apparently, recognizing that terrorism is a crime and not an act of international warfare.* The wars on which they embarked against Afghanistan and, shortly after, Iraq, succeeding initially in removing the ruling regimes, but failed to locate the chief suspects, Osama bin Laden and Saddam Hussein, while being less successful in establishing new governments of which they approved.

Saddam Hussein was captured in December 2003 and executed for war crimes, crimes against humanity, and genocide in 2006 after what many consider to be a flawed and illegally conducted trial. The aftermaths of these wars have been exceedingly distressing for the peoples of the countries concerned, and the process of restoring law and order is proving difficult, tardy and painful.

There has been much debate among the western nations concerning the "legality" of these wars, especially the one against Iraq. Security Council Resolution 1441 unanimously approved "serious consequences" if the Iraqi administration failed to cooperate with weapon inspectors which the Council then appointed, and the unanimity was conditional on the omission of any mention of immediate military action.

The inspectors within weeks reported that the Iraqis were being cooperative and that they were making what they described as significant progress; but the United States and Britain made strenuous efforts to persuade the Council to authorize immediate military invasion of Iraq. When they failed they went ahead with the invasion without further UN authorization, in violation of international law.

What all this shows more than anything else is the absence in international relations of any effective rule of law and the impotence of the United Nations to control and regulate the actions of its sovereign members (hampered as it is by Article 2 of its Charter that commits it to respect their sovereign rights).

Consequently it is not only the "rogue states" and dictators like Saddam Hussein that are intransigent, but also reputedly "law abiding" nations like Great Britain and the United States that interpret International Law to suit their own ends (e.g. claiming that they are acting in self-defence) and pursue their own policies irrespective of UN approval.

3.4   The Economic Scene and the Question of Federalism

MEANWHILE world economics are, with few exceptions, in the doldrums, even the economies of the US, Japan and Germany are feeling the pinch. The collapse of the communist states of Central Europe and of the Soviet Union left these countries in the direst straits, seeking for help from the West to reconstruct their industries and to establish a market economy where none (apart from the black market) has existed for decades. Their currencies were for the most part worthless and inflation was on the rampage.

In Russia the people who have benefited most from the change of regime have been the Mafia. The western nations, on the other hand, have been experiencing a stubborn regression which, despite constant predictions of recovery has refused to "bottom out" or else is bumping along the bottom with little, if any, sign of an upturn. Collapse of the Stock Markets has so far made at most only tentative recovery and the crisis has been exacerbated by the September 11th terrorism (which has deterred people from air-travel), by the immense cost of the wars in Afghanistan and Iraq, and continuing international uncertainties. To make matters worse, the convulsions in the Middle East combined with increased demand from China and the prospect of reduced production in Russia have sent the price of oil soaring.

Consequently, there is no great hope that the West can do much to give assistance to developing lands or alleviate the strains and pressures experienced by third world countries burdened by intolerable debts. The World Trade Organization and the General Agreement on Tariffs and Trade have been struggling for years to create a viable world economic order, but until now disagreements between developing countries, the United States and Europe on farm subsidies and other issues have frustrated all efforts at an accord, although attempts to span what seem to be unbridgeable gaps continue.

The Germans are still struggling with the costs and administrative difficulties of unification, and like the French along with other countries are faced with problems of inflation, unemployment, and consequent growing resentment against immigrant workers and refugees seeking asylum. The flood of asylum seekers has been increased after the conflicts in the Balkans, by those in the Middle East, and by the conduct of military dictatorships elsewhere, creating a serious and virtually insoluble problem, especially for Great Britain.

Nations of the European Community have moved towards closer association and the new nations of the former Warsaw Pact have been admitted. The admission of those of the Free Trade Association has been approved, with the drafting of a new Constitution for Europe; but this has not escaped controversy between Britain and her neighbours. A unified currency has been introduced (the Euro), which Britain and some Scandinavian countries have not yet adopted. And in Britain there is as yet much dispute between Eurosceptics and Europhiles over future relations with the nations across the Channel: every suggestion of anything like a federal unity is deplored, for fear of losing the sovereign right of Parliament to make its own independent decisions and of the British Government to pursue its own chosen policies.

There is considerable confusion of thought about federal union among politicians and populace in the European Community. Resistance to closer unification derives from a natural fear of outside interference in domestic affairs, which, however, is just what genuine federal government is designed to avoid. The structure set up by the Treaty of Rome was not federal, nor was that proposed by the Maastricht Treaty. Resistance to closer union, in consequence, arises from the lack of democratic control over such institutions as the European Commission and the Council of Ministers.

Pressure for reform would be more appropriate if it concentrated on giving the European Parliament more power and making the executive bodies more responsible to it. What is also indispensable for proper federal government is a clear demarcation of matters of purely domestic concern that should be reserved to the states' jurisdictions from those of common interest to be taken over by federal authority.

A somewhat distorted recognition of this requirement is reflected in the talk of "subsidiarity"; nevertheless, deprecation by Eurosceptics of a United States of Europe, like the United States of America, is largely unreasoned and uninformed. Moreover, there are other federal models to be followed if need be, such as Switzerland, Canada and Australia; and there is nothing to prevent the adoption of new devices to meet special needs and local demands.

Meanwhile, present strains within the Community are prompted by devotion to what is really an outdated nationalism and an ill-founded belief in national independence which really no longer exists, *for in this century no nation is independent, economically, ecologically, or culturally.*

The undeveloped countries are economically in grave difficulties even greater than those experienced by economically more advanced nations—difficulties exacerbated by overwhelming debt, the interest on which alone is crippling their exchequers, even when they are not wracked by civil wars, debilitating poverty, or environmental chaos.

The drugs traffic defies all attempts to arrest its activities, and is, in some cases, closely bound up with the economic survival of the producing countries. As we have seen, many attempts to introduce change have a seriously detrimental effect on the environment, creating new threats to human survival.

There can be no question but that none of these difficulties can be averted, and none of the problems solved, without widespread cooperation between the presently established sovereign states, none of which, by itself, has either the jurisdiction, or the capacity to cope with them on its own. The likelihood and effectiveness of such cooperation is a matter we shall shortly discuss.

3.5 International Flashpoints

WHILE the relations between the greater powers have, since the late 1980s, become greatly improved, there are still dangerous tensions in different parts of the world. Relations between the now independent republics of the former Soviet Union are not yet by any means clear or satisfactory: occasions for violence and strife persist especially in Chechnya, Georgia, the Ukraine and their neighbors. The entire question of the command of the former Red Army and the organization of the previous Soviet defense system is still uncertain. Meanwhile, all the republics of the new Commonwealth and their neighbors who have not yet joined it have been suffering the most acute economic crisis, and have numerous potential causes for conflict and dispute.

In the Middle East, as has been noted above, acts of conflict and defiance recur and despite Presidents Bush and Obmana's "road map for peace" there is continuing and increasing violence between Israelis and Palestinians in a never ending circle of suicide bombing and disproportionate reprisal, rendering hopes of peace between Israel and her neighbors forlorn. The Israeli Prime Minister, Ariel Sharon, announced his intension to remove Israeli settlements and withdraw from the Gaza Strip, on condition that the illegal settlements on the West Bank remain and are augmented, and his successors Olmert and Netanyahu have continued similar policies. President Bush, with questionable wisdom or legitimacy endorsed this policy in flagrant violation of United Nations resolutions, while in Israel itself the policy has excited considerable controversy.

Subsequently the Israeli government has engaged in further unrestrained violence, bulldozing Palestinian homes and killing numerous civilians on the pretext of eliminating secret tunnels from Egyptian territory allegedly used by the Palestinians to smuggle in arms. President Obama continues to uncritically support Israel in spite of his claims to want peace. Elsewhere in the Middle East problems of settling the chaotic civil conditions in Iraq so far from having been solved have been made more acute by the revelation of gross maltreatment by American soldiers of Iraqi prisoners. Internal contradictions and conflicts in Iran still present the West with questions affecting relations with that country (unrelieved by the fact that George W. Bush has accused it of being one of "the axis of evil"), and what the future holds for Afghanistan is as yet highly questionable.

The most ominous threat, however, to the security not only of the Far East but to the world at large is the intransigent attitude of North Korea to the demand from America to refrain from developing nuclear weapons, which would threaten her immediate neighbour, South Korea (closely allied to the United States) and

Japan, along with others further afield.

The situation in Cambodia is extremely uncertain and perilous, and in Myanmar, where the tyranny of the military dictatorship seems to be quite unconscionable, there is repression and strife, while conditions for those in opposition to the government appear to be altogether appalling. Meanwhile Syria has exploded into civil war, generating immense suffering, many refugees, and civil chaos. In the Horn of Africa there has been continuous disastrous fighting and a very real threat of widespread famine.

In southern Sudan, the civil war has raged for many years and the condition of the surviving Christians and others is desperate. The Democratic Republic of Congo persists in the grip of violent civil strife, while President Mugabe of Zimbabwe reduced his country to economic collapse and his people to dire destitution by using the most extreme and barbarous methods to bring about land reform and of tyranny and dictatorship to cling on to power.

3.6 Persistent Perils

WHAT all this amounts to is that there are still many potential flash-points around the world where warfare already in progress could escalate, or could flare up where it is not yet occurring. That nuclear weapons, and certainly the threat of their use, might be involved is evident from the current anxieties of the major powers (repeatedly expressed by the American President, the British Prime Minister and Foreign Secretary), and the worries of the United States Administration about proliferation.

So while the arms race between superpowers has eased for the present, and has even, for a while, taken on the appearance of a competition between them to reduce arsenals, there remain prospects of new threats that might induce them to reverse this process of relaxation. The peace is threatened, not just by rogue nations, but by the anxiety and eagerness of the United States, the British and other governments to counter international terrorism, which they claim has become the most immediate, frightening and widespread danger of the modern world.

Moreover, governments change and with them policies; unexpected and unpredictable coups may at any time overturn existing well-intentioned regimes; so the nations continue to hold on to their military power and their ability to augment it. They profess and loudly advertise the need to keep up their guard.

Speaking on the Today Program of the BBC (August 22,1991) The then British Prime Minister, John Major, said: "The military defense of our own interests is of first importance to any government, and especially to a Conservative government." And his successor, Tony Blair, was equally convinced that any threat to Britain's security is to be met at all costs. The continuing militarist policies of Britain and the United States show this to be the case.

While economic difficulties are at the moment forcing some of the major powers to consider reducing their expenditure on defense, and the prevailing relaxation of tensions between superpowers following upon the end of the Cold War enables them to do so with comparative safety, if conditions change for the worse, against which there is no guarantee, this trend towards disarmament and *detente* may well be reversed. It is therefore not surprising that the foremost nations retain large numbers of nuclear weapons, quite sufficient, if they are ever used, to bring about disaster beyond what has ever been envisaged.

Accordingly, the threat of wholesale nuclear destruction (so appalling when considered in detail), although now less apparent, has not been removed, and the prospect for the human race remains as bleak as it ever has been since the Second World War. To discount or ignore this fact, simply because it is not at the moment obvious and seems to be more remote than it has been hitherto, would be as rash and as foolish as to dismiss, or be dilatory about, the environmental threat of ecological breakdown and climatic disaster. In this connection also, we should not forget the plight of the frog becoming comatose in water the temperature of which is gradually rising.

3.7 Obstacles to Amelioration

NEITHER of the above menaces can be adequately countered within the limits of jurisdiction of national sovereign states, a fact not always readily admitted by politicians; and when it is recognized, the resort is taken to diplomacy and international agreement.

This has the disadvantage that agreements are always between sovereign governments, which interpret their terms as they wish, often in conflicting and controversial ways (for instance, the Japanese insistence that their whaling is purely for scientific purposes), and always in accordance with what is seen by the party concerned as its national interest, so that the intended effect of the agreement is often nullified.

Even worse is the possibility that the parties to the agreement are free at any time to renounce it, and there is no lack of cases in which commitments have been simply ignored and treaties violated as happened to suit anyone of the signatories. In particular, the problem is ever-present how to supervise and detect infringements, which occur with abundant frequency even among apparently trustworthy parties.

Here the authority of the United Nations should come into play, though indeed in the past few years its influence seems to have been less effective than ever before. During the period of the Cold War, it could hardly ever perform its intended (or for that matter any significant) function, because resolutions of the Security Council, the main executive body, were constantly liable to the veto of one or other of the five permanent members, who belonged to opposing blocs on the political front.

So frustrating was this practice that many nations had desisted altogether from appealing to the Organization in cases of dispute or in circumstances of crisis. Since the cessation of the Cold War, the five permanent members of the Security Council have sometimes been in substantial agreement and have cooperated in an unprecedented manner, with the result that concerted action could be taken, for instance occasionally in dealing with Middle Eastern problems like those of the first Gulf War and the Palestinian predicament (both of which, however, have since deteriorated spectacularly). At other times, as when Britain and the US tried to get agreement on a second resolution authorizing war in Iraq, it was not forthcoming.

With the decline of the Soviet Union and Gorbachev's revolution in foreign affairs, the Security Council has become virtually an instrument of American foreign policy. Its members followed the recommendations of the United States Administration almost slavishly in the affair of the first war in the Persian Gulf, even when opinions differed between the members.

When it came to the determination of President Bush to attack Iraq on the pretexts that Saddam Hussein was defying Security Council resolutions and abetting terrorism, the Chinese, the Russians and several European countries (France, in particular) were far less bellicose than were President Bush and Tony Blair, and would have preferred to wait longer for weapons inspectors to report before resorting to force. The American and British determination to do so, however, led to military action irrespective of Security Council decisions. In the opinion of many, for what it is worth, the wars were waged more to serve American interest in the unhampered supply of oil than for the liberation of Kuwait or the discovery of weapons of mass destruction (which have not been found). Much the same happened in the dispute with Libya over bringing to trial suspected terrorists.

The demands of the United States, Britain and France prevailed over the objections of the Arab League and Third World states that supported Libya. The suggestion that the suspects should be brought before an international court (similar to that set up in Nuremburg after the Second World War) was scouted, and resort taken to sanctions, in preference to negotiations and conciliation. Eventually Gadaffy (hoping for the lifting of sanctions) gave in and handed over the suspects to be tried by a Scottish Court sitting at The Hague. He since went further (for much the same reasons) and renounced the use of weapons of mass destruction. In spite of Libya's cooperation in these matters, the western powers, led by the US, attacked Libya on the pretense of protecting human rights, driving the civil order of the Gadaffy regime out of power and introducing internal chaos and civil war to that country.

Consequently, the professed function of the United Nations, that of the peaceful settlement of disputes, has, in effect, been forsworn. The first major "success" of the United Nations after the end of the Cold War was the conduct of a war against Iraq to liberate Kuwait, which caused thousands of Iraqi and other Arab casualties, brought disaster to the immediate environment (from the burning of hundreds of oil wells), and left the main culprit, Saddam Hussein, in power to ravage the local Shiite and Kurdish populations. The use of military force with so-called "authorization" can hardly be described as peaceful, and without "authorization" (as in the more recent case) can neither keep the peace nor eliminate terrorism.

There is, however, no other way to enforce upon sovereign states either the rules of International Law, or the resolutions of the Security Council, than by war. Economic sanctions have to be backed by force if they are to be made effective and states seeking to break them can be prevented only by military threats. So in the last resort war is the only means to which recourse can be had. If Saddam Hussein had been a private miscreant acting illegally under municipal law, he could have been arrested, tried and dealt with according to its rules. But as the President of a sovereign state against which no such legal action is possible, he could be removed only by invading his country. The outcome has been that if his annexation of Kuwait as a fifth province of Iraq was to be opposed by more than words, or his suspected hoarding of mass-destructive weapons prevented, it would have to be by military conquest.

The other significant action of the United Nations since the end of the Cold War has been to convene the Middle East peace conference; and that was fraught throughout with disagreement between the parties and had scant prospect of success, largely because the United Nations' authority cannot effectively be exercised against the sovereign claims of Israel, which it is, by its Charter, committed to respect, and Israel continues to be intransigent about Palestinian representation, while the Palestinians and the Arab states demand the return of occupied territory (to which Israel refuses to agree) in return for peace. The facts that there is a strong Jewish lobby in America and that the United States is a firm ally of Israel, have not been inconsiderable in preventing the United Nations from taking the same kind of action when Israel has refused to respect Security Council resolutions as it has done against Iraq and Libya.

The success of negotiations for the release of Western hostages in Lebanon, conducted with the good offices of the Secretary General of the United Nations, was the result of several factors. First, the Western governments could not negotiate directly, for they had abjured all negotiation with terrorists; so a neutral intermediary was indispensable. Second, the national interest of Iran, whose influence with the hostage holders was paramount, required better economic and diplomatic relations with the West after the withdrawal of support by the Soviet Union. It is significant that these negotiations produced little result by way of the release of Lebanese hostages (in particular Sheikh Obeid) held by Israel, whose perceived national interests lay elsewhere. Neither the United Nations nor any state government has been able to prevent hostage taking in Iraq nor to save the victims from the most savage forms of murder.

The United Nations can sponsor international conferences on the environment as well as on the settlement of disputes, and occasionally it does so, but whatever is agreed in such conventions is subject to the limitations that we have already noticed. Much the same applies to even more authoritative scientific conferences, the recommendations of which are seldom met with any very enthusiastic response by governments; and even when some deference is paid to them the action taken is usually niggardly and insufficient, as exemplified by the United States' reluctance to accept the recommendations made by the Intergovernmental Panel on Climate Change with respect to carbon dioxide emissions.

The reason for this is that perceived national interests are always given precedence over global needs by the governments affected, especially where industrial lobbies are strong and active. The much publicized agreement on climate change reached to boost the Earth Summit in Rio was lamentably deficient in its failure to set any date for the stabilization of CO_2 emissions, and inasmuch as it was not legally binding, it was virtually useless. The subsequent environmental summits in Tokyo, South Africa, and Copenhagen have produced nothing better.

At the 1992 summit meeting of the Security Council proposals were made clearly aimed at restoring some of the almost forgotten aims of the United Nations. President Mitterand of France proposed the establishment of an international rapid deployment army to be used in cases of threatened conflict. The suggestion, which, after all, is only a reminder of what the Charter originally laid down in Articles XLII-XLV, was not received by other members of the Council with any great enthusiasm, and if it had been, it may have raised awkward questions. First and foremost, one might ask, how would a rapid deployment military force prevent conflict otherwise than by threatening conflict, supposing, as is necessary, that it is to be deployed against sovereign nations?

Next, it should be questioned, under whose command and direction would such a force be employed? Long ago, soon after the United Nations had been founded, I suggested that the "teeth" with which its original founders were reputed to provide the Organization (and which never were provided) could only be false teeth, because their provision would be at the discretion of its sovereign members, who could be forced to comply only by the means they themselves agreed to supply. I predicted that, for this reason, no international force would be forthcoming,[3] a pre-

---

[3]See *The Survival of Political Man*, pp. 106f

diction that proved to be correct. Perhaps, then, we should not be very surprised that President Mitterand's proposal was not endorsed, and that once again the emphasis has been given to the old (and somewhat outworn) idea of "collective security."

In this connection Boris Yeltsin proposed that the nuclear nations should cooperate in the development of space-based defences against the use of ballistic missiles, and the merging of developments already made by Russia and the United States. Once again, his proposal was not taken up, least of all by President Bush (Snr), who had evident interest in retaining an exclusive hold on the American SDI.

But if the idea had been accepted the question would remain whether such a system of space-based defence were really as purely defensive as is professed, or if it might not become an even more potent means of first-strike offence against any who could not take advantage of it. Moreover, the further question of how, and by whom it would be controlled and used, remains to be answered.

John Major declared that the United Nations should henceforth take steps to prevent situations of tension from developing into open conflict. This was its original purpose, and its Charter provides the means, although seldom, if ever, has it succeeded in the past in nipping critical situations in the bud. It is not clear even now how Mr. Major's demand could be met, or what new provision he had in mind.

Various reforms of the Security Council have been adumbrated: the inclusion of Japan among its permanent members, the admission of Germany, and an Indian proposal for further changes in the permanent membership. These suggestions were all provisional, and only the future could determine whether any of them would be implemented, or what effect, if they were, they would have on the operation and effectiveness of the international body. Their reception was somewhat half-hearted, and what is fairly patent is that they all derive from the assertion by the nations most closely affected Gapan, India, and any others that may be similarly concerned) of their national interests and presumed rights. They would not have affected the veto right of the permanent members, unless it were intended to extend it to others as well, which was hardly likely.

There does not appear to be any great prospect of significant change, therefore, in the effectiveness of the United Nations with respect to peace keeping and the pacific settlement of disputes, apart from advantages gained from the (temporary?) rapprochement between the super-powers. But, if the ultimate threat of nuclear disruption of the environment and even of final holocaust is to be effectively countered, some greater assurance than the United Nations has hitherto offered is urgently needed and absolutely indispensable.

Undoubtedly, some of the critical situations existing around the world can be mitigated by means already at hand. It has been possible, for example, to end the conflict in Mozambique by measures similar to those that ended the civil war in Angola, and similar mediation has been able to bring peace to Somalia. The Yugoslavian civil strife has been pacified by the intervention of peace-keeping forces from both the European Community and the United Nations.

Nevertheless, many of the minor issues are closely connected with latent, or overt, power struggles between the major powers, which cannot themselves be so easily resolved. This review of the state of the nations makes it clear that war is still raging in many parts of the world, is commonly resorted to by nations that feel their "vital interests" to be threatened, and that wherever it occurs there is potential risk of escalation—a risk that in these days we cannot afford to take, because the ultimate outcome may involve the use of weapons of mass destruction including nuclear bombs. If that happens there is likely to be only one outcome: the total destruction of human civilization and possibly even more, the extinction of life on the planet. War of any kind, therefore, ought to be avoided like a plague, and some means of peaceful settlement of international disputes has become indispensable if survival is reliably to be assured.

Further, it should be clearly apparent that the chief problems of maintaining world-peace, and of conserving the environment cannot be met except by global action and international cooperation, which is so difficult to come by that efforts to secure it seem almost always to end in frustration. Why should this be so?

The answer lies in one word: Sovereignty. Because nations are sovereign, they view their national interests as paramount, and for each these take precedence over global requirements that are seldom fully appreciated, are often controversial, and are only vaguely, if at all, recognized. Consequently, agreements are reached, when they are, only with difficulty, and they are always precarious, for reasons some of which have already been indicated. The problem is so deep-seated, and is so rarely understood or admitted, and its necessary consequences are so grave, that it deserves separate treatment in a special chapter devoted to a detailed discussion.

Chapter 4

Sovereignty and Power Politics

4.1 The Aim of the Discussion

THE object of this chapter is not simply theoretical, it is to make clear the implications and practical consequences of the universal claim by the nations of the world to sovereign independence and the aspiration to it of peoples of kindred ethnic origin—Bosnians, Serbs, Croats, Scots, Kurds, Chechnyans, et al.—in an age when no nation or ethnic group is independent, economically, culturally, linguistically, medically, or for that matter, politically. Of course, the nature of sovereignty is not wholly independent of past theoretical ideas and postulations, but my purpose is to draw attention (nowadays sorely lacking) to the practical consequences of a political reality.

To guard against diversion of attention to side issues, therefore, and distraction by red herrings, it is best to state at the outset just what is the aim of this discussion—not just its primary aim, but its sole aim. Having reviewed the state of the planet and of the nations by whom it is inhabited, and having found that mankind is facing the most dire prospect of decimation from environmental catastrophe, if not from the apocalyptic ravages of nuclear war, (or possibly from both), our object is to discover what feasible remedy is available to the people of the world for the ills that threaten this denouement to the history of the human race.

It is clear that the measures to be adopted must be global in scope, and that nothing less will avail. It is equally clear that nothing national sovereign states can do will be sufficient and that the least that has any promise of success can be achieved only through comprehensive international action; the measures to be adopted must be global in scope. So our central question is how this can be brought about, not just eventually in the distant future, but immediately.

For deterioration of the environment has already advanced so far, and its reversal is already so precarious, that the time at our disposal is extremely limited and the urgency of the problems is acute.

4.2 Sovereignty

IT is not my intention at this juncture, therefore, to discuss at any length the theory of sovereignty, which has a long history, and many versions of which have been proposed in the past. I shall not recall them now, nor any, such as may be, that are entertained at present. I have done this before in *The Survival of Political Man* and in *Annihilation and Utopia*[1] All that needs mention here are the salient points:

> (1) Every organized social system, to be effective and successful, requires the observance of laws regulating the conduct of its members.
>
> Such laws must be known, administered interpreted and enforced, and any disputes concerning them must be adjudicated by an impartial authority, which is paramount and whose pronouncements and decisions are final.

---

[1]*The Survival of Political Man*, Ch.II, and *Annihilation and Utopia*, Ch.III.

> Every such society, therefore, must be ruled by a sovereign body, be it monarch, president, assembly, or some constitutional order involving several such institutions, which legislates, promulgates, adjudicates and enforces the law.
>
> (2) The sovereignty of such a body involves two essential features: (a) power, unchallengeable by any private person, individual or corporate; and (b) authority derivative from the consent, the approval (tacit or overt), or at least the acquiescence of the majority of its subjects.
>
> The condition of such approval is, in the long run, the service by the policies of the government of the interests of the nation, among which security is universally taken to be one of the most vital. These two aspects of sovereignty I have in the past called the juristic and the ethical.[2]

Law, to be real and effective, must be enforceable. It is not sufficient merely to pronounce and codify rules if there are no sanctions applicable when they are transgressed. However reasonable and law-abiding most people may be, they are always subject to the temptation to prefer their own advantage to that of others, there are always differences of opinion about the interpretation (and so about the requirement) of the law, and there are always those who, even if a minority, will attempt to evade or to violate the law in what they take to be their own interest, and so to hold others to ransom. Accordingly, if the law is to serve its purpose efficiently, some degree of force is needed to ensure compliance.

There can be no doubt that at the present time the independent nations of the world arrogate to themselves sovereign jurisdiction, and the international community recognizes a nation as independent only when it can be seen as competent to maintain law and order among its people, that is, when it is clearly sovereign.

In this respect, its sovereignty is viewed as paramount There is no internal authority that can rightfully challenge it, and none that can, without insurrection, resist it. Its supremacy in law is not questioned, and the hold on power of the government of the day

---

[2]Cf. Ibid.

is dependent ultimately only on acceptance by its subjects and the adequacy of its defence against invasion by which alone it can be threatened from without.

This is the firm view adopted in International Law, as has been stated by Dr. H. Lauterpacht: "The sovereign State does not acknowledge a central executive above itself; it does not recognize a legislation above itself; it owes no obedience to a judge above itself.[3] And in judgment of the Palmas case (1928), we have the following definition:

> Sovereignty in the relations between States signifies independence. Independence in regard to a portion of the globe is the right to exercise therein, to the exclusion of any other State, the functions of a State....

Should anybody object that these pronouncements are more than half a century old, we need only point to the practices of contemporary states and their attitude to any attempt to interfere in their internal affairs (for instance, China, with respect to its action in Tienanmin Square; Iraq, with respect to its annexation of Kuwait, or its treatment of its Kurdish and Shiite subjects; Israel, with respect to its treatment of Palestinians and the establishment of settlements in the occupied territories) to show that the judgments are not out of date.

Such developments as the European Parliament and the EEC Commission in Brussels do not contradict them, for the submission by member states of the European Community to the decisions of these institutions follows upon treaty arrangements, agreed by the sovereign nations concerned, and are enforced only by their own governments subject to such qualifications as their sovereignty demands.

---

[3]Cf. H. Lauterpacht, *The Function of International Law in the International Community* (Oxford, Clarendon Press 1933), p. 64

4.3 Security and Vital Interests

IT is obvious that the government of every state with sovereign independence will give precedence, in fact, will devote itself exclusively to the furtherance of its national interests, and as it can do so only as long as the state remains independent, its first and overriding concern must be its means of defence against attack and aggression from foreign sources.

Security, therefore, is always the paramount consideration of independent sovereign nations, and each attempts to acquire and to maintain as strong a military capability as it can. Other states are, for reasons which will presently become progressively more apparent, potential opponents, especially those closest to the home state's borders. Hence Pakistan's hostility to India, India's to China, Indonesia's suspicion of Australia, and China's uncertain relations with Russia.

When wealth or population is inadequate for any state to maintain from its own resources sufficient forces for its safety, it seeks to ally itself with some stronger power, with which its interests most nearly coincide. The structure of alignments, in consequence, tends to take the form of opposing blocs, each regarding the other as the potential enemy.

4.4 The Balance of Power

THE natural consequence is a continual effort in international relations to maintain a balance of power, such that each state, or each bloc, is able to threaten the other just sufficiently to deter attack, and when any power seeks to increase its military strength and to aggrandize itself sufficiently to seem able more easily to overpower its rivals, its potential opponent immediately seeks to increase its own power to prevent this. The inevitable result is an arms race to which there is no reliable antidote.

Even the persisting need merely to keep weapons up to date stimulates competition, scientific and technological advances fuel the rivalry still further, and tensions are always, in consequence, liable to rise, and crises to recur, until finally the ever-teetering balance is upset and the nations are engulfed in conflict.

The history of the past two centuries copiously illustrates the truth of these statements. It has been one of successive great wars, interspersed with crises, threats, and innumerable minor wars, always, in one way or another, aiming to maintain the balance of power, a balance which is constantly unstable and always threatening to break down, because one side or the other is forever seeking to gain an advantage. So Europe went from the Napoleonic wars (to go back no farther) to the Balkan wars, to the Crimean war and to the Franco-Prussian War, and thence to the Great War involving most of the important nations of the world. What was called "the war to end all wars" proved to be no more than the curtain-raiser to a fresh period of minor conflicts and crises, that eventually sparked off the Second World War.

Since then, the pattern has not really changed; there have been more than 150 wars the world over since 1945, and between the superpowers and their respective allies a so-called cold war varying from time to time in intensity. That, for reasons largely economic, has now come to an end, at least for the present, but there is by no means any reliable assurance that the general pattern will not continue.

The new name for the balance of power policy is "deterrence" implying that the possession of nuclear weapons has somehow made a difference. But this is by no means the case. The aim is still to maintain a balance, now recognized as a balance of terror, which is, as ever, unstable and is apt to be upset not only by political changes but even by a technical breakthrough in weaponry; so "deterrence" is never a guarantee against the outbreak of war. If the weapons of the combatants happen to be those of widespread destruction, so much is the danger of world-wide catastrophe increased.

No doubt, the threat of a nuclear onslaught may make nations more reluctant to resort to force if that is avoidable, but the possession of nuclear weapons does not prevent them from using that threat in the conduct of their affairs whenever they think it necessary.

That is precisely what the policy of deterrence amounts to. And no threat is credible unless there is a firm intention to carry it out. So what is called deterrence only makes the outbreak of nuclear war more probable rather than less, if resort to conventional weapons should prove insufficient to procure victory or to avert defeat.

The assumption frequently made that the possession of nuclear weapons by the major powers is what has prevented the outbreak of another world war is specious. Although we have been spared that cataclysm for over sixty years, that is no historical precedent. Nearly a hundred years intervened between the battle of Waterloo and the First World War, during which nobody had dreamt of nuclear weapons. Of the numerous wars that have occurred since 1945 any might have escalated into a major conflagration, and no country possessing nuclear capability will refrain from using it if it is attacked and is unable to prevail with the use of conventional weapons alone.

In the sixties writers like Hermann Kahn sought to make it credible that a nuclear war could be won and survived, contradicting the assumption that the prospect of nuclear retaliation would always deter a prospective aggressor; and the strategies worked out by the Pentagon in Washington contemplated preventive strikes which brought the world perilously near the fatal brink.

Moreover, the technologies involved in the delivery of the weapons has become so sophisticated and sensitive that the accidental triggering of a nuclear attack has been made ever more likely, be the supposed deterrent effect what it may.

4.5   Treaties

THE validity of treaties and the assurance they might offer is profoundly affected by the sovereign independence of their signatories. Never have treaty obligations been respected beyond what the participants consider is in their national interests. The most respectable statesmen have declared that the violation of treaty requirements is justified whenever necessary to preserve the "vital interests" of the nation;[4] both Presidents Theodore Roosevelt and Woodrow Wilson maintained that a nation could renounce a treaty at any time it thought fit, and the pages of history are littered with examples of wanton transgression and abrogation of treaties by signatories who no longer found them advantageous, as well as of arbitrary interpretations of the terms of a treaty by the participants to suit their own interests. In the seventeenth century, Charles II of England, having made an alliance with Sweden and the Netherlands in 1688, in 1771 signed the secret Treaty of Dover and in the following year joined with Louis XIV of France in a war against Holland. In 1818 the Quadruple Alliance of Russia, Prussia, Austria and Britain solemnly declared an "unchangeable resolution never to depart, either among themselves or in their relations with other states, from the strictest observations of the Principles of the Law of Nations."

But in 1831 the Czar suppressed the Kingdom of Poland which had been set up at the Congress of Vienna by a treaty of which Russia was a signatory. Later Britain destroyed a Turkish fleet without any declaration of war, and Prussia overran the Duchies of Schlezwig and Holstein without pretext or title. These are not isolated examples; since then, treaties have repeatedly been decried and treated as "scraps of paper" when they became an embarrassment or a hindrance to any signatory. Kaiser Wilhelm II of Germany tore up the treaty obliging him to refrain from invading a neutral Belgium, and Hitler's disregard of treaty obligations

---

[4]Cf. the public statements of prominent political figures quoted in *The Survival of Political Man*, p.53.

was notorious, when he reoccupied the Saar, invaded Czecho-Slovakia (having acquired the Sudetenland, which included the natural defences of the country) after undertaking to respect its independence, and attacked the Soviet Union after having signed a non-aggression pact with Stalin in 1939. Other similar cases are plentiful enough and would not be difficult to cite. But let these suffice.

However law-abiding and trustworthy the government of any country may seem, a change of regime, a coup, or a revolution can at any time transform its attitude to its past commitments; so treaties are always precarious and their observance can never be relied upon.

The hallowed principle in International Law, *pacta sunt servanda*, thus becomes a dead letter. It always was in any case qualified by the proviso that all conventions were to be understood as holding only if "things remained the same." Nor is there any sanction that can be applied against sovereign states in cases of violation except retaliation, reprisals of some kind, with or without military action. Treaties are thus never a reliable hedge against war and are little more than a provisional and temporary resource for the procurement of advantage among parties whose national interests happen, for the time being, to concur. There can never be any assurance that agreements between sovereign states, even although they are reached only when the interests of the parties are served, will be observed in the future.

Although all treaties are supposed to be registered with the United Nations, that cannot guarantee that they will be observed, because the parties are always sovereign states that have absolute discretion to interpret the terms as they think fit, or to abrogate the treaty at will, and have no compunction, when they consider their sovereign interests to be threatened, about simply ignoring their acknowledged commitments, usually on some pretext alleged to be permitted by International Law. Because the United Nations Charter is itself no more than a treaty, it cannot prevent these blatant aberrations from the professed norm, the more so in that, like

International Law itself, it acknowledges the sanctity of sovereign rights and is committed (by Article 2 of its Charter) to uphold and to respect the sovereign independence of its members.

4.6   Disarmament

THE implications for disarmament of this unreliability of the sanctity of treaties are momentous. Disarmament is practicable in the circumstances we have outlined only by means of international agreements. Unilateral action, were it to be taken, would leave the country concerned vulnerable to attack by any aggressor that felt strong enough to invade it. In short, it would expose itself to the risk of losing its sovereign independence. Disarmament by states remaining sovereign and independent, therefore, can only be brought about by treaty arrangement. But conformity with treaties can never be ensured unless by the threat or exercise of military action. Other forms of "pressure" are always liable to prove ineffective if they are not backed by force, and that requires the maintenance of arsenals.

But if the treaty concerned is designed to limit the very instruments of applying such force, it cancels out the only means at the disposal of the parties of ensuring its observance. The natural result is that never in history had any genuine disarmament treaty been concluded until the 1980s, when Gorbachev and Reagan agreed to dispense with their intermediate ballistic missiles; and even that accord has been criticized as an agreement to do no more than forego the use of weapons already obsolete and dispensable in the strategies currently being adopted by their military advisors—as if the prospective combatants in the First World War had agreed to abolish the use of flintlocks.

Disarmament treaties are, therefore, self-stultifying. If they are concluded, observance can never be confidently anticipated, and the only available method of providing against their violation is what the treaties themselves seek to restrict or abolish.

4.7 International Law

THE insecurity of international agreements has far-reaching effects upon the relations between states. By it, International Law is rendered nugatory whenever vital national interests come into play. International law, has no firmer status than that of a treaty, for its foundation is no other than the Hague and Geneva Conventions.

Learned treatises on the subject, from Grotius to the present day, are often brilliant, ingenious, and instructive, but they give the law no force, and even when deference is made to them by the sovereign powers it is entirely conditioned by the purpose it may (or may not) serve for immediate national interests.

International law, therefore, is not effective (positive) law, and is observed only when perceived vital national interests are not infringed, or when reciprocal benefits are expected.

Moreover, the very idea of international law is a standing contradiction, because, as we have seen, sovereign nations are, by their very sovereign nature, subject to no law superior to their own (and they can alter that, or even contravene it at will, if external affairs make demands at variance with those of internal policies), they cannot then be subject to International Law.

Yet the Permanent Court of International Justice, advising the League of Nations in 1923, stated that the recognition of sovereign independence of states was "a fundamental principle of international law"; and it is a primary stipulation of International Law itself that its sole subjects are sovereign states. Thereby it renders itself ineffective.

It is not surprising, then, that its provisions are disregarded by the nations whenever they find them inconvenient or disadvantageous, and that international courts can operate only when the parties to any dispute submitted to them agree to abide by the court's decisions (which is not often); and even then, if any of the litigants decides that the verdict goes against its national interests, it will reject the final judgment.

South Africa and the United States, to name only these, have at various times refused to respect the judgment of the International Court of Justice, or even to agree in advance to submit to its jurisdiction; and many disputes over what are primarily legal rights (like that between Great Britain and Argentina concerning the Falkland Islands, or Malvinas) so far from being submitted to the International Court of Justice, are settled in preference by resort to war. In short, international law does not and cannot regulate the conduct of states, except when it suits them; so, in international relations the Rule of Law does not and cannot prevail.

The authority of the United Nations suffers accordingly, for its Charter too is no better than a treaty, and it lays down in the first two of its Articles that it is "based on the sovereign equality of all its members." The resolutions of the Security Council are subject to the veto of anyone of its permanent members, and when that has not nullified its operation, its decisions have been treated with contempt, whenever it has suited the purposes of those affected (for example, the United States, Israel, Iraq, Iran, South Africa and others).

In consequence, during the Cold War period, the influence of the United Nations was reduced to insignificance, and even after the tension between the Soviet Union and the West had come to an end, was defied by Saddam Hussein until one devastating war forced him to submit and another forced him out of power.

4.8   Power Politics

BECAUSE of its impotence to regulate effectively the conduct of international affairs, the activities of the nations under the eagis of the United Nations is what has been described as power politics in disguise.[5] This is an apt description, for its transactions, especially in the Security Council, are simply the manoeuvring of the sovereign powers in the pursuit of their national interests.

---

[5]Cf. *The Survival of Political Man*, Ch. V.

Schwartzenberger has given a detailed account and analysis of such moves, and the recent events in the Gulf present a typical example, where American, British and European interests in the supply of oil and the support of Israel demanded by the powerful Jewish lobby in the United States dictated the policies pursued by the coalitions that conducted the wars against Iraq. In fact, the main function of the United Nations is to provide a forum for negotiation rather than a court of appeal for the adjudication of disputes, or for the implementation of legal requirements.

These negotiations are no different from what goes on habitually under the name of diplomacy in all international affairs. And that is simply power politics—to which Clausewitz referred when he declared that "war is politics carried on by other means." We might say with equal truth that international politics are war carried on by other means.

The question might be raised why the original founders of the United Nations would have gone to so much trouble to constitute the organization if it could provide nothing better than common diplomacy. The answer is largely historical. The shock of the First World War induced the great powers to establish some kind of treaty arrangement that might possibly prevent the recurrence of so debilitating a conflict. President Wilson, in particular, sought to set up an international body that would direct the influence of the stronger nations to the deterrence of aggressive acts by the smaller powers such as might spark off larger conflicts, as had the tensions between Austria and Serbia in 1914.

So the League of Nations was conceived and constituted. But Wilson was seen in his own country as a starry-eyed idealist, and the succeeding United States Administration reverted to a more isolationist policy, refusing to join the League that had been created in large measure through the influence of its former President.

Then, when in 1939 the League finally and signally failed of its purpose, critics concluded that the causes were, first, the absence of the United States from among its members, and, secondly, the

League's lack of means to enforce its decisions. These were not the real causes of its failure, which was due rather to the exercise of the sovereign rights of its members.[6]

After the Second World War, a fresh determination to outlaw aggression and the resort to force in international disputes issued in the repetition of the same sort of undertaking, with strong American backing and the proposal of an international military force provided by the members to give the organization "teeth" with which to enforce observance of its decisions.

But these "teeth" never materialized for predictable reasons, and the veto provisions in the Security Council subjected it to frustration at the will of any of the major powers. In truth, the states by whose agreement the Charter was endorsed never intended to abjure their sovereign rights, and so could be persuaded to join nothing better than a treaty organization such as the United Nations has proved to be.

In its subordinate institutions the international organization does much valuable work, and at times agreements involving peace-keeping forces are reached that are helpful in cases of local conflict (as, for example, in Cyprus); but the United Nations, as long as its members remain sovereign and while its Charter commits it to uphold and respect their sovereign independence, is powerless to interfere in their internal affairs. Accordingly, it cannot legislate or enforce its resolutions (of whatever kind) to ensure the adoption of global measures capable of averting either planetary ecological and climatic disaster or serious threats to world peace.

The character of power politics follows from the facts and circumstances that have thus far been set out. Because states are sovereign and are therefore not subject to any superior regulation or enforcement, there is strictly no such thing as international order, but properly speaking only anarchy and disorder, in which, as

---

[6]Cf. G. Schwartzenberger, *Power Politics* (London, Stevens and Sons Ltd., 1951), Second Ed., Part II; *The Survival of Political Man*, Chs. IV, V, and VI; *Annihilation and Utopia*, Ch. VI.

Thucydides expressed it, "The question of justice arises only between equals in power, the strong do what they can and the weak
suffer what they must."[7] For the balance of power is perpetually
changing and unstable, treaties are unreliable, and alliances are
untrustworthy.

The awareness of these facts is always present, consciously or
unconsciously, to the minds of politicians. They are therefore always suspicious of the policies of foreign nations and always in-
sistent upon the need to maintain their armaments and look to
their defences. All other states are regarded, in varying degrees,
as potential enemies; even present allies may, in the event of a
coup, a revolution, or simply a change of government, come to be
hostile. Consequently, as Thomas Hobbes recognized long ago:

> ....in all times, Kings and Persons of Sovereign Author-
> ity, because of their independency, are in continual jeal-
> ousies, and in the state and posture of Gladiators; hav-
> ing their weapons pointing and eyes fixed on one another;
> that is their Forts, Garrisons and Guns upon the Frontiers
> of their Kingdoms; and continual Spyes upon their neigh-
> bours; which is a posture of War.[8]

This opinion has been repeated by Spinoza[9] and Hegel[10], and
at the present time by theorists such as Hans Morgenthau,[11] and
the conditions they describe persist to this day. The relations
between states may thus rightly be described as power politics.
In such circumstances no independent nation can afford to neglect its defences and the first obligation of its leaders is to look
to its moat. The overriding consideration of governments and
the main aim of their policies is the acquisition, or the maintenance of power. Their motives in all international transactions are

---

[7]Thucydides, *The Peloponnesian War*, Ch. V.

[8]Thomas Hobbes, *Leviathan*, Ch. XIII.

[9]Cf. B de Spinoza, *Tractatus Politicus*, Ch. III, 13.

[10]Cf. G.W.F. Hegel, Grundlinien der Philosophie des Rechts, Sections 330-
350.

[11]Cf. Hans Morgenthau,*Politics Among the Nations*(New York: 1960).

governed by strategic considerations, and, in their anxiety to secure themselves against aggression, they continually prepare for war. History throughout the past five centuries proves the truth of these contentions, but most decidedly in the last.

Consistent support given by the United States Administration to the white (apartheid) regime in South Africa was largely premised upon assessment of the strategic importance of the Cape of Good Hope, and similar considerations undoubtedly influenced its decisions to invade Grenada and Panama. Acquisition of colonies has always been largely for strategic as well as economic reasons, and since nuclear weapons have changed the nature of warfare and made colonies more of an embarrassment than a strategic advantage, imperial nations have been much more ready and eager to grant their colonies independence.

By and large, foreign and defence policies are driven simply by the requirement to maintain the power balance; this and the arms race with the recurrent tensions so engendered, renders fallacious the much vaunted proverb that the best way to ensure peace is to prepare for war. So far from providing conditions in which means could be found for safeguarding the human race against nuclear war or environmental catastrophe, the present absence of order and impossibility of international regulation, create the very conditions that make both of these eventualities more likely. The inescapable conclusion is that, as long as the nations remain sovereign and independent, intermittent minor wars are inevitable, and in the long run, a major war very probable.

If this view seems, at first sight, somewhat extreme, the facts of history, past and present, are enough to confirm its truth. It does not follow, of course, that ordinary diplomacy cannot ever achieve anything salutary. As has already been conceded, whenever so-called vital interests are not involved, or the issues concerned are relatively minor, helpful and pacific arrangements are often made.

But the crucial matters are those affecting peace and war, which inevitably involve vital interests, and global problems are not minor but impinge directly on, and frequently require restriction of, national interests, and these problems are of the utmost weight for the survival of the race.

Vital national interests are almost always closely entangled with such issues, provoking the assertion of sovereign rights. Thus, like so much else, matters affecting the environment no less than those concerning security become the counters and playthings of power politics.

It is for this reason that the solution of global problems cannot be found in the conduct of diplomacy, any more than it can be achieved by the independent action of sovereign states. Where global interests should prevail, national interests ought not to be given preference; but the converse is what invariably happens in transactions between sovereign states.

At the present time, despite the activities of the United Nations, there is no such thing as international order, because power politics universally prevails, even within the United Nations, which in fact is no more than a forum for the conduct of customary diplomacy. That, as we have seen, offers no way of preventing war (for the waging of which Chapter VII of the United Nations Charter actually provides).

There is inevitably only international anarchy, because sovereign states are subject to no superior legislation, and could not be sovereign if they were. Consequently, the Rule of Law in international relations cannot be established and the normal world situation is always a form of "cold war" (as Hobbes, Spinoza, Hegel, and Clausewitz contended).

It is then clear that some effective world governance must be established if modern war, with its unavoidable prospect of escalation and the ever-present threat of nuclear holocaust, is ever to be reliably prevented.

This being the case, what is urgently needed if mankind is to be saved from final calamity is a new world legal system. Recently this phrase has been on the lips of politicians and the promise of a new dispensation has been held out to the listening public. But the new world order so far offered is no more than what the United

Nations, either in its present form or reformed in some respects, can provide; and we have seen strong reason to believe that the United Nations, as an association of sovereign states, cannot accomplish what is required.

Some other institutional form is, therefore, essential, and careful consideration must be given to the sort of new world order that could appropriately and competently achieve the required end.

Chapter 5

Impracticable Alternatives

IT should now be clear that the international anarchy resulting from the sovereign independence of the nations is the main source of conflict and an insurmountable obstacle to world peace as well as to environmental conservation, posing an intolerable threat to the survival of civilized life. How then may it be surmounted? Whatever remedy is adopted must be applied as soon as possible, because time is running out. We have no time to lose.

5.1 Has Anything Changed in the Conduct of International Relations?

SINCE the dissolution of the Soviet Union and the revolutions in the Central European countries, journalists and politicians have spoken of a new world order as already having sprung into being; but the analysis of the international situation so far given shows that nothing of the sort has really happened. There has been no change in the world order, only in the balance of power.

That change, however, does offer an opportunity for the establishment of a new world order, if only the nations can be persuaded to embark upon it. What is needed is first to decide what

85

can be effective in remedying the desperate global ills that now beset all peoples the world over, then to consider what sort of new order is desirable and what is practicable.

5.2 Proposals for Change

IT is not only now that proposals for a new world order have come to the fore. Ever since the end of the Second World War and the establishment of the United Nations political theorists and jurists have felt that the institutions provided for the pacific settlement of disputes between nations were unsatisfactory and unable to perform their intended function. Four different types of proposal have been made that merit consideration:

1. Reform of the United Nations,

2. Obligatory legal adjudication ("peace through law"),

3. The fostering and growth of an international civil society, and

4. World federalism.

In this chapter we shall be mainly concerned with the first three of these proposals, and our aim will be to discover whether any of them could really deliver the promised result.

5.3 United Nations Reform

PROPOSED reforms of the United Nations have included the enlargement of the Security Council, the abolition of the veto by its permanent members, direct election of representatives to the General Assembly, or to a second Assembly with advisory function, and the removal of the present prohibition against interference in the internal affairs of members. None of these reforms, however, would materially change the international system in a way that could ensure the pacific settlement of disputes, because all of them retain intact the sovereign rights of the nations and the obligation laid down in the Charter to uphold the sovereign independence of member states.

In fact, the proposal to remove the prohibition of interference in internal affairs is self-frustrating in that context, because sovereign states will never brook outside interference in their internal affairs, and any attempt to adopt such measures by the international body could well be viewed as a hostile act and might even be militarily resisted.

Increasing the size of the Security Council would make no significant difference, beyond satisfying the aspirations of the minor powers to participate in discussion and decision-making. Abolition of the veto prerogatives of the permanent members of the Council might facilitate action to some extent, but even that would be doubtful, because a great power which had been overruled could easily act to obstruct the implementation of a resolution it had opposed so as to nullify any decision.

Even now, minor powers like Israel and Iraq, are quite capable of defying Security Council decisions, and ignoring its resolutions. Imagine, for instance, what could have been done about the Iraqi occupation of Kuwait if the United States had opposed the decision to move against Saddam Hussein, and had been outvoted in the Security Council. Without the cooperation of the most powerful nation, it would have been very difficult to take effective action.

When the United Nations was first established its founders defended the veto provision on the ground that nothing could ever be accomplished unless the major powers were in agreement. But the essential point is not so much whether action could be taken at all, as what sort of action would be possible; and it is obvious that there could be no other than the application of sanctions, which, of whatever kind they might be, could be made effective only if backed by military force, or the threat of its use.

No dispute can be settled peaceably if the recalcitrant disputants are sovereign nations. Kuwait could not have been liberated without war as long as a sovereign Iraq resisted. In fact, every positive and effective action authorized by the Security Council since its inauguration has involved military conflict, in Zaire, in Korea, in Somaliland, and in the Persian Gulf.

Quite apart from these considerations it is far from likely that all five (if any at all) of the permanent members would agree to the proposed reform, and the disagreement of only one would itself be an exercise of the veto.

Direct election of the members of the General Assembly would increase the democratic character of the representation in that body, and might improve the kind of decisions reached. But, as the Assembly is in any case only an advisory body, its recommendations could not have any other than a limited influence upon the decisions of the Security Council. Here again the question is one of principle. What, or whom, would the delegates represent? Would they simply be delegates of the states the people of which had elected them, or would they represent the population itself? If the latter, how would they relate to the ambassadors of their governments who are supposed to represent them in the Security Council?

What political party or opinion in the country concerned would they speak for? If the delegates still represent their countries as sovereign states, no difference in principle would have been made. If they were to be regarded as representing other constituencies, let us suppose the majority opinion in their homelands (if that could be clearly demarcated), could their decisions affect any positive action taken by the Security Council, which would still be controlled by the governments in power?

The answer to the last question is almost certainly negative, and to the earlier ones highly dubious. It is also improbable, except in special cases, (perhaps, like Iran, and more recently not even there), that the political alignment of the whole people of any country would be one and the same, and if, as is very likely, it were not, the voice of its representatives in the General Assembly and the Security Council could hardly be decisive. So the proposed reform is unlikely to produce any useful result, and would not cure the ills to which the international comity of nations is subject.

The alternative suggestion of a popularly elected second chamber with advisory function is similarly otiose. The General Assembly, as it is, has no more than advisory powers, and another chamber with no powers beyond advising an advisory body would be little more than supernumerary. Neither of these assemblies have, or could have, legislative power as long as the members of the Organization are sovereign, because to be so they must be subject to no superior legislation.

Removing the prohibition against intervention in domestic affairs would certainly make a considerable difference to the kinds of action that the Organization could take, but would hardly make it easier to implement them, because if the state concerned did not consent, its government would almost certainly resist the interference and would have to be coerced, again involving the use of military force.

The legal right of the United Nations to intervene in civil conflicts might well have a salutary effect; but to resolve civil issues by means of foreign intervention, as the recent conflict in Yugoslavia testified, is extremely difficult and has never yet been accomplished without the use of military force and excessive loss of life; long-term enforcement would require nothing less, involving occupation, tantamount to conquest and subjection, which few peoples would stomach, as the recent events in Iraq have convincingly shown.

It follows that such reform of the United Nations as has been proposed could not alter the overall situation materially in any way that would satisfy contemporary needs. What is required is some effective method of outlawing war, because, apart from the human misery it causes, and the disastrous environmental effects of modern warfare, the risk that it would escalate and involve weapons of mass destruction cannot be tolerated.

As long as such weapons exist and are stockpiled, the imminent danger of accidental devastation remains, with the accompanying menace of environmental catastrophe. That, moreover, may be caused by warfare even if no nuclear attack is contemplated, as was the case in the first Gulf War. Further, the means of combating environmental deterioration (quite apart from the possibility of nuclear explosions) because they are not available within the limited jurisdiction of national governments, require the conclusion of treaties; and some reliable assurance of the observance of treaties is, therefore, essential.

Yet, while nations remain sovereign, no such assurance is to be had, and it cannot be provided by the United Nations, for the reasons already given. The only really effective reform, therefore, would have to abolish sovereign rights. Most peoples will probably react adversely to that suggestion on first consideration; but if it proves to be the only way to avoid the extinction of the race, it would be the preferable option.

5.4 Peace Through Law

THE second type of world order that has been advocated, mainly by international lawyers, is that the Court of International Justice should have mandatory jurisdiction in all disputes—that the rule of law should be made to prevail in international affairs as it does (or can be made to do) in domestic affairs. That is a consummation devoutly to be wished. But there are some crucial questions that cry out for answers.

First, a very awkward and unsatisfactory doctrine of International Law as at present interpreted would have to be overcome. That is the doctrine of so-called nonjusticiability of certain cases. In metropolitan law, every case is justiciable—that is to say, a binding decision can be given on any case by some court. If ever any case is regarded as non-justiciable, it is only by certain special courts designed to adjudicate special classes of litigation (as, for example, those in France which hear only cases on Administrative

Law). There are always other courts competent to pass judgment on other matters, even if there is no provision in statute law that covers the particular situation under scrutiny, for then the judge is usually empowered to decide on grounds of equity.

In International Law a case is held to be non-justiciable if any of the parties affected refuses to submit to the court, or to accept the court's jurisdiction—an exemption unheard of and altogether impermissible in domestic law. Sovereign states are entitled to withhold their consent and thus to nullify the jurisdiction of the court whenever they choose. If the rule of law is to prevail, no such privilege is tolerable, yet while states remain sovereign this resistance to adjudication cannot be overruled.

Further, cases are considered non-justiciable if they concern conflicts of interest rather than "legal rights." Now, in international affairs legal rights are sovereign rights, and interests are national interests, and it is the sovereign right of every independent nation to pursue its national interests. Accordingly, conflicts of legal rights are inevitably conflicts of interest.

At all events, it is virtually impossible to distinguish between the two categories in practice. So whatever a court may decide as to the justiciability of a case, any of the parties (being sovereign states) can easily decide otherwise. Once again, the doctrine of non-justiciability defeats any attempt to maintain the rule of law.

Another criterion offered to determine justiciability has been the exclusion, as non-justiciable, of cases that concern sovereign rights, and the permission, as justiciable, of those which concern only minor matters. It is clear, however, that minor matters are unlikely to upset the balance of power, or to threaten hostilities between disputants, whereas sovereign rights cover virtually any action that a state may take. Only the latter are ever likely to threaten world peace, and they are excluded from justiciability. Accordingly, this provision puts the maintenance of the rule of law altogether out of the question.

A fourth distinction between justiciability and non-justiciability is that the former includes cases that can be decided under existing rules of the law, and the latter those which are not covered by any existing rules. It is here that in the internal law of states considerations of equity become relevant. In international cases, it seems, no such considerations are likely to be heeded.

As there are larger gaps in the coverage of International Law than in any other legal code or system, the cases ruled out by this criterion are bound to be numerous, and once more the rule of law will be defeated. It may be argued that this hiatus could easily be filled simply by ruling that where the law is defective equity should be invoked, and then to allow as justiciable cases which are now excluded.

But this could be achieved only with the agreement of the subjects of the law, who are, by the provision of the law itself, sovereign states, and may well refuse to give their consent in any instance where their national interests are at risk. Nor would the obstacle to justiciability have been removed which is presented by the sovereign prerogative of refusing recognition of the Court's jurisdiction; nor can it be removed simply by fiat. States cannot forego their sovereign rights and remain independent, so the main problem persists.

Yet another distinction is made between cases that involve change in the existing law and those which do not, only the latter being justiciable. In no instance can any change in the law be made by the Court, for changes are subject to international agreement and require what are called law-making treaties. So if circumstances bring states into dispute because of issues that the law does not cover, there should be some other method of changing the law if violent conflict is to be avoided.

In the international sphere, however, the only method of doing this is by agreement and the signing of a treaty and that assumes that the dispute has already been settled without any intervening litigation. If it is not settled the defective law cannot be invoked. So if the law is to be made relevant to the dispute it can only be by a means that the dispute itself rules out of consideration. Moreover, the presumption of the principle *pacta sunt servanda* is that the rule of law prevails ensuring the observance of treaties, but this is precisely what is lacking in the relation between sovereign states.

A prior question is what law the Court is to administer. Among the existing international institutions at present none has the power of legislating world law, and none could as long as the nations are sovereign. Accordingly, the only law adjudicable by the International Court of Justice can be International Law as currently recognized. But that upholds the sovereign rights of independent states, which, as sovereign, cannot be subjected to any superior law.

How then are they to be compelled to submit to the jurisdiction of the Court, if they do not willingly agree to do so beforehand and to abide by its decision? If they can be so compelled only by military force, or by sanctions that are backed by military threat, the situation would not in the least have been improved.

On the other hand, if the law to be administered were not International Law as it is now understood, what is to be its source? How and by what authority is it to be legislated? What would be its status, other than that of a treaty, the limitations of which we have already pointed out? In fact, if the attempt were made to persuade all states always to submit their disputes to the International Court of Justice, and if it were to succeed, it could only be by interstate agreement enshrined in a treaty.

But, alas, sovereign states observe treaties only on condition that they serve their national interests, and it is notorious that they ignore them whenever they think fit. More than once the United States has refused to submit to the International Court of Justice on the grounds that it would not be in its national interest to admit its jurisdiction in the type of case concerned; and no sovereign state is ever likely to do otherwise.

Again, how could the decisions of the Court be enforced if any of the litigants sought to resist or to disregard them? There would be no alternative to the use of force, which, if exercised against a sovereign power, could only be the waging of war, and that is just what the rule of law is designed to prevent.

Peace through law, therefore, cannot be achieved unless there is some form of world government to legislate, and unless the law can be enforced, not upon sovereign states (which is impracticable without threats to the peace), but upon individual persons who infringe its provisions and who can be prosecuted as they are by domestic law enforcement agencies, and compelled without excessive violence to submit.

The proposal for a new world order consisting in the demand for peace through law, then, will not serve to provide the conditions in which the human race might save itself from final destruction, unless it goes further and includes the establishment of an authority superior to what now rank as sovereign states, one capable of making and enforcing law on individuals unprotected by a sovereign national government, of whatever nationality they might be. In short, if it is to fulfill the function of maintaining the rule of law in the comity of nations, it will have to abolish state sovereignty.

5.5 An International Civil Society

LET us then turn to the third suggestion, which is much more subtle, and also more intricate and complex. It is based on the distinction sometimes made between the state and civil society.

Our main purpose will not be well served by entering into detailed discussion of the theories of political philosophers, like Hegel and Ernest Barker,[1] who have made this distinction, important and perspicacious though they are; but some understanding of the terms is essential if we are to be able to assess the proposal of at least one contemporary writer on the subject of a new world

---

[1]Cf. G.W.F. Hegel, *Grundlinien der Philosophie des Rechts,*dritter Teil, zweiter Abschnitt; Ernest Barker, *Principles of Social and Political Theory*(Oxford, at the Clarendon Press, 1951), Books I and II.

order, namely Richard Falk.[2]

According to Falk, the prospect of a new world order rests upon the rejection of what he calls Modernism and the ascendancy of what he terms Postmodernism. He gives these names meanings different from those usually assigned to them by contemporary philosophers and literary commentators.

For Falk, Modernism consists of the combination of statism, militarism, and industrialism, the exploitation of science and technology. By and large, the influence of these tendencies is (he holds) destructive. Postmodernism, on the other hand, is constructive in his view, and is rooted in personal relations, conscientiousness, and feminization.

It displays a trend against secularism and in favour of religion; it appeals to normative considerations, and reacts against and rejects the intolerable (terrorism, torture, public deception, and the like), and it includes a willingness to project into and plan for the future.

Falk is cognizant of the evils and dangers of the present world situation and he attributes many (though not all) of them to what he calls statism, a term that he does not define but which seems to refer to the working of governmental bureaucracy in the service of nationalism [national sovereignty?]. He is also aware of the problem of discovering an alternative to the present dispensation. He explores at considerable length and in some detail the influences that oppose the ill effects of "Modernism" and the prospects they offer of a new world order. This, he believes, will emerge as the result of the efforts of people who see themselves as "pilgrim-citizens" and who do not limit their vision to the confines of the national state.

They are pilgrims because they actively seek an ideal order. It is not sufficient, Falk maintains, to try to develop merely psychological attitudes without taking practical action of some sort (in the form of non-violent protest). Concurrently, he believes, there

---

[2]Cf. Richard Falk, *Explorations at the Edge of Time: The Prospects for World Order* (Philadelphia, PA, Temple University Press, 1992).

is a developing global civil society, embodying all these features and tendencies, on the strength and efficacy of which the new order will depend.

The distinction between the state and civil society is one that has certainly some foundation in fact, yet it is also very difficult to define and maintain. The state is the familiar system of institutions exercising the legislative, executive and judicial functions of government, and whatever pertains to their operation is usually described as political. More private social activities, associations, and movements are ascribed to the civil sphere.

Falk does not follow Hegel's use of the phrase, *beurgerliche Gesellschaft*, which refers to the economic system, including craft guilds and police administration; he seems to have in mind something more like Ernest Barker's use of the term Society.[3]

As opposed to the State, Society (for Barker) is the network of associations, coterminous with the nation, each formed spontaneously for a special purpose. Membership of these associations is optional and observance of their rules is voluntary, no other means of coercion being exercised by (or available to) them than expulsion.

The State is the system of governmental institutions exercising compulsory legal authority over all the members of society within the scope of its jurisdiction; that, likewise, is coterminous with the nation. So one body of people organizes its activities in two concurrent and complementary ways: voluntarily and spontaneously in Society; legally and compulsorily as the State. Normally, but not necessarily, Society is confined to the same limits as the political unit, or the nation; although frequently special societies have links with similar associations beyond the borders of their own State. What Falk envisages is a wider, global, society, giving allegiance to worldwide objectives and taking transnational action.

The organizations contributing to a global civil society, in Falk's opinion, are such as Greenpeace and the international Peace Movements, Amnesty International, Pugwash, the Sanctu-

---

[3]Cf. Barker, op cit., pp. 2ff.

ary Movement, Liberation Theology, and Ground Zero. Similarly, voluntarily formed associations serving normative principles, like that which prepared and circulated the Nuremberg Pledge, create a favorable moral aura.

The Nuremberg Pledge commits lawyers and officials to abide by the Nuremberg Principle of responsibility—the principle, established in the trial at Nuremberg of war criminals after the Second World War—it is the principle that responsibility for international crimes cannot be excused by the fact that the perpetrator was obeying orders from superior authority.

Another such example is the Permanent People's Tribunal set up by citizens and legal specialists drawn from different nations, who met in Rome and Algiers in 1976 to draw attention to, and condemn, abuses committed anywhere in the world: for instance, Indonesian oppression of the people of East Timor, Turkish massacres of Armenians, United States aggression in Latin America, and so forth. Also, multinational "blue-ribbon" commissions like the Palme Commission on East-West security arrangements represent international effort to bypass statism.

The emergence of a global civil society is undoubtedly of the utmost importance, and the influence of the associations that Falk enumerates as contributing to it are indicative of a growing awareness that human interests in peace, justice, and social welfare transcend state boundaries. This fact, we shall discover, is fundamental to the establishment of any desirable new order.

Nevertheless, Falk is compelled to admit that the results voluntary organizations have been able to produce have been disappointing and insufficient. Non-violent civil resistance movements succeed, when they do, only if the regime against which they are directed is relatively benign. Gandhism, for example, succeeded in India against the British Imperial government, because the tradition of the British Empire was democratic and its professed aim was to prepare its colonies (India especially) for eventual self-rule.

It was not successful in South Africa, where the government's discriminatory policy was entrenched and there was no commitment to enfranchise the subject races. It is significant, all the same, that apartheid has now succumbed as a result of outside pressures exerted by what may loosely be called the international community, even if it is a community far from united or unanimous. This is an aspect of the matter to which we shall presently return.

Religious movements, to which Falk points as contributory to the global civil society, he admits can pull in opposite directions, as when Liberation Theology excites opposition from the Papacy. Fundamentalism can, and usually does, militate against democratic principles, is apt to engender fanaticism and to fuel, rather than to extenuate, strife. This we have seen not only in Iran and Algeria, but even in the United States. It also opposes liberalism in religion and is a further cause of tension in consequence.

Even when contradictions of this nature are absent, the influence of the movements listed frequently proves to be limited and unrewarding, except perhaps to the relatively few individuals directly involved. The valiant attempts of Greenpeace, for example, to interfere with whaling activities by the Japanese and the Icelanders have had very limited success; but quite apart from that, their aim is to ensure the observance of a treaty already signed, which the offending countries are simply interpreting to suit their own interests, claiming that whaling for scientific purposes is permissible.

Similar attempts to persuade the nations to agree to abstain from exploiting Antarctica are perpetually stymied by the pursuit of national interests on the part of the sovereign states concerned. And were they to succeed, the result would still be no better than a treaty, the observance of which would always be in jeopardy, for the reasons we have already noted.

Valuable and important though these civil movements may be, there are other contradictions endemic in many of them. The determination to abide by the Nuremberg Principle and to ensure its wider recognition is fraught with difficulty, due entirely to the nature of both sovereignty and International Law.

National law in every sovereign state makes disloyalty (especially in time of war) a heinous offence. If it consists in the disobedience of military commands it can amount to treason and may be subject to the death penalty. But the Nuremberg Principle requires servants of the state and military personnel to hold themselves responsible for the effects of carrying out the orders of their superiors.

If they entail the committal of war crimes, and the requirements of International Law are to be respected, then national law must be broken, and the individuals concerned are placed in the intolerable position of risking self-incrimination whichever law they seek to observe. Moreover, International Law is supposed to uphold the rights of sovereignty, which, in this instance, it is explicitly denying. Movements to secure the recognition of the Nuremberg Principle, in consequence, are asking those to whom they appeal to pledge to put themselves in a new species of double jeopardy—an impossibly contradictory position.

The Permanent People's Tribunal may have succeeded in giving publicity to deplorable practices, but its remedial effects have not been spectacular, and Falk admits "that its judgments cannot invoke any coercive apparatus of the state system, not even of the United Nations, and the claim of representativeness on a popular basis is always controversial and difficult to investigate."[4]

Likewise, Amnesty International, a most excellent and commendable organization that does invaluable work in exposing violations of human rights, is hampered by lack of all means to bring to book the culprits it detects, who, being sovereign governments, are able to deny, or merely to brush off the accusations with impunity, alleging that Amnesty has produced no reliable evidence.

The existence of a global civil society is essential to the establishment of a new world order, and it is not without import that already talk of "the international community" has become common. International public opinion, engendered by the media throughout the world, is also proving increasingly influential on the conduct of national governments; and those who advocate reform of

---

[4]Falk, op cit., p. 94.

the United Nations have suggested that a new Assembly elected by non-government organizations should be added. This would, in effect, represent the world civil society.

These developments are the result of a growing awareness (still rather unorganised and undirected) that people all over the world and of whatever nationality have common interests that are ultimately so vital that they should override national concerns.

But such common interests are, as yet, not embodied in any institutional establishment; consequently, the beneficent influences Falk emphasizes are still rather minimal, and they are unlikely to be much more as long as the "vital interests" of national sovereign states take precedence, as at present they are bound to do, in international affairs.

All the factors so far discussed which tend towards the emergence of a global society, when they do not cancel one another out (as in the case of some religious movements), are countered and rendered ineffective by their lack of coercive force, not merely against individuals, but more especially and necessarily against state governments that wield sovereign power. Civil societies can never exert more than moral influence over their own members— and scarcely that over others who reject their norms and professed principles.

The civil society in national communities is coextensive with the state, and so far as it succeeds in getting its ideals recognized, it is only the legal order of the state government that protects their recognized rights and gives the accepted norms coercive effect. If this is to come about in the international sphere there must be a corresponding legal order parallel to and coterminous with whatever global civil society effectively exists.

Falk, as we saw, admitted the absence of any coercive apparatus for the Permanent People's Tribunal, as if deprecating the fact; yet he is opposed to the operation of "statism" in civil affairs. He does not seem to notice that without the coercive operation of the law, both criminal and civil, society would degenerate into anarchy and no social order could survive.

On the other hand, statism, if that means state sovereignty, is a constant impediment to the regulation of international affairs in any orderly and pacific manner, and the lack of a genuinely effective legal structure in this sphere is, in the circumstances mankind now finds itself, little short of calamitous.

We have seen that, without war, or the threat of war, legal enforcement is not possible against sovereign states, but a legal system enshrined within a political constitution which itself exercised sovereign authority, could be made effective. It must, however, exercise its jurisdiction over persons, for it cannot do so over states that are sovereign; and the persons concerned cannot be allowed to appeal to their national governments for protection from world law.

What this means is that the nations of the world will have to unite under some kind of federal constitutional structure if any global civil society is to be sustainable. Yet Falk brushes aside world federalism, without any discussion of the pros and cons, as "a failed social movement fashioned by reason and constrained by deference to the legitimacy of the existing order."[5]

Why reasonableness should be regarded as a disadvantage is not apparent, and the legitimacy of the existing order is something that needs looking into (as we shall do in the next chapter). If the idea of a World Federation is held to be merely academic and utopian (as it so often is), the practical conditions and requirements for a new world order may not be disregarded.

These conditions and requirements are what we have been examining, and we have found that none of the expedients (such as they are) that have so far been recommended can be made effective. None is either practicable or sufficient. Yet, oddly enough, none of them is castigated, even by its critics, as academic or utopian.

What Falk means by saying that federalism is "constrained by deference to the legitimacy of the existing order" is difficult to guess, for world federalism, so far from deferring to the legiti-

---

[5] Op. cit., p. 71.

macy of the existing order, if that means national sovereign independence, would do away with it altogether. If all he means is that constraints are put upon the idea by the deference to sovereign independence of its opponents, then the grounds and the justification of that deference have to be investigated.

We have already found that national sovereign independence is a persistent obstacle to any world order yet devised or proposed. Our next task then will be to examine the fourth option, and to consider whether the constraint alleged is either warranted or legitimate. The three proposals we have so far examined have proved unavailing and impracticable, and the predicament we face is urgent and insufferable because it threatens to be terminal.

We are therefore constrained to reflect carefully and immediately on the one remaining, to see whether that might possibly deliver results, rather than to reject it in deference to what is impeding progress towards salvation; and we may not summarily reject it as merely theoretical, or simply distasteful, without examining the principles on which it rests, the implications embodied in it, and the prospects it may hold of practicability and help in removing the existing threats to human survival.

Chapter 6

Federalism

6.1 The Evil Genius and its Exorcism

L AW Professor G. W. Keeton wrote that national sovereignty is the evil genius in the forest of international relations.[1] Indeed it has been the source of wars for centuries—and war has now become so widely destructive that we can no longer afford to regard it as a viable instrument of policy. Further, we have discovered that national sovereignty has presented obstacles to every attempt to create an international organization that can maintain world peace and ensure the pacific settlement of international disputes. Every proposal for a new world order that has so far been examined is rendered impracticable by its inability to overcome the effects of the exercise by the nations of their arrogated sovereign rights.

How, then, are these obstacles to be circumvented, or their source to be removed? One way of eliminating national sovereignty, of course, would be some sort of Alexandrian world conquest to bring all nations into subjection under a single imperial power—establishing a new version of the *pax Romana*. But today any such adventure is ruled out, because it entails a world

---

[1]Cf. *National Sovereignty and International Order* (London, 1939)

103

war in which nuclear weapons would almost certainly be employed; for no nation that possessed them would refrain from using them if it were threatened with defeat and total subjection to a foreign invader. The result would be so catastrophic that no contestant could be victorious and the entire enterprise would be self-defeating.

It may be suggested that now, with the demise of the Soviet Union, the United States has emerged as the sole superpower, and can exert irresistible influence the world over. But although this is to some extent the case, it is hardly a desirable disposition, for the foreign policy of the American administration is often far from what other nations can approve, and at the present time it is so unacceptable to many that America has become a prime target for terrorism by those who hate her hegemony. It is far from true that all other countries will meekly obey American behests.

Japan and the European Community are quite strong enough to pursue their own ends, in resistance to pressures from the western hemisphere, nor are Russia, China or India likely to become totally subservient. At all events these and all other nations that remain independent are still sovereign, and they will continue to claim and to exercise their sovereign rights, as far as their actual military strength gives them scope.

They will cooperate, if at all, only to the extent that their sovereign national interests require, and they will continue to give these precedence over global considerations. Consequently, any attempt to deal with an international crisis or the defiance of Security Council resolutions by a rogue state will, in the last resort if not sooner, involve war. Concurrently, the advance of global warming cannot be slowed down without concerted international action, always frustrated because sovereign nations give priority to their own national interests.

The overriding need is for some political structure superseding the national state that is capable of maintaining the rule of law worldwide, and the only such structure available—the only practicable alternative to anarchy, on the one hand, and to one-nation hegemony, on the other—is federation, constitutionally established and freely entered into by the nations of the world.

What the present world situation requires is a democratically elected authority constitutionally empowered to legislate and administer genuine World Law that could be enforced on individual persons without resort to military might, as no law (be it called international or what you will) can be enforced upon sovereign states. We must first consider the principles, philosophical and legal, on which any such regime could be based; then we must assess the prospect of its workability, and finally the means and conditions of its being established.

First, however, let me state clearly the indispensable conditions on which any such world federation can be acceptable.

1. It cannot be imposed by force or fiat on any nation; it can be established only by popular consent.

2. Accordingly, it must be democratic in form and practice.

3. The Federal legislation must be confined entirely to matters of common (i.e., global) interest, such as cannot be adequately regulated by the national governments of its members. In all other matters the local powers of the member states must be preserved and protected. World Federation, therefore, if it is to be acceptable to the peoples of the planet, can never be over-centralized, can never be authoritarian, and need not be excessively bureaucratic.

6.2 The Necessity and Proper Role of Sovereignty

BEFORE proceeding further it must be noted that the evil genius to which reference has been made is not sovereignty as such, but is its exercise by national states, or states assumed to be national even when their populations are multinational, in a world which inevitably brings them into mutual relations. No state can be completely self-sufficient within its own borders, so the existing nations are necessarily involved in mutual intercourse which is what we know as international relations. It is in the conduct of their transactions that the claim to national sovereign independence becomes the evil genius.

A collection of sovereign states in mutual relation thus constitutes an association or a confederation, but it can never form a *community*, because sovereign independence entails giving precedence to national interests over all others, while the defining characteristic of a community is that its members subordinate their own individual advantage to the demands of the common good.

It is in the nature of the case that sovereign states should consider their national interests paramount, for every organized society involves the regulation of the conduct of its members so as to make ordered cooperation possible, and that requires the imposition upon them of laws that must be promulgated and made known, must be impartially interpreted, and must be duly enforced upon the recalcitrant.

All this implies the necessary exercise of supreme power by a ruling government with sovereign authority. The exercise of that power, however, is legitimate only if it is exerted in the common interest and as long as it sufficiently promotes the common welfare. It is proper and inevitable, therefore, that a sovereign government should regard the national interest as paramount and should act accordingly.

Within the nation the common interest takes precedence, and for that very reason, in external affairs, international accommodations are subordinated to national advantage. In principle, then, the nation is a community, but the so-called comity of nations, while they remain severally sovereign, cannot be.

As essential to the existence of social order, sovereignty is legitimate and indispensable. Without such supreme authority, empowered to enforce law, anarchy would prevail and people would be in the condition described by Hobbes as the State of Nature. But in the international sphere, because states are sovereign and independent, that condition is precisely what does prevail, and that is how national sovereignty becomes an evil genius. The only way to avoid this hindrance to any really salutary international order is to *internationalize* sovereignty, which cannot be done except by uniting the nations in a federation.

6.3 Philosophical Considerations

THE absolute supremacy of the sovereign in internal affairs is the juristic aspect of sovereignty. The requirement that it exercise its power in the common interest, what legitimises it and gives it authority, is its ethical aspect. In the present world situation, the relation between these two features of sovereignty has become of the utmost importance and constitutes the theoretical basis for fundamental change in the international order.

There can be no doubt that the nations of the world at the present time have overpowering common interests in the conservation of the environment and in the maintenance of world peace. There is also widespread interest in the protection of human rights, and it is unquestionably desirable that they should be universally respected. As Falk has demonstrated, there is also plentiful evidence of the emergence of a world civil society drawing its consensus from an increasing realization of the importance of these common interests; and there is also a growing recognition of the existence of a *world community*.

A community, however, as has been said, implies not only the existence of common interests, but also that they be given precedence over sectional and individual concerns. It is, then, pertinent to consider what authority is capable of defending and upholding such global common interests, and is thus entitled to legislate for their advancement and to be empowered to enact and enforce the law. That the United Nations is not, and why it cannot be, such an authority has already been demonstrated.

Also, it should now be apparent that national sovereign states are incapable of serving this purpose. So far from being able to maintain world peace, their activities are what perpetually upset the balance of power and render precarious the pacific settlement of disputes. Conservation of the environment demands urgent measures on a global scale which transcend the limits of national sovereign jurisdiction. Diplomacy and international agreement cannot be relied on to ensure the action necessary.

So the national sovereign state is clearly no longer competent to secure the welfare even of the community over which it rules, for that is obviously dependent on the conservation of the planetary ecology and the maintenance of world peace, both of which are also interests common to the whole of humanity. It follows that the national state is no longer rightfully entitled to wield sovereign power. By its inability to serve the common interest it forfeits its authority and thereby its legitimacy.

With this legitimacy forfeited, there is clearly no call upon anybody to pay it deference in opposition to the idea of world federalism, as Falk claims to be inevitable. On the contrary, it is essential and urgently necessary to establish an institutional structure that can enshrine and exercise such power as is legitimized by its competence to serve the interests common to mankind as a whole, and nothing less than a world authority can do this.

6.4   Legal Principles

IN law, the theoretical background for any such authority is the doctrine of Natural Law, dating back to the Romans and the Mediaeval Church, a doctrine for the revival of which there are nowadays good grounds.[2] It was on the basis of this doctrine that Grotius initiated the idea of International Law, but as that was designed to regulate the conduct of sovereign states, it inevitably fails and lamentably falls short of what is now required.

---

[2] Cf. E.E. Harris, *Cosmos and Theos* (Humanities Press, Atlantic Highlands, NJ. 1992), Ch. 3.See also John Finnis, *Natural Law and Natural Rights.* Oxford, Clarendon Press, 1980.

The idea of a Law of Nature is not to be despised. It was traditionally and still should be understood as the law of reason: namely, what prescribes the rational requirements of social living; for it is only the rational capacity of human beings that makes civilized society possible (whatever other propensities and characteristics human nature may include). It is just so far as human beings are rational by nature that they become political animals. The law of reason, therefore, in as far as it is the law of human nature, is indeed the Law of Nature. But the doctrine of Natural Law has always presented difficulties, both in theory and in practice.

To explore and discuss the issues in dispute would not serve our present purpose; suffice it to say that the idea is far from dead and has been resuscitated in a new form by several eminent international jurists under the guise of what goes by the name of legal monism. This is the conception of all law as belonging to one universal system, applying to the international (or better, world) community as well as to all subordinate communities included within it.

The doctrine is explored and criticized in *Annihilation and Utopia* (Ch. XIII), as it has been advocated variously by writers such as Leon Duguit, Paul Laband, and Georg Jellinek, and has exercised influence on the works of Harold Laski, H. Krabbe, Hans Kelsen and Georges Scelle. [3] The argument of all these thinkers converges upon the notion of a single legal system, which, whether they admit it or not (and most of them do), implies a single sovereign legislating authority with power to enforce the law. Apart from that, as they all acknowledge (either

---

[3]Cf. H. Kelsen, *General Theory of Law and the State* (New York, 1961); H. Krabbe, *The Modern Idea of the State* (D. Appleton and Co, New York, London, 1922); G. Scelle, *Precis de Droit des Gens* (Paris, 1923-24) 2 Vols.; H. Lauterpacht, *Private Law Sources and Analogies of International Law* (London and New York, Longmans Green,1927), *The Function of Law in the International Community* (Oxford, Clarendon Press, 1933); Clark and Sohn, *Peace through Law* (University of North Carolina Press, 1944); W. Schiffer, *The Legal Community of Mankind* (Columbia University Press, 1954); P.C Jessup, *A Modern Law of Nations* (New York, Macmillan, 1952); E.E. Harris, *The Survival of Political Man*, Ch. VIII; *Annihilation and Utopia*, Ch. XIII.

explicitly or tacitly by implication) that so-called "international law" cannot be regarded as "positive" or genuine law.[4] Without enforcement it cannot be made effective.

The implication of the doctrine is, for the most part, clearly stated by its proponents. It is that there is one universal world community, but that it is as yet inadequately organized. It still lacks, and requires, institutional representation, which, when established, would amount to a world federal state, with power to legislate, and enforce law upon individuals. Several of the writers (Krabbe and Scelle in particular) repudiate the idea of national sovereignty explicitly, and declare that the ideal form of international government would be federal. Perhaps the most interesting and instructive discussions of the whole question in its various ramifications are to be found in Walter Schiffer's book, *The Legal Community of Mankind* and in Philip C. Jessup's *A Modern Law of Nations*.[5]

6.5 Practical Requirements

THE crying need for the establishment of a world constitution to objectify the common interests of the world community now requires no further demonstration. The questions to be answered are simply: What conditions would make the establishment of such an authority acceptable to the peoples of the world? And how can it be brought into being?

The only feasible form of world government, and the only one that could be made acceptable to the world community is federalism. Unitary government, concentrating all power and administrative control in the hands of a central administration would not only be too cumbersome, and, in all probability, too bureaucratic, but would also too grossly override the separate interests of the associating nationalities.

---

[4]*Annihilation and Utopia*, loco cit, and Ch. III; *The Survival of Political Man*, Ch. III.

[5]Cf. Schiffer, op. cit.; Jessup, op. cit.

Historically diverse national regions would, therefore, have to be left autonomous, so far as is permissible by the demands of their own common welfare and that of the global community; and only those issues which cannot effectively be controlled by regional authorities would have to be invested in the central federal government.

6.6 Objections and Their Refutation

A common objection to the idea of world government is that it would be too concentrated a centralization of power and would be (or become) totalitarian and oppressive. This is, of course, a hazard for any and every form of government, and in national regimes the antidote to it is democracy and constitutional safeguards against the infringement of personal liberties. There is no obstacle to the entrenchment of similar safeguards in a world constitution, and indeed they would be a necessary condition of its acceptance by its prospective subject peoples. It should, in fact, include a Bill of Human Rights and civil liberties, which the world authority would be committed to respect and to protect.

Likewise, national communities are apprehensive of the submergence and loss of their national identity and traditions, which they fear may wither away unless they can be self-determining and independent. National identity, however, is no very definite conception, and the unit for which independence is being sought, when a right to national self-determination is claimed, is difficult to distinguish. None of the criteria of nationality that have been suggested apply with any exactitude to what have, in different Federalism cases, been identified as nations, whether it be common descent, common language, common religion, or common culture. In fact, national identity usually turns out to be quite literally mythical: that is, the belief by people with a common culture in their descent from a common ancestor, for which there is no good historical evidence.[6]

---

[6]For a fuller discussion of the right to national self-determination see *Anni-*

The truth is that national traditions are usually hybrid, rather than exclusive to one group. They are amalgams of cultural habits and institutions derived from numerous culture contacts and combined in one societal group. Social anthropologists agree that thriving civilizations are, and always have been, those exposed to contact and interrelation with other cultural traditions, while societies which become isolated decline and become degenerate.

At the same time, many nationalities have remained distinct and vital that have not coincided with any independent sovereign state. The several nationalities in the Swiss federation have retained their distinctive identities for centuries without dilution, while Jews, Kurds, Armenians and many Asiatic nationalities have kept their heritage intact even though they have been scattered among many different states.

According to circumstances, national consciousness can work in either of two opposite ways. It may tend towards separatism where a national group has suffered discrimination and oppression at the hands of another dominant nationality, as has happened to the Armenians and the Kurds, or among the nationalities of the former Soviet Union which were subjected to a dictatorial central government.

Or it may bring together into closer unity peoples of different nationality but sharing a common tradition and recognizing a common interest, as within the European Community, and the associations of Baltic or of Scandinavian states. A like affinity between different nations is expressed in transnational movements such as the Pan-African and Pan-Slavic.

Where the sense of common interest is very strong, however, the overriding force is gravitation towards union. The nearest approach to a definite meaning for nationality would be one that applied the term to a population with interests in common, who

---

hilation and Utopia, Ch. XI.See also Benedict Anderson, Benedict,*Imagined Communities: Reflections on the Origin and Spread of Nationalism*. New York, Verso, 2006.

live under a government that serves those interests. But then the common interest must take precedence over any so-called right to self-determination on the part of any subordinate groups within it.

National differences need not be weakened by inclusion within a federal union. In a federal system the specific characters of nationalities can be protected by the federal constitution and are safeguarded by the fact that purely local concerns and the conduct of local affairs are reserved for the provincial and regional authorities, and only those departments of government responsible for overriding interests common to all national groups are assigned to the central federal administration. In short, federalism is the primary example of devolved administration and is the diametrical opposite of centralized government.

It is quite unlikely that the administrative systems at present in operation in national communities would be very much affected by their unification under a federal authority. They would lose certain departments of government responsible for such matters as, for instance, conservation of the environment (over which, in any case, they have never had exclusive power, and could not exercise effective control). They would no longer need departments of foreign affairs or defence and would not miss them, because disputes would be settled by courts of law and diplomacy would have become obsolete. What immediately concerns the territories over which they preside would for the most part remain in their hands.

Despite disputes and constitutional crises in Canada, this has been true of the province of Quebec, which has always remained predominantly French and has retained its national traditions within the federation. The states of the Union that followed the victory of the British American colonies in their war of independence have not lost their local autonomy, and where, as in Puerto Rico, there is a dominant national character, membership in the Union has not obliterated it.

More conclusive than any of these considerations, however, is the fact that contemporary world conditions have made national independence itself obsolete. No nation today is independent in any real sense. Economically every nation is dependent on many, if not all, others to an extent far exceeding what has been the case hitherto. The activities of the stock market in New York affect those in Britain, Europe and Japan, and *vice versa*. The average wage paid in the United States and in Europe compared with that paid in the Far East affects employment in the West.

Transnational corporations conduct their business indifferently in every country, adjusting their operations to conditions all over the world. More significant yet is the fact that health, welfare, and the very survival of all peoples the world over now depend on what happens and what is done in any and every country, for that has effects on soil, water and air, the food supply and the climate over the entire globe. *Unless and until this common destiny of all nations is widely recognized and is reflected in political institutions,* the hope of resolving the difficulties and removing the environmental perils now threatening mankind will continue to be very dim—if any at all can be entertained.

The main misgivings about unification in a world federation, therefore, are largely groundless, and even although risks would have to be taken in embarking upon so far-reaching a change, the disadvantages anticipated are only speculative, whereas the real and acknowledged risks already threatening mankind are immensely greater and the real dangers are vastly more formidable.

It is now apparent that these dire prospects cannot be removed by any of the other expedients hitherto proposed, nor can any of the remedies presently contemplated for the deterioration of the environment succeed without universal compliance with rules legally enforced; and as only globally applied remedies can be sufficient, no such enforcement is possible under the present system.

There are, no doubt, many who will object that, even if one admits all I have so far said of the possible acceptability of the idea of world federation, it is hardly likely to recommend itself to many nations. Would powerful nationalist nations like the US,

Russia or China, for instance, be willing to submit to any sort of world authority other than the United Nations?

The answer, surely, is that if her rulers could be persuaded of the dire and virtually inevitable consequences of permitting the present international anarchy to persist they would be more amenable to the idea of world federation. All governments today have to be shown that the continuance of sovereign independence among the nations promises only final disaster and that the one alternative to world government is wholesale catastrophe, either nuclear or climatic, or both.

6.7 Al Gore's Fatal Error

AL GORE has written a book remarkable for its acute awareness of the dangers and the predicament faced by humanity at the present time, for its insights into the causes of present problems and the changes in global thinking and policy-making needed to meet them.[7] But it has one fatal defect; Gore sweeps aside the idea of World Government as impracticable and undesirable, without the least consideration or apparent awareness of the massive evidence I have assembled here and elsewhere that none of the other options are workable.

Gore himself admits that the United Nations is unlikely to be able to help significantly to extricate the world from its present conflicts of interests; he sees that what is necessary for remedies to be global is that all nations should act in concert; he calls for "agreements that obligate all nations"; but he fails to explain how such obligation is to be made effective, or what sanctions, short of war, have ever been, or can ever be, brought to bear upon sovereign states, that will compel them to keep the agreements they have entered into when their national interests are at stake.

Gore, while he recognizes and insists that we must fundamentally change our modes of thinking if the world is to be saved from

---

[7] Al Gore, The Earth in the Balance: Ecology and the Human Spirit (Boston, New York, London, Houghton Mifflin Company, 1992).

disaster, cannot free himself from the inveterate habit of viewing (even if only tacitly) international relations in terms of national sovereignty. So he declares that, in their inability to relinquish their interest in national sovereign independence, and the freedom which is alleged to accompany it, no people will ever accept the idea of World Government. In actual fact, power politics among sovereign states, with its constant threats of war and violent conflict, and its neglect of the global common interest in the balance of nature, is perhaps the paramount obstacle to *real freedom* in modern times.

So while Gore rightly identifies the strategic goals at which we should aim, the Global Marshall Plan that he offers as the solution to the world's ills is fatally flawed by the absence of any known means to induce sovereign governments to agree to it where it is not obviously to their own national advantage, and the lack of effective means of regulation and enforcement of any agreement that might (problematically) be reached.[8]

The Marshall Plan adopted in the aftermath of the Second World War was accepted and implemented, as Gore himself recognizes, for the strategic reason that America feared the Soviet Union's ability to capitalize on the economic distress and disarray in Europe.

His own proposed Global Marshall Plan is of a different kind and is designed to achieve different aims. It cannot be financed or directed by any one nation (although Gore clearly expects and urges the United States to take the lead); nor is its object to strengthen the strategic advantages of any one bloc—as, indeed, it should not be.

He recognizes and insists that it can be carried out only with the full and determined cooperation of all or most of the nations of the world. As he says: "We must negotiate international agreements that establish global constraints on acceptable behavior but that are entered into voluntarily albeit with the understanding that they will contain both incentives and legally valid penalties

---

[8]Cf. op. cit., Part III.

for noncompliance."[9]

He does not tell us what these penalties could be, other than economic sanctions or the military threats without which economic sanctions seldom prevail, nor does he say how they are to be made legally valid, nor does he disclose by what means agreement is to be reached on such far-reaching measures as he proposes, many of which would inevitably put strains on the national interests of the several independent states.

It is already clear that the nations, especially the United States, are reluctant to finance the operations of the United Nations, or to fix dates for the stabilization of C02 emissions, much less a global plan as comprehensive and demanding as Al Gore proposes.

The plan itself includes admirable suggestions of ways to meet current needs, none of which, however, are strikingly new, and all of which could easily have been put into operation before now. But they have not been, and we should ask why not. The technology is for the most part already available, but no significant move has yet been made to apply it.

The need and its urgency is widely known, but it is not being met. Gore is entirely right to insist that it should be, and his analysis and assessment of the world situation could hardly be bettered. But he gives no indication how the obstacles are to be overcome which have hitherto prevented the proposals he makes from being adopted, or how independent sovereign nations are to be persuaded to carry them out, nor yet how to compel them to abide by their agreements if they are ever made. He confesses that without legislation his Global Plan would hardly be possible, yet he does not say who will legislate.

No national government has wide enough jurisdiction, and if this responsibility is to fall to the United Nations, what better means than heretofore are to be found to make the resolutions of the Security Council effective? Gore is fully aware and gives ample evidence of the difficulty of getting his own country's administration to adopt the desired policies.

---

[9]Op. cit., p. 302.

How then does he expect them to be implemented globally? For, as we have already established, international agreements will not and cannot achieve what is necessary. Gore knows what should be done, but he rejects the one and only precondition that it ever could be.

6.8   Realists and Utopians

TO castigate the proposal of world federation as merely academic and utopian should thus be seen as ludicrous. What is utopian is visionary and impracticable, but that federalism as such is neither is made blatantly apparent by the existence and successful working of numerous actual federal states in the world today, notably the Swiss, the Australian, the Canadian and the Indian, and most prominently of all, the United States of America. It is curious that writers like Al Gore should dismiss world federation as unfeasible while they recognize without hesitation the success and stability of the American Constitution, a governmental system which Gore himself admires, praises, and in which he has effectively served.

In the eighteenth century there were many who castigated the idea of federalism as impracticable and undesirable—witness the arguments that Hamilton and Madison were constrained to advance to allay such fears and to recommend union—yet the United States has been a spectacular example of the practicability and resilience of federalism.

World federation would, indeed, be more complex and would present greater problems of organization. But that these could not be overcome will be disproved in the following chapters.

Surely, what must be identified as utopian are those proposals which, as has been shown above, could not possibly work in an association of sovereign states, and the true visionaries are they who imagine that peace can be preserved by reliance on treaties and the good faith of national sovereign powers, which history has consistently shown to be fickle.

That organizations like the League of Nations and the United Nations, whatever advantages they can provide, are incapable of preventing wars and are seldom able to pacify determined combatants has time and again become dismally apparent. That they cannot ensure the observance of treaties is equally manifest, and they certainly could not underwrite or maintain any Global Plan that would be adequate to save the Earth's ecology from disruption.

It is, then, clearly only delusory complacency and visionary optimism that can persuade politicians and academic theorizers that contemporary problems can successfully be met through the agency of such organizations. The only realistic and shrewdly practical reformers are those who advocate world federation, the one and only expedient that has any real chance of success, and one, examples of which on a smaller scale are plentiful, have proved impressively and stably democratic, and are practically effective.

6.9 Conditions of Federation

STATES are persuaded to unite under a federal government for diverse reasons. Sometimes it may be that they are jointly subject to some external threat, and seek to unite for mutual protection. In the ordinary way, a military alliance, or at most a confederation would be sufficient to meet that need if other pressing conditions did not demand a closer union.

But if external danger is considered a necessary condition for federation, it is undoubtedly one now present to the Earth as a whole. There can be no doubt that the nations of the world at the present time are under a threat more terrible and less liable to mitigation than any mere augury of military invasion.

The prospect of destruction now imminent cannot be averted by any military alliance, and a confederation, (under which classification the United Nations would fall) is manifestly inadequate, so the one remaining course is federal unification.

Another appropriate cause for federation is the interdependence of neighbouring states who find that their sovereign separateness creates tensions and confusion in their mutual relations, as occurred among the newly liberated British colonies in North America after their revolutionary war against the British Crown.

This again is precisely the situation in which modern nations find themselves. They are all mutually interdependent, yet their interrelation, both economic and political, is marred by constant tensions and disputes, by threatened conflict, and fatal contradiction (as when loans from the IMF and World Bank encourage economic policies that are environmentally destructive and saddle the poorer nations with crippling and intolerable debts, or when food surpluses build up excessively in some regions, while starvation ravages others). The European Community is clearly in this situation, being a sort of confederation with persisting strains and difficulties, which it is seeking to overcome by uniting its members more closely.

Old-fashioned ideologues like Margaret Thatcher and some of her successors inveighed against this trend, but they failed to distinguish between dictatorial centralized government which she feared and democratic federalism which she should have welcomed. Instead of fulminating against the latter, she would have done better, in her speech at The Hague, to urge more democratization of the Community's institutions by making the Commission an elected cabinet responsible to the European Parliament, and giving that elected body proper legislative powers.

The republics of the former Soviet Union are in the same condition of mutual strain and conflict, with no effective federal constitution for the so-called Commonwealth to provide the means to resolve the differences and disputes between its members. The reluctance of the separate states to federate is to be attributed to the fact that they had been long held together by a dictatorial and tyrannous regime, a revival of which they would naturally deprecate. Nevertheless, the solution to many of their problems quite obviously lies in some more democratic form of federation.

Another precondition favourable to federation is that the nations uniting should previously have belonged to some other form of union, either a colonial empire or a confederation of some sort. The states that federated to form the United States of America had been in both these situations. Many, if not all, of the states of the Earth today have similarly experienced some form of looser association, first in the League of Nations and then in the United Nations. Further, in recent decades, various regional alliances and economic groupings have come into being (such as BRICS, the economic association of Brazil, Russia, India, China, and South Africa), which might well prepare the ground for closer association.

6.10 Hypothetical Transformations

THE existence of a world community has now become unquestionable. It is what the jurists cited above have recognized and what Falk calls the global civil society. It makes itself visible in the activity of numerous nongovernmental organizations (NGOs), in the response of world public opinion to violations of human rights or unjustifiable conduct on the part of ethnic groups (as, for instance, the behavior of the Serbs in the former Yugoslavia), and in the massive popular demonstrations in many countries against the war in Iraq. Once this world community with the global common interests that unite it is given institutional expression in a democratic federal structure of World Government, the political crises that are now so frequent and ubiquitous will either disappear or be totally transformed.

In a federation the member states will require no military forces, because their rights will be enshrined in the Federal Constitution and will be upheld by the federal courts. Military coups like those in Chile, Burma, Nigeria, Thailand and elsewhere, could not then occur.

Legal defence of civil and human rights would prevent terrorist freedom fighters from resorting to violence, and there would be no more popular uprisings against despotic governments: disputes unresolved and grievances unaddressed by state governments could be submitted for settlement to the federal courts, providing an ever-ready hedge against internal unrest. Those resorting to violence of any kind could be arrested and prosecuted under federal criminal law as they are now under municipal law without the need to resort to excessive force.

Such conditions would eliminate the causes and provide solutions of ethnic conflicts like those that have arisen in Kosovo and East Timor. If civil strife were to break out, the control of the arms trade and of the supply of arms in general would effectively prevent the violence from spreading and the world government would be empowered to send in, not just peacekeeping, but peacemaking forces.

In short, the carnage and misery lately witnessed in Bosnia, Rwanda, and still raging in Israel, Syria, Iraq, Sudan and elsewhere, could hardly have arisen, because the ethnic conflicts could easily have been equitably settled under federal law and brought to an end. The frustration hitherto experienced in dealing with international terrorism could no longer hamper those who wish to see the culprits brought to justice. There would be no sovereign regimes (so-called rogue states) to shield and protect them or prevent their apprehension.

Had Libya been a member of a world federation, no Colonel Gadaffy could have stood in the way of the arrest, on the warrant of a federal Attorney-General, of suspected criminals; nor could the Taliban in Afghanistan have protected Osama bin Laden. Economic sanctions harmful to the welfare of entire populations would not be called for, nor any military threat—nothing more than firm action by the federal police.

Where relief from famine and other distress is needed, it could be organized and provided without fear of obstruction by civil wars. Ethnic groups (Kurds, Armenians, Tamils or whoever) could appeal to the federal courts for protection of their rights and could be given autonomy within the federation without need or pretext to fight for sovereign independence. Disputes such as those between the republics of the former Soviet Union would not arise, as they have done over the possession of the Black Sea fleet (which would have been abolished and replaced by a coast guard), over responsibility for nuclear armaments (which would have been transferred to the World Disarmament Agency), or over the command of the army of the new commonwealth, for which there would be no further use.

The armed struggle that raged over the Nagorno-Karabach region between Armenia and Azerbaijan need never have happened if the dispute could have been submitted to a world court, defiance of whose ruling could have been dealt with as an ordinary criminal offence committed by the individuals concerned, who could have been arrested by the federal police and prosecuted by the federal courts. In fact, even now, if the Commonwealth of Independent States could agree upon a federal constitution under which they could unite, these excesses might be overcome. The main reason, it would seem, why they do not is their fear of a centralised tyranny such as the Soviets imposed; but a genuinely democratic constitution properly authorised by the people and observed by their elected officials could obviate that.

Once the political battles and entanglements are eliminated that are generated by the relations between sovereign independent states, or communities seeking sovereign independence, the real and most pressing menaces to human survival could be addressed without constant distraction of attention by local disputes and belligerence, and plans could be made to meet them without the need to conclude treaties between states whose good faith is never wholly reliable. The plans once made and endorsed by the federal legislature could be enshrined in statutes; their implementation could be backed by legal enforcement as required, and progress could be made where today valuable time is lost in wrangling and vacillating without any reliable outcome. In a federated world the entire international prospect would be transformed.

There would indeed be a new world order, one in which war

would no longer be "politics by other means," for the political troubles and civil strife that are now plaguing the nations would have disappeared, and the urgent problems facing the human race as a whole could be addressed with some hope of solution.

6.11 Logistics

THE complex organization of a world federation would require an efficient logistical base—world-wide communications and transportation. Today the elements of such logistics are all spectacularly available. There are far swifter and longer-ranging methods of communication than existed in the North America of the late eighteenth and early nineteenth centuries, when, even before the conquest of the far west, two months had to be allowed for newly elected senators and representatives of the states of the Union to travel to Washington. Nowadays the whole Earth can be encircled in a time-span measured in hours, rather than days. Radio, television and the internet put peoples of the antipodes in mutual touch by the tap of a key, or the turn of a knob, or they can communicate yet more directly through satellite technology.

Politicians can talk to one another from points widely separated and can address millions of potential constituents scattered over thousands of miles. Debates on crucial issues can be conducted between speakers separated by oceans and can be heard and seen by audiences across continents. Information can be transmitted and publicized the world over, in any desired number of languages, and political leaders can confer together from opposite ends of the Earth. Today, in all respects except political organization, the world is a unified whole, and its peoples are potentially a single community with the weightiest interests in common.

6.12 The Obvious Conclusion and What Obscures It

THE necessary and sufficient conditions for world federation are therefore at hand, and the pressing need for an authority that can legislate measures to combat the desperate global problems facing humanity is unquestionable. All that remains to be done is to persuade the peoples of the world of the danger they seem so reluctant to acknowledge, and of the one course of action prerequisite to dealing with it, so that they will take the necessary steps to establish appropriate legislative institutions. It is not that a federal structure of international government will automatically solve all difficulties.

It is only the precondition, the administrative structure, that will permit the necessary expedients to be put into practice. That it is the necessary precondition is made plain by the stubborn obstacle to the solution of world problems presented by national sovereignty and the failure of all the other options available.

The global problems are complicated and immense and they will require all the ingenuity and effort that the best minds can devote to them if they are to be solved. But what is, or should now be, clear as daylight is that no effort or ingenuity can succeed as long as national interests divert their course into the wrong channels, and sovereign governments frustrate the implementation of the best laid plans. It should likewise be obvious that diplomacy, international agreements, and treaties entered into by sovereign states, but observance of which cannot be enforced, do not help.

Why is it that so few people nowadays are able to recognize clearly the nature of the predicament in which the human race is now placed, let alone the path by which to extricate it? In part, perhaps, it is because we have become so mesmerized by the achievements of modern science that we convince ourselves of the ability of scientists to resolve the problems and provide the means of escape from the consequences of their own technology. In this we may not be altogether wrong, but scientists, however authoritative their advice may be and whatever their skills, cannot, on their own initiative, take the necessary steps to effect the remedial measures.

This requires government action, and there is a prevalent failure to realize that whatever the remedies may be, they cannot be applied without legal enforcement, which is insufficient within national boundaries; and, as things now stand, no authority, other than national governments, is available beyond those limits that has the power to enact the means of application. This again is due to our preoccupation with the indispensability of national independence, a fetish devotion to which in the present age threatens our very survival.

What then should we do? How should we proceed? What may be learnt from the history of past federations? Let us brush away the scales from our eyes, remove our blinkers and consider urgently the practical steps immediately necessary.

Chapter 7

The Precedent

TO answer the questions with which the last chapter ended, it would help to look back at the history of the foundation of the most impressive and successful of existing federations. In 1774, when resentment against the government of George III was reaching boiling point in the thirteen North American British colonies, the colonists called together the First Continental Congress to coordinate their resistance.

It was no more than a Convention and it produced little beyond determination to cooperate in defiance of the autocratic imperial rule, and one or two high-sounding documents (like a Declaration of Rights). At the outbreak of War in the following year (May, 1775) a Second Congress was convened, but it too was no more than a convention of delegates, without executive power.

The Congress did its best to direct the War of Independence that ensued, but it was not much more than a forum for debate, with few or no powers from the start, which exercised less and less influence as the war continued. Mutual jealousies surfaced among the emerging states, and economic crises loomed. Monetary contributions to the running of the Congress was voluntary and seldom forthcoming. Paper-money was freely issued, which depreciated to worthlessness ("not worth a Continental"); individual states began issuing their own currency, which also depreciated; families became destitute, and confusion rife. When the war ended, disregarding its undertakings in the Congress, the legislature of Virginia independently ratified the peace treaty with England and concluded an alliance with France.

In order to stabilize the situation, in 1776 the Congress appointed a committee, which drafted the Articles of Confederation that it adopted in the following year, but it was not until five years later that all the states had agreed to ratify them. Even then, as the Confederacy had no executive head and no legal means of enforcing its decisions, its members continued to pull in different directions and to ignore its ordinances.

Again the states bickered over, and sometimes refused to pay, their financial contributions to the running of the Congress. (Compare the reluctance of the U.S. to pay dues to the U.N.) They quarreled over boundaries and came near to open warfare; they levied customs dues on one another's exports and entered into mutually contradictory relations with foreign powers. Once more, several began to issue paper money of their own which rapidly became worthless.

The effects inflamed tempers and instigated Shays' rebellion in Massachusetts, which momentarily threatened to escalate into civil war. Nine of the states mustered their own navies, yet none of them could command respect abroad: Barbary pirates decimated American trade in the Mediterranean and the disunited navies were powerless to prevent them, while the disagreement and disarray among the states, and the weakness of the Confederacy, excited little more than contempt from Britain and the older regimes. Their very existence and independence seemed threatened by anarchy and chaos.

In miniature, the situation on the American seaboard in 1786 foreshadowed the international scene of the 20th and 21st centuries, first under the League of Nations and then under the United Nations. The problems faced by the ex-colonies were similar to, if more restricted in scope, than those by which the western nations were beset in 1919, and the whole world in 1946; though by then they had become immeasurably more menacing. A similar state of affairs is now prevailing in the former Soviet Union, and the conduct of some members of the United Nations at the present time is reminiscent of what occurred in America in 1786. But the newly established American states recognized their predicament and took the necessary step to extricate themselves, as the nations of the world have yet to do.

Virginia called a convention at Annapolis, which agreed only to meet again at Philadelphia in the following year. Those who assembled there became the Constitutional Convention, authorized solely to revise Articles of Confederation; but the delegates were acutely aware that something more drastic was needed if the union was to become viable. So they drafted a federal Constitution, which was eventually adopted as the Constitution of the United States of America under which the greater part of North America has been governed to this day.

Let me here quote Al Gore once again:

> The world as a whole has now arrived at a watershed comparable in some ways to the challenge that confronted the founders two hundred years ago. Just as the thirteen colonies faced the task of defining a framework to unite their common interests and identity, the people of all nations have begun to feel that they are part of a truly global civilization, united by common interests and concerns— among the most important of which is the rescue of our environment.[1]

But then he rejects out of hand the natural and obvious conclusion, that the world as a whole must now take the same step as the founding fathers of the United States then did. Why, indeed, should Gore think this appropriate for America but not for the wider global community, when he so perceptively understands the analogous situations?

---

[1] Al Gore, op cit., p. 204.

The Fathers of the American Constitution had to solve the problem of maintaining states' rights and, at the same time, ensuring central coordination. They had to establish on a firm basis a federal executive and a judicial system that could settle disputes between the states and enforce federal law upon individuals, as one of them, John Fiske, put it:

> When an individual defies the law, you can lock him up in jail, or levy an execution upon his property, and he is helpless as a straw on the billows of the ocean. He cannot raise a militia to protect himself. But when the law is defied by a state, it is quite otherwise. You cannot put a state into jail, nor seize its goods; you can only make war on it, and if you try that expedient you find that the state is not helpless. Its local pride and prejudices are aroused against you, and its militia will turn out in full force to uphold the infraction of law

This neatly states the antithesis that persists even now, and is at the present time much more dangerous in its practical implications. Yet, at the same time, the states were jealous of their rights as independent states, and that aspiration had also somehow to be satisfied. The same problem faces would-be World Constitution framers today.

The Philadelphia Convention had no precedent to go upon and had to work out the solution by patient and laborious negotiation. Today there is a precedent, and better, there is an actual draft *Constitution for the Federation of the Earth* already drawn up, which needs only ratification by peoples and governments to become operative.

In the 1950s there was considerable interest in the idea of world government. The Second World War had left the nations exhausted, many of them almost mortally crippled, and the advent of atomic weapons made the prospect of any repetition of the conflagration too shattering to contemplate.

The idea of world federation has been ably discussed and persuasively advocated in a number of excellent books on the subject.[2] But neither the peacemakers nor the mass of the people seemed able to grasp the crucial issues nor the conception of world unity. In all probability the major stumbling block was the mutual opposition and implacable hostility of the two main ideologies, each of them a self-styled "democracy", one liberal and the other communistic.

Nationalism, however, quite independently of ideology was a potent factor; so the prospect of world government faded and throughout the Cold War era the idea was castigated as visionary idealism. In 1945 a conference held in Dublin, New Hampshire, considering the prospects of atomic warfare, declared that a world federation capable of preventing war and with genuine legislative power, responsible executive, and adequate tribunals to enforce enacted law, was the sole means of averting global catastrophe. There was (declared the delegates) no time to be lost—"the necessity of immediate action is urgent. There is not a moment to lose." Since then we have lost more than half a century! If we delay any longer we are in danger of losing everything.

Nevertheless, at that time several associations and societies were founded to argue and campaign for world unification, each supporting different versions of the way to attain it. Several draft world constitutions were proposed and published, but only one

---

[2]Cf. W.B. Curry, *The Case for Federal Union* (Harmondsworth, Penguin Books, 1939); Emery Reves, *The Anatomy of Peace* (New York, Harper Bros. 1945, London, G.Allen and Unwin, 1946); Clarence K. Streit, Union Now, *A Proposal for an Atlantic Federal Union of the Free* (New York, Harper Bros., 1949), *World Government or Anarchy? Urgent Need for World Order* (Chicago, World Citizens Association, 1939); Harris Wofford, *It's up to Us: Federal World Government in Our Time* (New York, Harcourt Brace, 1946); Ralph Barton Perry, *One World in the Making* (New York, Current Books, 1945); Oscar Newfang, *World Government* (New York, Barnes and Noble, 1942); Lionel Curtis, *The Way to Peace* (London, Oxford University Press, 1941); R.M. Hutchins, *Preliminary draft of a World Constitution* (University of Chicago Press, 1948); E.E. Harris, *The Survival of Political Man* (Gohannesburg, Witwatersrand University Press, 1950); Jerry Tetalman and Byron Belitsos, *One World Democracy: A Progression Vision for Enforceable World Law* (San Rafael, CA, Origin Press, 2005); Glen T. Martin, *Ascent to Freedom: Practical and Philosophical Foundations of Democratic World Law* (Appomattox: IED Press, 2009); and many others.

was backed by any practical measures towards implementation. One body of federalists decided to take positive action and to go ahead not only with the framing of a federal constitution for the peoples of the Earth, but to take practical steps towards its ratification.

This was the World Constitution and Parliament Association (WCPA). It drew up an Agreement in 1958 to call a World Constituent Convention and circulated it world wide, with a request to both national governments and the people of each state to send delegates. Several thousand prominent persons signed the agreement and supported the project.

In 1961 a definite call to a World Constituent Assembly was drafted and sent out, which again secured thousands of signatures, including those of the Presidents and Prime Ministers of five countries. A first preparatory congress was held in Denver, Colorado, in 1963 repeating the call for delegates. Two years later, a second preparatory congress met at Milan in Italy (in 1965), and, in 1967, the outline of a constitution was drafted and circulated for discussion.

At the same time, it was decided to plan for a Peoples' Parliament to meet concurrently with the World Constituent Assembly and a revised call attracted yet more signatories. At a third preparatory meeting, in 1967, in Geneva, Switzerland, it was decided to go ahead and convene a World Constituent Convention whether or not any governments participated; and 300 people's delegates pledged themselves to attend. At Interlaken and in Wolfach (West Germany) the Convention met and in June of the next year began work on drafting a Constitution. Today this 1968 meeting is known as the "First Constituent Assembly."

A first draft was completed in 1973, printed and circulated for comments, and a second session of the Constituent Assembly was called for 1977. It met in Innsbruck and debated every paragraph of the draft and adopted amendments. The document was signed by 138 participants from 25 countries in six continents. Although no governments had sent representatives, a call was issued for ratification of the draft Constitution by the nations and peoples of the Earth

A third session of the Assembly took place in Colombo, Sri Lanka, in January, 1979 and issued a further appeal to national parliaments to ratify the Constitution provisionally—that is, with the reservation that the draft would be reviewed and further amended if necessary.

Subsequent international meetings have been held in New Delhi, New York (where a copy of the Constitution was distributed to delegates to the United Nations, many of whom were also entertained by the Association to a luncheon, when copies of the Constitution were distributed and its aims and rationale were explained), in Washington, D.C., Goa (India), Tours (France), and elsewhere; and a fourth session of the Assembly took place in Troia, Portugal, in 1991, from which a new call was made for a world-wide campaign for ratification.

Meanwhile, the Assembly called into being the provisional World Parliament, which has met at a number of times and places: in India (several times), England, the United States, Spain (Barcelona), Malta, Bangkok, and Libya, and has drafted and approved a number of bills dealing with world problems, including world finance, climate change, and the elimination of nuclear weapons.

None of this spectacular, professional and devoted work, conducted over the past fifty-six years, is official, in the sense that it has any legal force, but it is obviously representative of a considerable body of opinion derived from a large number of different nations the world over.

I have recounted all these various occasions in order to make plain the care, industry and effort that has gone into the drafting of the *Constitution for the Federation of Earth*, the international character and extent of the representation among the delegates who took part in its production, and the effort and length of time spent on getting it right.

The Association is genuinely international, and the persons

who have been active in drafting the Constitution include the most eminent international lawyers and professors of law and politics, drawn from many countries.

Moreover, it could all become official if ratified by a sufficient number of organizations and governments, a ratification that need commit nobody to anything more than the principle of world government, leaving the details to be finally decided by a World Parliament properly elected as the Constitution provides.

Some world federalists have criticised this Constitution as undemocratic because it was not drafted by a popularly elected constituent assembly—but this criticism is misguided. What makes a constitution democratic is not who drafted it but that it should be accepted by the peoples who are to live under its provisions.

This Constitution is an admirable document on which it would be difficult to improve and it provides (in Article 18) for its own amendment as soon as it becomes operative, either by petition or as required by a democratically elected world parliament, and for periodical special sessions thereafter to reconsider its details. So nobody who objects to its details need be reluctant to ratify it provisionally.

A constitution for world federation cannot be imposed on any nation by any means. What has been drawn up is a draft offered for approval and willing adoption by people who see the urgent need for establishing a new world order, in which genuine world law can be made and administered as the one and only means of ensuring the Rule of Law world-wide, the adoption of effective remedies for the deleterious environmental disruption now taking place, and of perpetuating a peaceful and law-abiding world community, free from the fear of nuclear disaster.

In 1787 the Philadelphia Convention was called only to examine the shortcomings of the Articles of Confederation. However, the delegates from South Carolina came with an almost complete draft of a federal constitution drawn up by one of its members, Charles Pinkney, who argued that amendment of the Articles of Confederation could not serve to remedy the situation in which the states then found themselves, and which, as I have tried to show, was similar to that in which the world as a whole finds itself today.

After spending two months in debate, the Convention submitted twenty-three amendments to a five member Committee of Detail, of which the chairman was John Rutledge of South Carolina, who presented the committee with Mr. Pinckney's draft.

The committee, when it reported, presented the Convention with a complete draft (Mr. Pinckney's, with some additions) for a federal Constitution of the United States of America. This is what has now been done for the Earth as a whole by the World Constitution and Parliament Association. All that is needed today—we cannot afford to wait until tomorrow—is the ratification of the instrument that has been produced by the federating nations.

The arduous work of the Convention that framed the Constitution of the United States two centuries ago, has now already been accomplished for the Earth as a whole. The fact that the need is urgent and that time presses for the solution of the most menacing global problems, makes this preparatory work especially valuable and propitious. Time need no longer be spent on working out the difficult details, or on wrangling over states rights, or similar controversial issues.

All that is now required for genuine progress is that what has so far been accomplished should be universally endorsed and that the Constitution that has been drafted be adopted. Those who advocate a more indirect course of progress through reform of the United Nations until its Charter can be converted into a world federal constitution (and there are many) fail to consider how urgently this conversion is needed and how long the process they recommend is likely to take, if it can ever be accomplished at all.

Let us then examine the Constitution and consider its suitability for the purpose for which it is designed, its viability as a practical institutional form, and its probable efficacy in accomplishing the end at which we aim—namely, to maintain world peace and to stave off the threat of wholesale destruction of the planet's ecology and the consequent extinction of human civilization, or possibly of mankind and of all living species.

Chapter 8

The Structure of World Union

THE essential condition of the establishment of world government must be fundamental constitutional law enacted by a democratically elected world parliament and enshrined as statutory. This constitution must ensure the protection of communal and individual rights, both human and civil, for everybody on earth, all who will henceforth be world citizens as well as the citizens of their own national heritage.

Once the Constitution has been ratified by a prescribed sufficient number of national governments it will become operative and the world parliament can be elected according to its provisions henceforth to be recognized as legally empowered (i) to amend the Constitution if the majority of its members so desire, or to consider amendments suggested by petition from among its electors; (ii) to consider and debate, and if approved by the required majority, to enact into world law measures passed by the Provisional World Parliament prior to the ratification of the Constitution; (iii) forthwith to function as the final World Legislature.

8.1   Electoral Divisions

THE first requirement of a democratic world administration is the division of the Earth into electoral areas, so as to ensure equitable representation. The Constitution provides for distribution of voting power by denominating five continental divisions (but not necessarily limited to five, if at any time more should be thought desirable). These are then divided into Magna-Regions, in which are grouped contiguous electoral and administrative regions, which are again subdivided into electoral and administrative districts.

The districts are to be the electoral units. There are not to be more than 1000 of them and they are to be as nearly as possible equal in population. Their boundaries are to conform as nearly as practicable and desirable (though not necessarily) to the national boundaries at present prevailing. One can imagine that circumstances may make it desirable for some relatively small areas to be included in the same electoral district, where the people have national affinities or other interests in common with those in areas overlapping national boundaries.

Or again, an ethnic group now included within certain national boundaries along with other such groups, could be included in a different electoral district for the purpose of voting for representatives in a World Legislature if there were no other way of equalizing constituencies. The main consideration is to make representation as fair and equal as possible.

8.2   The Structures of Government

CLEARLY, the first necessity is a democratically elected Legislature. Next, there must be an Executive to carry out the enacted laws, with an Administrative branch to apply and enforce them. There must also be a Judiciary to interpret the law and to adjudicate in cases of infringement or dispute. Finally, but far from least in importance, is an Ombudsmus to protect individuals and legitimate associations from maladministration, and to eradicate corruption.

This is not the only feature of the constitution, although it is perhaps the most important, which provides safeguards against the abuse of power and surveillance for the maintenance of justice by government with the consent of the governed throughout the world. The Constitution, accordingly, sets up a Parliament, a Presidium with a cabinet, and an elaborate Administrative system under a Secretary General consisting of 28 Departments, with an Integrative Complex comprising seven Agencies to coordinate the various functions of administration and to keep Parliament and the Presidium informed of its progress.

1. The Legislature: The Parliament is to be tricameral—a significant feature. The House of Peoples is to represent the populace voting with universal suffrage directly for representatives from each electoral district.

The second House gives equitable representation to the different nationalities, members being elected or appointed as decided by each national government. To this House of Nations each nation with population of between 100,000 and 10,000,000 is to send one delegate, each nation with population between 10,000,000 and 100,000,000 will send two delegates, and nations with larger populations than one hundred million will each send three delegates.

The system of representation is similar in principle to that in the United States, where the people are directly represented in the House of Representatives and the states are given equal representation in the Senate. But here more consideration is given to the proportion of population comprised in each national group.

In this way a balance would be maintained between the interests of mankind as a whole and of particular national groups, without sacrificing either unduly to the other. On the one hand, national interests would not be allowed to impede measures needed to ensure world common interests, and on the other hand, nations need not fear arbitrary neglect or override of those matters of special interest to themselves. So here is the first safeguard of national freedom and self-determination within a community the common welfare of which should take precedence if the two come into conflict.

The third House, the House of Counsellors, is to consist of 200 members, ten from each of the 20 Electoral and Administrative Regions. They are to be nominated by the convocations, students and faculties of universities, colleges, scientific institutes and academies within each region, and elected by the members of the other two Houses, voting as representatives of each of the respective regions for its own Counsellors.

The function of this House is to provide the other two legislative Houses with expert information and advice. The House of Counsellors will not itself vote on Bills before the other two Houses, unless there is deadlock between them, but it may initiate legislation for submission to the other two Houses, or introduce opinions, or proposals into their deliberations which they must then consider and vote on. The influence of the Counsellors, besides being instructive and helpful in the working of the two main legislative bodies, preventing rash, ill-advised, or misinformed legislation, should exercise further restraint upon possible abuse of power, or unwarranted sacrifice of special interests.

2. The Executive: The Presidium is not to be in the hands of any single individual, but is to consist of a committee of five, each member from a different Continental Division. The chair of the Presidium is to be taken by each member in annual rotation, who will for the term be designated President, the other four being Vice-Presidents. Decisions will be taken by a majority vote of the five. The term of office for the Presidium is to be five years, running concurrently with that for members of the World Parliament, and no incumbent may serve for more than two terms. There is thus little or no danger of any personality cult or domination by one dictatorial figure, while all the main regions and divisions of peoples and nationalities of the world would be represented.

The United States Constitution is based on the principle of balance of powers between the Executive, the Legislature and the

Judiciary. In Britain and many other European countries, constitutions are framed on the principle of responsible government: that is, the executive is responsible to the legislature, and judges are appointed by the executive (as in the United States). While the structure of the World Parliament, with respect to the first two Houses, follows the American pattern, the relationship of the three functions of government is similar to the British, the executive being elected by the legislature, which also elects the judges, as will presently appear.

The members of the Presidium are to be nominated by the House of Counsellors from among the members of the three Houses of Parliament, no more than one third being from the House of Nations or from the Counsellors themselves, and elected by all three Houses sitting together.

At the same time there is an element in this World Constitution resembling the American model, in that the Executive is forbidden by the law of the Constitution to act contrarily either to the Constitution or to the enacted laws of the World Parliament. It cannot dissolve Parliament or any of its Houses, nor can it veto legislation properly enacted, nor can it declare a state of emergency and suspend the Constitution, and it may not flout the decisions of the World Courts.

At the same time, the World Supreme Court, with whichever of its subsidiary courts may be appropriate, has jurisdiction over issues arising from the provisions of the Constitution, which would include any actions *ultra vires* by the Executive branch. Here are further safeguards against authoritarianism or arbitrary rule. There is to be an Executive Cabinet of twenty to thirty members, at least one from each of the ten World Magna-Regions and not more than two from anyone nation. There may not be more than one member in the Executive Cabinet from any nation from which a member of the World Parliament is serving in the Presidium.

Members of the Cabinet will be the Ministers in charge of departments and agencies of the World Administration. As thirty-four of these altogether have been designated in the Constitution, the Vice-Presidents will also rank as Cabinet Ministers heading specific departments or agencies. The members of the Presidium will nominate at least twice as many persons as are necessary for the rank of Cabinet Minister, and from the list of nominees, the three House of Parliament sitting together will elect the cabinet.

Ministerial portfolios will be assigned by the Presidium, but not more than three may be held by any one cabinet member. It is explicitly stated in the Constitution that the Presidium and its Cabinet are to be responsible to the World Parliament, both individually and collectively.

The powers of the World Executive are limited by the Constitution, as has already been outlined, to guard against the possibility of arbitrary and dictatorial rule. Further in several Articles the Constitution provides for the removal from office, by an absolute majority vote of all three Houses in joint session, of any member of the Executive or official of the Administration, for good cause (e.g. corruption, malfeasance or abuse of power).

3. The Administration: To implement World Law and the policies determined by the World Executive, there are to be 28 Departments and 7 World Agencies. These are listed in Section 3 of Article 7 of the Constitution and Section 1 of Article 8.

The seven agencies are collectively called the Integrative Complex, their joint function being to coordinate the working of government, to administer its finances and to conduct research and planning, as well as to carry out other tasks detailed in this Section and in Section 2 of Article 8. Each agency is to be headed by a Cabinet Minister and a Senior Administrator, together with a Commission appointed by the Presidium.

One very important function that will be performed by one of the Agencies (the Institute on Government Procedures and World Problems) will be to instruct World Government personnel and delegates in the nature and interrelation of the various organs of Government and to give them expert information on world problems. If properly used, this educational function, especially as relating to the World Civil Service could help to eliminate bureaucratic inefficiency, one of the disadvantages feared by many opponents of world federation.

Another very significant provision appears in Section 8 of Article 8, which sets up a Commission for Legislative Review to examine the laws passed by the World Parliament or adopted from presently existing International Law to see that they are appropriate and serve the purposes intended, and to recommend amendment or repeal when necessary. The Commission is to consist of twelve members, two elected from each of the Houses of Parliament and the Presidium, from among the World Judges, and the Ombudsmus. Here is yet another safeguard against rash, inequitable or invasive legislation that member nations might resent, an issue taken up again more specifically in Article 14.

The first of the agencies in the Integrative Complex is the World Civil Service Administration, the duties of which are to select suitably qualified persons for appointment to a World Civil Service to carry out the provisions of World Law and the decisions of the Presidium and Cabinet, to define standards and devise tests for such personnel, to fix their salary scales and to employ those appointed as required by the various executive departments and agencies.

The World Civil Service Administration is to be headed by a ten member commission as well as the appropriate Cabinet Minister or Vice-President and Senior Administrator. There is to be one commissioner from each of the ten World Electoral and Administrative Magna-Regions. As before, they will be nominated by the House of Counsellors, but they will be appointed by the Presidium, not elected by the World Parliament, for five year terms, of which they may serve more than one consecutively.

4. The Judiciary: We have observed that International Law, because it lays down from the outset that its only subjects are sovereign states, renders itself impotent, because sovereignty, by definition can be subject to no higher law. Sovereign governments submit to the judgments of the International Court of Justice only if and when they are prepared to recognize its jurisdiction, which they do only when it suits their national interest; and even then they are able, if they dislike the final decision, to repudiate their previous agreement to accept the decision of the Court.

International law is thus rendered ineffective and ceases to be law in anything but name and theory. In contrast, the *Constitution for the Federation of Earth* gives mandatory jurisdiction to a World Supreme Court in all cases arising under its provisions, and makes its decisions binding on all the parties involved.

Further, a fatal weakness of International Law as it is presently conceived is that its interpretation is left to scholars, who have no political power, or to the International Court, whose rulings are unenforceable, or to the arbitrary and self-interested dictum of sovereign governments, who are supposed to be its subjects and are the parties to the disputes submitted (if they are) to its judgment. The World Supreme Court, in contrast, would be authorized by the World Constitution to interpret the laws enacted by the World Parliament, and its judgments would be final for all parties, thus providing an impartial arbiter disinterested in the issue subject to dispute.

According to the World Constitution, a collegium of World Judges is to be established by the World Parliament, consisting of a minimum of twenty judges, which may, if occasion arises, be expanded to as many as (but no more than) sixty members. They will be nominated by the House of Counsellors and elected by majority vote of all three Houses in joint session. The nominees must exceed in number two or three times that to be elected, and an equal number of judges is to be elected from each World Electoral and Administrative Magna-Region, to ensure equitable distribution and national impartiality.

The qualifications for judges are laid down in Article 9, Sec. 4.9 of the Constitution. They will hold office for a ten year term, but may be reelected for successive terms without limit. The Collegium will elect a Presiding Council of five members, one from each of the five Continental Divisions, who will serve for a term of five years and may not serve for more than two successive terms. One of the members of the Presiding Council will be designated Chief Justice, but no one may serve in that capacity for two successive five year terms. The duties of the Collegium will include assigning judges to the various Benches of the World Supreme Court, at least three to each, except those on constitutional issues and international disputes, and the Appellate Bench, which are to have at least five.

The World Court set up by the Constitution is initially to consist of eight Benches, with more to be established if recommended by the Collegium of World Judges (Art. IX, Sec. B). On their recommendation also, the World Parliament may combine or abolish any new Benches thus established, but none of the original eight, except by amendment to the Constitution. Each Bench will annually choose its own Presiding Judge and will decide cases in specific classes, criminal, civil, constitutional, and so forth; and each, for its own class of cases, is to be the court of highest appeal, except for matters deemed to be of extraordinary public importance ¡/SPAN ¿that are to be referred to a Superior Tribunal of the World Supreme Court consisting of the Presiding Council of World Judges together with one member of each Bench named by its Presiding Judge.

This would establish a genuinely effective Judiciary for the whole world, with mandatory jurisdiction, that can adjudicate in any cases of dispute between nations, or about human rights, or concerning infringements of World Law, breach of agreements, or failure to carry out decreed measures of universal benefit. Means are to be provided for the effective enforcement of the Courts' decisions, as will next appear, an indispensable condition (now so frustratingly lacking) of coping satisfactorily with world problems.

5. Enforcement System: No law is really positive law, unless it is effective; that is, unless it can be enforced. For this reason the International Law now in vogue is not really positive law; for it has no better status than an international treaty and cannot be enforced except (as in the case of any treaty) by military action on the part of one or more of the parties in dispute. Its subjects are sovereign states, and in no other way can a sovereign state be coerced than by defeat in war. That is why International Law can never be a means of maintaining world peace.

International Law is in effect an agreement, or convention, a sort of contract, between states. In Municipal Law a contract can be enforced by the courts, but for International Law there is no enforcement provision that is not dependent on military force. Even the International Criminal Court (ICC), which opened its doors in 2002, is dependent on the nations signatory to its Statute to indict, arrest or prosecute individuals.

World Law as enacted by a properly constituted and democratically elected World Parliament, on the other hand, can be enforced (as is stated in Article 10, Sec. 1 of the *Constitution for the Federation of Earth*) directly upon individuals, who are held responsible for compliance, even if they are acting as officials or agents of an autonomous national government.

No problem arises in enforcing law upon individuals. They can be coerced without resort to military action, and under World Law they are not put into the impossible situation, that results from applying the Nuremberg Principle in current (or possible) international practice, of being held responsible for breaches of International Law while owing allegiance to a sovereign government whose laws or edicts may require action contrary to what International Law lays down.

The non-military character of enforcement is explicitly ordained by the World Constitution (Art. 10, Sec. 1.4-6), which, at the same time, provides for the devisal, by the World Parliament in consultation with the members of the Judiciary and the Enforcement System, of means to cope with actual or potential riots or insurrection. The emphasis is placed on the prevention of outbreaks of violence, which would obviate the need to suppress them after that has occurred. But should such prevention fail, the means of suppression will be decided as set out above. Further, assurance of fair hearings and due process is given for any persons concerned (Art. 10, Sec. 4).

The enforcement system is to be headed by an Office of World Attorneys General and a Commission of Regional World Attorneys. The first of these is to consist of five members, a World Attorney General and four Associate World Attorney Generals. They will be nominated by the House of Counsellors (three from each Continental Division) one of whom from each Division being elected by the vote of the three Houses of the World Parliament sitting together.

The Commission of Regional World Attorneys will have twenty members nominated from the twenty World Electoral and Administrative Regions (two or three from each) from whom the World Parliament by the usual procedure shall elect one for each Region. Article 10, Sec. 2 of the Constitution sets the terms of office for these officials and defines their functions as investigation, apprehension and arrest, prosecution of suspected law-breakers, correctional action against the persons accused, and conflict resolution. As for Judges, the Constitution sets out the required qualifications for Attorneys General and Regional Attorneys (Art. 10, Sec. 2.9).

One section of the staff of the Office of World Attorneys General and its Regional off-shoots—that responsible for the apprehension of violators of World Law—is to be the World Police. It will be divided by Regions, each having a Regional World Police Captain appointed by the regional World Attorney, while the Office of World Attorneys General will appoint a World Police Supervisor in charge of those police activities that transcend regional boundaries. Searches and arrests will require warrants issued by one or other of the Offices of the Attorneys General and the Police will be armed only with weapons sufficient and appropriate for the apprehension of individual law-breakers.

As with other officials and delegates of the World Government, World Police Supervisors or Captains can be removed from office for good cause by the World Parliament in joint session of all three Houses.

A world federation would thus be provided with an enforcement system adequate to maintain World Law without resort to excessive force, without danger of war, and without the frustration of defiance by sovereign states. Violators can be detected, arrested by the World Police and arraigned directly by the World Attorneys General, taking action against individuals, who are powerless to resist, and who will be committed only by due process of law, in which they can be assured of legal defence and a fair and impartial judgment.

An important question, however, now arises. Of the numerous powers of World Government listed in Article 4 of the Constitution, the first is to prevent wars and armed conflicts among the peoples of the earth. The second is to supervise disarmament and to prevent re-armament of the nations. Clearly this poses an immediate problem.

True it is that the Constitution will become effective only after full ratification and that implies that the ratifying governments will agree to its provisions. Article 17 of the Constitution stipulates that ratification carries with it an obligation to turn over to the World Government all weapons of mass destruction and a commitment never to use any armed forces against other members of the Federation. But if the federating nations are armed and if they are required to disarm, there must be some way of enforcing conformity upon any that proves recalcitrant.

What is it to be? This is a question to which we must return; but once it has been settled, there still remains that of quelling any possible insurrection that may occur after federation. The framers of the Constitution have recognized that prevention is better than cure. Nevertheless, the cure must be ready at hand and (except for non-military sanctions) is not obvious from the provisions as at present set out.

Non-military sanctions, as we have already insisted, are unlikely to be successful without at least the threat of forcible backing. It is, therefore, necessary that the Federation of Earth should have at its disposal some force, under the control of the World Parliament and its Executive, that is unchallengeable by any other power. This is a matter to which the World Constituent Assembly needs to pay attention, as it could prove crucial for the success of the Federation.

6. The Ombudsmus: As defender of the public against abuse of power, discrimination, or deprivation of rights, the Constitution sets up a Council of five World Ombudsmen, one of whom is to be the Principal World Ombudsman, and the other four are to be Associate World Ombudsmen. They are to be appointed by the same procedure as for other officials, one from each Continental Division, and are to be assisted by a Commission of World Advocates of twenty members nominated by the Council from the twenty World electoral and Administrative Regions.

The principal office of the World Ombudsmus will be located at the seat of the World Government and there will be an office in each of the regions in parallel with the offices of the World Attorneys General. Each regional office is to be headed by a World Advocate and supervised by an Associate World Ombudsman. The Ombudsmen and advocates will be qualified lawyers with at least five years' legal experience.

The Ombudsmen will be the watchdogs to ensure the welfare of all peoples, on the alert for perils from technical innovations and environmental disturbances. They will also receive and pursue complaints from citizens about any misconduct or abuse of authority, or neglect of duty, by World Civil Servants or other World Government officials. They will maintain surveillance over human and state rights; see that they are protected and defended by the World Courts, initiating litigation when deemed necessary; and they will keep watch over the functioning of departments, agencies and commissions of Government in all areas, to see that they are properly and efficiently executed. They will also report to the World Parliament and Presidium annually on the activities of government and make recommendations for improvements that need legislation.

A World Ombudsmus is an obvious necessity if justice is universally to be done, and to be seen to be done. It is equally a necessary safeguard against official misconduct, abuse of powers, and arbitrary action on the part of government agencies. The provision of this protection of citizens and social groups against the violation of their legitimate rights is a strong reason for commendation of the Constitution and a solid reassurance for any who may still have misgivings about the need for, and efficacy of World Government.

8.3   Bill of Rights

HAVING laid out the structure and composition of the institutions of World Government, the Constitution enunciates the rights universal to all people, legal, civil, political, intellectual, human and personal. They cover the rights to protection by the law against discrimination of every kind, of equality before the law, of *habeas corpus*; the rights to personal privacy, to family planning, to safety from threats to the peace, and to property free from arbitrary seizure; rights to freedom of travel, to freedom from military conscription; rights to protection from mental or physical violence, torture, duress, arbitrary arrest, detention and cruel or unusual punishment; rights to protection from slavery, peonage and conscription of labour; to freedom of conscience, of speech and expression, of publication; rights of assembly, peaceful demonstration and petition, freedom to organize politically, to campaign and to vote; rights to religious freedom, and to intellectual and academic liberty. This list of common rights is set out in Article 12, and some critics contend that they should be given more prominence, say, in the Preamble or in the opening Articles.

But that would be to put the cart before the horse. It is not realistic to declare the sanctity of universal rights before any authority with power to protect them is properly constituted. The Charter of Human Rights was approved by the United Nations over half a century ago, yet to this day there are nations that have not signed it and many more that constantly and flagrantly flout its principles. It has amounted to little more than a pious gesture, valuable only for the indication it gives of a general recognition of what ought to be, without any assurance that it will be. The violators are all sovereign governments, upon whom no effective compulsion can be imposed, and against whom, for the most part, non-military sanctions have either not been invoked or have been ineffective.

In a World Federation violators could always be identified as individuals and brought to book, could be prosecuted and punished as common criminals, by a government that has received its authority by popular consent and election to exercise power that no individual can resist, yet without the use of excessive force. Under such conditions rights can be protected, can be legally and practically ensured; and these conditions must first be established before the definition of rights can have practical significance.

The *Constitution for Federation of Earth* does not stop at enshrining common civil, political, personal and human rights under legal protection; it goes on in Article 13 to specify further aims and define further rights and freedoms as Directive Principles for World Government.

Article 13 declares that the World authority will impose an obligation on all subordinate administrative authorities to pursue every reasonable means to actualize rights to full employment with adequate remuneration, freedom of choice of vocation, unrestricted access to legitimate information and acquired knowledge, free public education, free health services, adequate housing, adequate food and water supplies, social security, sufficient leisure, protection against hazards of technical innovations and against ecological disruption, and to the discovery and use of alternative energy sources. Here, following on the broad functions of the Federation in Article 1, protection of our planetary environment is built into the Constitution as a human right. It also sets up as mandatory goals the maintenance of cultural diversity, the decentralization of administration and the freedom of cultural minorities to self-determination. Once again, there is assurance and protection for national traditions and cultural self-identity.

The Constitution, further, envisages universal freedom of migration, and the protection of, and provision for, refugees (for example, from natural disasters), as well as the abolition of the death penalty. Clear as it is from all that has gone before that local communities and national identities are to be preserved and protected under World Government, the Constitution goes further and leaves the matter in no possible doubt, by stating additional safeguards in Article 14, to ensure that the legislation and legal procedures, the public acts and records, of member nations shall be respected, as long as they are consistent with the provisions of the World Constitution. It assures freedom of choice within member nations to determine their own internal political, economic and social systems consistent with the rights above set out.

It grants rights of asylum to persons (if any) fleeing from oppression in countries not yet within the Federation; and, within limits, it grants leave to any persons wishing to secede from the Federation to do so. This last provision seems somewhat unnecessary and, perhaps, otiose; for it is hardly conceivable that anybody or any group of people would wish to escape from the security and freedoms assured by the World Constitution.

However, the presence in the Article of this provision can but serve to increase the confidence of any still hesitant about its liberality. Finally, in 14.2, it is plainly stated that all powers not delegated to the World Federal Government are to be reserved to the nations and peoples entering the Federation. Nothing could be more explicit or unambiguous.

8.4   Geographical Distribution of Seats of Government

TWENTY Federal Zones are to be distinguished in which the various organs of World Government are to be located, first within the five Continental Divisions, but later as the needs and resources of the Administration dictate. The precise divisions are to be determined by the World Parliament.

In each zone, a World Capital is to be established, one of which will be designated the Primary World Capital, where the primary seats of the several organs of World Government will be situated, and the other four will be Secondary World Capitals, where other major seats of government will reside.

Proposals for Zones and Capitals will be made by the Presidium, and decided from among these proposals by a simple majority vote of the three Houses of the World Parliament in joint session. The Presidium and Cabinet will then propose which of the five Capitals shall be Primary, and the choice again made by Parliament in the same manner.

Sessions of the World Parliament may be held, if it so decides, in rotation in each of the World Capitals. Relocations of Zones or Capitals will require a two-thirds majority of the three Houses sitting conjointly, and additional zones may be established by the procedure already laid down. These are simply workaday provisions necessary for obvious practical purposes.

8.5 World Territory and External Relations

THE framers of the World Constitution have envisaged its coming into operation by stages, not all of the present sovereign states joining the Federation simultaneously. This half-way stage, however, can only be temporary (and should be as brief as possible); because until World Government has universal jurisdiction the primary purpose that it sets out to achieve cannot be realized.

The Earth's ecology is a single system and its balance can be upset by practices in anyone area so as to affect all others. The hydrosphere is a single system and the biological community by which it is inhabited is indivisible. Likewise the atmosphere is changed as a whole by any excessive gaseous emissions anywhere in the world.

It follows that any independent sovereign nation of any considerable size, may fatally hamper whatever measures are taken to protect the environment by a World Federal Government. Accordingly, to attain its goals it must have universal jurisdiction, and that means that it must be authorized to enforce its law throughout the entire world. As it could not do so upon an independent state without the use of military force, and as war has a disastrous effect on people, economies and ecological systems, the objects of the entire project can be defeated by one recalcitrant external sovereign government. With this caveat we may note the provisions of Article 16 and what follows.

Section 1 of Article 16 designates as World Territory those areas of the Earth not under the jurisdiction of existing nations at the time of the formation of the Federation of Earth, and also the Moon, to be administered by the World Executive as determined by the World Parliament.

It is to include all seas and oceans, together with sea-beds and their resources more than twenty kilometres offshore, excepting inland seas under traditional national ownership.

It will also include vital straits, channels and canals, the Earth's atmosphere more than one kilometre above the general land surface, man-made satellites, any unclaimed islands or atolls, and any independent countries that choose the status of World Territory. Such assignation is entirely reasonable, and (once the Constitution is operative) legitimate. More questionable, unless all independent nations have ratified the World Constitution, is the inclusion of colonies (presumably of existing sovereign states) and disputed lands, which may choose that status, and nonindependent territories under United Nations mandate.

If a sovereign state which claimed such territories had not ratified the Constitution, there would be no feasible way of implementing the status of World Territory in their case, as long as that state prevented their transfer to the Federation. Paragraph 3 of the same section stipulates that the population of any World Territory not designated a World Federal Zone may elect (by plebiscite) to become a self-governing member of the World Federation, either singly or in combination with other such Territories or existing self-governing members.

The next Section brings all exploration of outer space under the exclusive control of the World Government, and undertakes that the World Federation shall maintain peaceful relations with any inhabitants who may be discovered on any other celestial body. So far so good; but it also states that the World Government shall maintain external relations, as directed by the World Presidium instructed by the World Parliament, with nations which have not joined the Federation of Earth, and that treaties with such nations shall be negotiated by the Presidium and ratified by majority vote of the three Houses of Parliament.

No mention is made of how the sanctity of such treaties is to be ensured, and, for reasons already set out, if such external relations were not to be merely provisional and their duration was not very short, this provision could prove to be an Achilles heel for the whole undertaking. To avoid this weakness and to ensure the primary aim of World Federation, ratification of its Constitution will have to be widespread and immediate, an objective to be addressed in the following chapter.

8.6 Ratification

THE means, conditions and procedures for ratification are set out in the following Article (17), discussion of which may therefore be postponed until we consider the whole of that question. Three stages of implementation are foreseen, the first when the Constitution has been ratified by 25 nations each with a population of over 100,000, or by ten nations with more than 100,000 plus ratification by popular referendum within a minimum of fifty additional World electoral and Administrative districts, or simply by popular vote within at least 100 such Electoral Districts.

The second operative stage will be when the Constitution is ratified by 50% of the nations of the Earth, or by direct referendum, provided that 50% of the Earth's population is included.

The final and full operative stage will be reached when 80% of the nations, or 90% of the population of the Earth have ratified the Constitution.

It thus becomes apparent that the Constitution is offered for free democratic approval by the peoples of the world. There is no suggestion that it be imposed upon any nation without its free consent, and no attempt is being made (or could be made to foist it upon any association that did not recognize and accept its necessity and the wisdom of its provisions).

The keynote of the whole concept of world federation and of this Constitution is freedom: democratic choice of representatives and free decision on their own forms of government by member states are its aims and the medium of its operation.

8.7 Amendments

ARTICLE 18 lays down the procedure for amendments, which, during preliminary operative stages, may be by popular petition or by a simple majority of any House of the World Parliament, but shall require a two-thirds majority of each of the three Houses voting separately when the Constitution is fully in force.

If amendments are proposed by popular petition the House of the Peoples will be required to approve it by a majority vote before it is submitted for passage by a two-thirds majority of all three Houses. It is also laid down that the members of the World Parliament shall meet periodically, at 20 year intervals, in a special session to serve as a Constituent Assembly to review the Constitution and propose desirable amendments for action as prescribed. In short, ratification commits people only to the general principles and not to the details, which can be changed by recognized legitimate procedures thereafter.

8.8   Provisional World Government

THE Article (19) is concerned with the establishment and activities of a Provisional World Government for the preliminary operative stages, in which the work already done by the Provisional World Parliament can be confirmed and continued by the officially constituted World Parliament once it is fully operative. This Parliament has drafted and approved a number of admirable statutes dealing with the climate crisis, with world finance and credit systems, disarmament, and environmental protection, all of which remain to be upheld by the constitutionally established world legislature.

8.9   Additional Features

OTHER points of interest and import are that in Article 4, which defines the powers of World Government, particular mention is made of control of population growth in relation to the life-support capacities of the Earth, as well as the regulation of agricultural methods, crop management and soil conservation, along with the conservation and distribution of transnational water supplies Supra-national trade and industry is also to be brought under the control and regulation of the world body, which would supervise the operation of corporations and cartels.

Energy production and the discovery and use of renewable energy sources would also be brought under its jurisdiction, and ways would be sought to reduce and safely to dispose of waste of all kinds. Finally the Article includes the power to organize and deploy a non-military World Service Corps to carry out projects designed to protect nature and enhance human welfare.

In this way the conditions would be created that make it feasible to tackle all the world's major social and ecological problems, to find global solutions, and to legislate on measures that would ensure their implementation. No other suggested procedures can give any such assurance, and resolute action that is so urgently needed and is not now being taken could be expected and could go forward.

It should now be unquestionably apparent that World Government offers no threats to liberty or repression of national identity and tradition, that it can be organized in a manner that is unlikely to be unduly unwieldy, bureaucratic or cumbersome, that it provides sufficient safeguards against all these dangers as well as against authoritarianism and the abuse of power, while it offers the one and only hope of salvation from the predicaments that currently envelop mankind and the threats of impending disasters.

Chapter 9

Campaign for Ratification

9.1 Referenda and Sovereign Independence

THE draft constitution recognizes for the purpose of ratification the majority votes in referenda organized and conducted by the provisional World Parliament. But until the Constitution is fully operative, which can only be after ratification, the provisional World Parliament has no official status and its decisions can have no legal force.

If, therefore, the sovereign governments to which the people voting are subject are unwilling to heed the result of any such referendum, no effective ratification will be forthcoming; although the popular vote could give such governments powerful notice of the wishes of its constituents.

The only significant acts of ratification would be those made by the established governments themselves. If they are democratic regimes this can be brought about by the election to the legislatures and executives of representatives supporting World Government, and not really in any other way.

If the regime is not democratic, it can be moved to ratify only under unusual pressures from among the populace (much in the same way as the Communist dictatorships of Central Europe were forced to step down in the 1980s). There is, however, as yet, evidence of very few strongly influential political parties agitating for world federation, nor any popular movements campaigning for ratification of the Earth Constitution.

9.2 Mounting the Campaign

As the matter has now become extremely urgent, it is essential that a vigorous world-wide popular campaign be mounted for the ratification of the *Constitution for the Federation of Earth*. The World Constitution and Parliament Association (WCPA) has announced a campaign of this sort enlisting several hundred organizations to work, under the coordination of a network of organizations known as the Earth Federation Movement (EFM), to persuade national governments, parliaments, and peoples of the need to federate.

So far the results do not seem to have been very significant. Despite some publicity in certain areas of the world, there has been no evidence of the existence of the campaign in the mainstream media. The response to appeals for funding has been minuscule, and the idea is being ignored in domestic and international politics, if not actually decried and vehemently rejected by leading figures (like Al Gore).

9.3 The Race Against Time

MEANWHILE, the temperature of the water, in which the frog is swimming, is rising apace while the amphibian seems to be sinking into the predicted torpor. A report by an international group of scientists not long ago announced that global warming is likely within the next half-century to increase the number of people facing starvation (already in the billions) by one third. If humanity is to be saved from speedy and inevitable extinction through the destruction of the world's ecosystem, from which neither the action of national sovereign states, nor agreements between them can rescue it (as I have shown in earlier chapters), urgent efforts must be made to get people to realize both the plight in which the human race is now embroiled and the only means of extricating themselves. This book is one such effort.

Every organization working for nuclear disarmament and for world peace, or for conservation of the environment, or for the preservation of wild-life, or for the protection of people against the violation of human rights, or for the prevention of starvation in Africa and elsewhere, must include in their programs united support for world federation, because without it none of them can achieve its professed aim; and they must all mobilize their resources behind the campaign for ratification of the Earth Constitution already in excellent form and presently at hand.

9.4 The Missing but Indispensable Factor

THE peace movements and the Campaign for Nuclear Disarmament have been active and growing ever since the end of World War II. The reasons motivating their campaign are sound and compelling. The appalling threat, not merely of devastation and suffering, but of total disruption of the planet's ecology, posed by the possibility of nuclear war is widely admitted. The immorality of using the threat of nuclear attack or reprisal as a "bargaining counter" in foreign affairs and as an assumed deterrent is obvious, even if its futility is not recognized. The enormous and deleterious cost of the arms race, even now when it is being reduced after the end of the Cold War, at a time when millions are faced with starvation in the Third World, is as illogical as it is morally indefensible.

Nevertheless, these powerful reasons against nuclear armaments have had little or no influence upon governments, or their electorates; and peace movements, even while they have grown and have recruited many supporters, have had little or no effect on policies. Political parties supporting nuclear disarmament are seldom, if ever, returned to power, and when they are, as in New

Zealand, the implementation of their policy creates international difficulties with neighboring and allied countries, who retain nuclear arms, and this nullifies the effects of their more pacific intentions.

Meanwhile, peace demonstrators and anti-nuclear protesters have been treated by officialdom in many western countries as if they were criminals and traitors and have been unjustly defamed, without evidence, as subversive.

The cause of this mis-appraisal and failure should now be obvious. It is the fact that sovereign nations in a world of power politics are constrained to depend on their own armaments and those of their allies to defend their independence (and/or imperial hegemony), and are bound constantly to strive to maintain a balance of power that is constantly breaking down. Accordingly, any proposal that they should disarm unilaterally is automatically seen as an act of subversion and its advocates as disloyal. Those that support multilateral disarmament are more easily tolerated, but we have explained the futility of trying to conclude a genuine disarmament treaty, observance of which can only be assured by use of the arms the parties are undertaking to forgo.

Until these obstacles to peace and disarmament are surmounted, therefore, the peace movements can only beat their heads against a stone wall, and the obstacles can be surmounted only by World Federation. The Campaign for Nuclear Disarmament can never succeed until it also becomes a campaign for the ratification of the *Constitution for the Federation of Earth*, yet the leaders of such movements seem altogether blind to this fact and nothing has yet succeeded in persuading them to support the Earth Federation Movement campaigning for ratification of the Constitution.

The WorldWatch Institute does unrivaled service to humanity in monitoring threats to the environment and issuing warnings about destructive practices in every quarter, but WorldWatch cannot by its own activity or on its own authority implement the remedies it advocates. It can advise governments and the United

Nations; but the first will do nothing that does not accord with their national interests as they see them, whether economic or political, and will be more swayed by the lobbying of multinational corporations pursuing profits and dividends before planetary safety; the second may convene impressive looking conferences (as in Rio, Kyoto, Johannesburg and Copenhagen) but the agreements they will reach (if any) will most probably be nonbinding and are likely to be for action too dilatory and too niggardly.

These agreements, moreover, are such that conformity to their prescriptions cannot be guaranteed or enforced, the participants all being sovereign states that can be coerced only by the threat of military action. There is no way to overcome these frustrations other than World Federation; so, if WorldWatch is ever to achieve its aim of saving the ecology of the planet, it must advocate and support the campaign for ratification of the *Constitution for Federation of Earth.*

The World Wildlife Fund is pursuing a most important and necessary end. The identification and protection of endangered species is vital at the present time, not only to rescue the creatures in peril of extinction, but for the welfare and the means of survival of human kind itself. The loss of medicinal herbs, of food sources, of scientific data, and of creatures of rare beauty is deeply to be deplored, and will eventually have execrable consequences for mankind.

But the World Wildlife Fund depends entirely on private donations and is in no better position than World-Watch to instigate the global schemes essential to protect and conserve the species whose safety it seeks to ensure, because even those national governments willing to take appropriate action cannot legislate for regions beyond their own borders, within which the species are seldom confined, and action taken by one state will prove totally inadequate if it is frustrated by neglect or counter-action in another.

Whatever the World Wild-life Fund can achieve in Europe and

America will have little or no effect on (for instance) the conduct of people in Sierra Leone and other West-African countries, who hunt primates for food and sell their meat to earn a living. What is needed is world legislation, by an authority with global jurisdiction—legislation assured of enforcement—and that is possible only under a World Government. The World Wild-life Fund, therefore, must spend some of its resources on advertising and promoting the campaign for ratification of the *Constitution for Federation of Earth* if it is ever to get adequate action taken to attain its objectives.

Greenpeace has taken spectacular and courageous action all over the world to protest against practices harmful to living species and to the environment; to try to prevent excessive whaling, often forbidden by international agreement; to obstruct nuclear testing in the Pacific by the French, to whose state-organized terrorism they lost their ship, the Rainbow Warrior; to publicize and to campaign for a treaty preserving Antarctica from exploitation. Members of the organization have risked their lives in many of these ventures, and one life was lost in the explosion that sank the Rainbow Warrior.

These people are truly the soldiers of peace and champions of conservation. But for all their valor they seldom succeed. If the French government for the moment suspended nuclear testing, it was not because of Greenpeace, but as a domestic election tactic. The Japanese still kill whales on the dubious pretext of scientific research, and Iceland is still recalcitrant.

No Antarctic treaty has yet been concluded to preserve it securely from industrial exploitation, and if one were to be, its sanctity and its observance would always be precarious in the face of the national interests of the signatories and the predatory machinations of military-industrial complexes.

To succeed, Greenpeace should change its objectives from treaties to World Law, and should advocate a World Legislature with authority and power to maintain the provisions of that law. It will not attain its ends unless it joins forces with other nongovernmental organizations and with the World Constitution and Parliament Association in a campaign for the ratification of the Earth Constitution.

The Provisional World Parliament has already accepted the same goals as Greenpeace and has already drafted legislation to accomplish them. All that is lacking is the ratification of the Constitution that can enact the Bills already approved and give them the force of law.

One of the most respected and effective charitable organizations in Britain is Oxfam, active throughout the world in combating famine and distress, whether it is caused by civil wars, crop failures, or other man-made and natural disasters.

Oxfam has fund-raising shops throughout Britain, which by selling produce from the Third World, help the poorer economies at the same time as they raise funds for the relief of the hungry and deprived. There are few more admirable charities and none more worthy of support. But Oxfam cannot prevent or stop the wars that cause the distress it does so much to relieve; it can do nothing to check the creeping desertification that advances with climate change and global warming, driving out millions of subsistence farmers to exhaust richer soils and spread starvation further afield.

Oxfam can treat the symptoms but cannot address the causes of the troubles it seeks to abate. Actions by national governments are equally inadequate to remove those causes, and international agreements have not done so, and cannot do so without reliable means of enforcement.

The goals of Oxfam are already included among the Directive Principles set out in the *Constitution for the Federation of Earth*, and only an authority with global jurisdiction could effectively legislate to attain them.

Although Oxfam is today doing magnificent and admirable work, that all compassionate people are bound to approve and support, the only satisfactory cure for the ills that it is combating is world federation; so it too should include among its activities support and publicity for the campaign for ratification of the Earth Constitution. If it cannot do this formally for fear of losing its status as a charity, it can at least sell the supporting literature.

Amnesty International keeps watch over governments the world over to monitor their observance of human rights. It reports the many violations of the Charter, and draws attention to the most flagrant excesses. Imprisonment without trial, maltreatment of prisoners, torture, political and religious persecution, punishment without due process of law, are all quarry for its ubiquitous search and vigilance. It publishes periodical reports of malpractices and makes protests to the United Nations and to delinquent executives in the offending nations.

Such publicity may do much to influence world public opinion, and may prompt deprecatory resolutions from the United Nations Assembly and Security Council. It rarely, if ever, does more. The offending parties almost invariably, if they take any notice at all, declare the Amnesty report to be false, or exaggerated, or lacking in evidence.

Other nations do not take strong action unless their "vital" national interest compel them to do so (which is very rarely the case). As we said earlier, the Charter of Human Rights is more an expression of things hoped for than the prescription of action to be universally enforced. Amnesty International has no powers, nor even any legal status, so its valuable efforts are perpetually frustrated by the inaction and neglect of the major democracies as much as by the contempt and reneging of the offending governments.

The human rights that Amnesty espouses and defends and the surveillance that Amnesty so skillfully maintains are all embodied in the World Constitution, which provides for the protection of the first and the assurance of the second by the establishment of a World Ombudsmus to carry out precisely the function that Amnesty is now assuming.

The only difference is that under a world executive with power to enforce its laws, the Ombudsmen could legally compel a proper investigation into and prosecution of the detected cases of infringement, and a World Federal Administration could make its writ effective; whereas Amnesty is unable to compel even so much as an impartial enquiry into the cases that it reports. To achieve its aims, therefore, Amnesty International must join in the campaign to ratify the *Constitution for the Federation of Earth* and apply its skills and its energies as much to advertising that as to detecting violations of Human Rights. s

9.5   The Required Plan of Action

THE majority of people all over the world are so engrossed in the demands made on them by their proximal needs and interests, many are so desperately preoccupied by the effort to provide themselves with the common necessities of life, that they are unaware or unheedful of the global perils in which they all stand. The better off are mostly too involved with the furtherance of their own selfish aims to take cognizance of them, the worse off are under too much pressure merely to survive to attend to them.

Millions are not even aware of their existence and nature. Politicians are more concerned with the chances of re-election than with the necessity for World Government; and what the electors do not emphatically demand, the politicians will not volunteer to provide. In times of great stress, however, in times of war, or in the aftermath of some great natural disaster, people are apt to forget their conflicting personal objectives and to unite in their efforts to support and further the common welfare.

Today the threat to human survival is worldwide and is vastly greater than that of any prospect of military invasion, or localized natural cataclysm. If only the mass of the people can be apprised of their common danger and be persuaded that the only chance to overcome it requires the establishment of World Government, they should be intelligent enough to unite in their demand for it and to put pressure on their governments to ratify the *Constitution for the Federation of Earth.*

The quickest and most efficient way to establish world government would be for the United Nations Assembly to resolve to replace its Charter with the *Constitution for the Federation of Earth*. That would make the constitution operative at one fell swoop.

But as long as the members of the United Nations are sovereign states, and the general public fails to appreciate the enormity of the dangers threatening mankind today, that is hardly likely ever to happen. For this reason, all the Non-Government Organizations (NGOs) mentioned above, must now join forces with others of like kind, with World Federalists and with the WCPA in a vigorous campaign to put popular pressure on national governments to ratify and bring into force the Earth Constitution by every approved procedure.

In a combined effort they must bang on the doors of the media and persuade them to do what at present they refuse altogether so much as to contemplate—to publicize the Constitution, to invite discussion of it, both criticism and defence, and to report on the campaign for its ratification.

At the same time, fund-raising efforts for the campaign must be organized, and the WCPA should be enabled to emulate Greenpeace, by chartering one or more aircraft (rather than ships) in which it can send teams of lecturers around the world to alert people everywhere, more fully than is yet apparent, to the perils in which they stand, to explain why World Federation is the only path to the removal of threats to survival, and the only hope of the solution of world problems, to inform them about the Constitution, and to advocate its adoption.

Finally, they must exhort the people of the Earth to elect to their Parliaments representatives who support World Government and will induce their legislatures to ratify the Earth Constitution.

And if, in the countries where they live, there are dictators in power, they must agitate for World Government with such insistence that their rulers cannot safely resist the pressure to ratify the Constitution. The campaign must become widely audible and visible; it must be persistent and unflagging; it must be unified, determined and convincing.

Further, the ratification process once begun must be resolute and rapid, because the world cannot afford a protracted period of power politics which will inevitably persist as long as states remain sovereign and "independent." This is why schemes for the so-called reform of the United Nations that are both improbable of success and, if they were implemented, would require long periods of evolution before they approached anything like genuine world government, are of no avail.

A preliminary and incompletely comprehensive federation, moreover, would have the status and remain in the situation of a contemporary sovereign state until it could be enlarged to embrace the whole world. The ratification process, therefore, must proceed apace to bring all nations under the jurisdiction of the Earth Constitution and the World Judiciary with the least possible delay.

Meanwhile, in the preliminary stages, the Provisional World Parliament should press ahead with the demarcation of administrative and electoral regions and the organizetion of elections, to give the federal governing institutions the means of operating at the soonest possible moment.

9.6 The Price of Failure

IF the *Constitution for the Federation of Earth* is not ratified, if no world union comes into being, and if nations remain sovereign, no new world order capable of coping with current major world problems will arise. Even if regional federations are formed (the probability of which at present is not very high, and the prospects of agreement where the process has begun are not very bright), the essential relationship between sovereign powers will remain unchanged.

In that case, power politics will continue and the threat of war will be ever present, with a nuclear holocaust always looming in the background. Even without the use of nuclear weapons modern warfare can be fatally devastating to the whole world community through its impact on the environment as well as its potential for destructive civilized order.

Further, the present international dispensation gives no promise of concerted action to counter the rapid deterioration of the environment now in progress. Population will multiply uncontrolled, urban sprawl will overrun arable land, domestic and industrial waste, much of it lethal, will accumulate. Forests will continue to disappear; deserts will expand; rivers, lakes, estuaries and seas will become more and more polluted; wetlands will be lost; living species will become extinct; global warming will increase, augmenting atmospheric turbulence and the frequency and violence of extreme weather phenomena, and climatic catastrophe will approach at an accelerating pace; the protective ozone layer will dissipate and terrestrial life, vulnerable to ultra-violet radiation, will succumb; the food chain will disintegrate and the millions of people facing starvation will multiply.

For how long the human race, or any life at all, can survive such mutually exacerbating and augmenting destructive influences is more than doubtful. If all this is to be prevented, there is no viable alternative to world federation; so a vigorous and determined global campaign such as we have described above must be conducted without delay for the ratification of the *Constitution for the Federation of Earth*—a concerted campaign, in which all the appropriate organizations and societies must join—to inform and educate the peoples of the world of the enormity of the dangers and of the indispensability of the required world order.

Unless this can be done, and unless the population of the world can be made to see why it must be done, no legal machinery will be available to ensure that the critical problems of global warming, climate change, the poisoning of the hydrosphere and the atmosphere, the control of nuclear radiation, and the maintenance of world peace, can be addressed with any prospect of success. The water in which the frog had been lulled to sleep will boil and the poor creature will succumb in consequence of its own inactivity. Mankind will indeed face extinction, along with other living creatures.

The fruits of culture will be lost forever; the light of knowledge will be extinguished, and the discoveries of science will have been in vain; the illumination of consciousness will vanish from the Earth, abandoning it to oblivion as it becomes a dead planet, like Mars or Venus.

Federalists of the Earth unite: we have everything to lose if you fail!

Appendix A

The Constitution for the Federation of the Earth

Preamble

Realizing that Humanity today has come to a turning point in history and that we are on the threshold of a new world order which promises to usher in an era of peace, prosperity, justice and harmony;

Aware of the interdependence of people, nations and all life;

Aware that man's abuse of science and technology has brought Humanity to the brink of disaster through the production of horrendous weaponry of mass destruction and to the brink of ecological and social catastrophe;

Aware that the traditional concept of security through military defense is a total illusion both for the present and for the future;

Aware of the misery and conflicts caused by ever increasing disparity between rich and poor;

Conscious of our obligation to posterity to save Humanity from imminent and total annihilation;

Conscious that Humanity is One despite the existence of diverse nations, races, creeds, ideologies and cultures and that the principle of unity in diversity is the basis for a new age when war shall be outlawed and peace prevail; when the earth's total resources shall be equitably used for human welfare; and when basic human rights and responsibilities shall be shared by all without discrimination;

Conscious of the inescapable reality that the greatest hope for the survival of life on earth is the establishment of a democratic world government;

We, citizens of the world, hereby resolve to establish a world federation to be governed in accordance with this Constitution for the Federation of Earth.

Article 1   Broad Functions of the Earth Federation

The broad functions of the Federation of Earth shall be:

1.1 To prevent war, secure disarmament, and resolve territorial and other disputes which endanger peace and human rights.

1.2 To protect universal human rights, including life, liberty, security, democracy, and equal opportunities in life.

1.3 To obtain for all people on earth the conditions required for equitable economic and social development and for diminishing social differences.

1.4 To regulate world trade, communications, transportation, currency, standards, use of world resources, and other global and international processes.

1.5 To protect the environment and the ecological fabric of life from all sources of damage, and to control technological innovations whose effects transcend national boundaries, for the purpose of keeping Earth a safe, healthy and happy home for humanity.

1.6 To devise and implement solutions to all problems which are beyond the capacity of national governments, or which are now or may become of global or international concern or consequence.

Article 2 Basic Structure of the Earth Federation

2.1 The Federation of Earth shall be organized as a universal federation, to include all nations and all people, and to encompass all oceans, seas and lands of Earth, inclusive of non-self governing territories, together with the surrounding atmosphere.

2.2 The World Government for the Federation of Earth shall be non-military and shall be democratic in its own structure, with ultimate sovereignty residing in all the people who live on Earth.

2.3 The authority and powers granted to the World Government shall be limited to those defined in this Constitution for the Federation of Earth, applicable to problems and affairs which transcend national boundaries, leaving to national governments jurisdiction over the internal affairs of the respective nations but consistent with the authority of the World Government to protect universal human rights as defined in this World Constitution.

2.4 The basic direct electoral and administrative units of the World Government shall be World Electoral and Administrative Districts. A total of not more than 1000 World Electoral and Administrative Districts shall be defined, and shall be nearly equal in population, within the limits of plus or minus ten percent.

2.5 Contiguous World Electoral and Administrative Districts shall be combined as may be appropriate to compose a total of twenty World Electoral and Administrative Regions for the following purposes, but not limited thereto: for the election or appointment of certain world government officials; for administrative purposes; for composing various organs of the world government as enumerated in Article 4; for the functioning of the Judiciary, the Enforcement System, and the Ombudsmus, as well as for the functioning of any other organ or agency of the World Government.

2.6 The World Electoral and Administrative Regions may be composed of a variable number of World Electoral and Administrative Districts, taking into consideration geographic, cultural, ecological and other factors as well as population.

2.7 Contiguous World Electoral and Administrative Regions shall be grouped together in pairs to compose Magna-Regions.

2.8 The boundaries for World Electoral and Administrative Regions shall not cross the boundaries of the World Electoral and Administrative Districts, and shall be common insofar as feasible for the various administrative departments and for the several organs and agencies of the World Government. Boundaries for the World Electoral and Administrative Districts as well as for the Regions need not conform to existing national boundaries, but shall conform as far as practicable.

2.9 The World Electoral and Administrative Regions shall be grouped to compose at least five Continental Divisions of the Earth, for the election or appointment of certain world government officials, and for certain aspects of the composition and functioning of the several organs and agencies of the World Government as specified hereinafter. The boundaries of Continental Divisions shall not cross existing national boundaries as far as practicable. Continental Divisions may be composed of a variable number of World Electoral and Administrative Regions.

Article 3   Organs of the Earth Federation

The organs of the World Government shall be:

3.1 The World Parliament

3.2 The World Executive

3.3 The World Administration

3.4 The Integrative Complex

3.5 The World Judiciary

3.6 The Enforcement System

3.7 The World Ombudsmus

Article 4 Grant of Specific Powers to the Earth Federation

The powers of the World government to be exercised through its several organs and agencies shall comprise the following:

4.1 Prevent wars and armed conflicts among the nations, regions, districts, parts and peoples of Earth.

4.2 Supervise disarmament and prevent re-armament; prohibit and eliminate the design, testing, manufacture, sale, purchase, use and possession of weapons of mass destruction, and prohibit or regulate all lethal weapons which the World Parliament may decide.

4.3 Prohibit incitement to war, and discrimination against or defamation of conscientious objectors.

4.4 Provide the means for peaceful and just solutions of disputes and conflicts among or between nations, peoples, and/or other components within the Federation of Earth.

4.5 Supervise boundary settlements and conduct plebiscites as needed.

4.6 Define the boundaries for the districts, regions and divisions which are established for electoral, administrative, judicial and other purposes of the World Government.

4.7 Define and regulate procedures for the nomination and election of the members of each House of the World Parliament, and for the nomination, election, appointment and employment of all World Government officials and personnel.

4.8 Codify world laws, including the body of international law developed prior to adoption of the world constitution, but not inconsistent therewith, and which is approved by the World Parliament.

4.9 Establish universal standards for weights, measurements, accounting and records.

4.10 Provide assistance in the event of large scale calamities, including drought, famine, pestilence, flood, earthquake, hurricane, ecological disruptions and other disasters.

4.11 Guarantee and enforce the civil liberties and the basic human rights which are defined in the Bill of Rights for the Citizens of Earth which is made a part of this World Constitution under Article 12.

4.12 Define standards and promote the worldwide improvement in working conditions, nutrition, health, housing, human settlements, environmental conditions, education, economic security, and other conditions defined under Article 13 of this World Constitution.

4.13 Regulate and supervise international transportation, communications, postal services, and migrations of people.

4.14 Regulate and supervise supra-national trade, industry, corporations, businesses, cartels, professional services, labor supply, finances, investments and insurance.

4.15 Secure and supervise the elimination of tariffs and other trade barriers among nations, but with provisions to prevent or minimize hardship for those previously protected by tariffs.

4.16 Raise the revenues and funds, by direct and/or indirect means, which are necessary for the purposes and activities of the World Government.

4.17 Establish and operate world financial, banking, credit and insurance institutions designed to serve human needs; establish, issue and regulate world currency, credit and exchange.

4.18 Plan for and regulate the development, use, conservation and recycling of the natural resources of Earth as the common heritage of Humanity; protect the environment in every way for the benefit of both present and future generations.

4.19 Create and operate a World Economic Development Organization to serve equitably the needs of all nations and people included within the World Federation.

4.20 Develop and implement solutions to transnational problems of food supply, agricultural production, soil fertility, soil conservation, pest control, diet, nutrition, drugs and poisons, and the disposal of toxic wastes.

4.21 Develop and implement means to control population growth in relation to the life-support capacities of Earth, and solve problems of population distribution.

4.22 Develop, protect, regulate and conserve the water supplies of Earth; develop, operate and/or coordinate transnational irrigation and other water supply and control projects; assure equitable allocation of trans-national water supplies, and protect against adverse trans-national effects of water or moisture diversion or weather control projects within national boundaries.

4.23 Own, administer and supervise the development and conservation of the oceans and sea-beds of Earth and all resources thereof, and protect from damage.

4.24 Protect from damage, and control and supervise the uses of the atmosphere of Earth.

4.25 Conduct inter-planetary and cosmic explorations and research; have exclusive jurisdiction over the Moon and over all satellites launched from Earth.

4.26 Establish, operate and/or coordinate global air lines, ocean transport systems, international railways and highways, global communication systems, and means for interplanetary travel and communications; control and administer vital waterways.

4.27 Develop, operate and/or coordinate transnational power systems, or networks of small units, integrating into the systems or networks power derived from the sun, wind, water, tides, heat differentials, magnetic forces, and any other source of safe, ecologically sound and continuing energy supply.

4.28 Control the mining, production, transportation and use of fossil sources of energy to the extent necessary to reduce and prevent damages to the environment and the ecology, as well as to prevent conflicts and conserve supplies for sustained use by succeeding generations.

4.29 Exercise exclusive jurisdiction and control over nuclear energy research and testing and nuclear power production, including the right to prohibit any form of testing or production considered hazardous.

4.30 Place under world controls essential natural resources which may be limited or unevenly distributed about the Earth. Find and implement ways to reduce wastes and find ways to minimize disparities when development or production is insufficient to supply everybody with all that may be needed.

4.31 Provide for the examination and assessment of technological innovations which are or may be of supranational consequence, to determine possible hazards or perils to humanity or the environment; institute such controls and regulations of technology as may be found necessary to prevent or correct widespread hazards or perils to human health and welfare.

4.32 Carry out intensive programs to develop safe alternatives to any technology or technological processes which may be hazardous to the environment, the ecological system, or human health and welfare.

4.33 Resolve supra-national problems caused by gross disparities in technological development or capability, capital formation, availability of natural resources, educational opportunity, economic opportunity, and wage and price differentials. Assist the processes of technology transfer under conditions which safeguard human welfare and the environment and contribute to minimizing disparities.

4.34 Intervene under procedures to be defined by the World Parliament in cases of either intra-state violence and intra-state problems which seriously affect world peace or universal human rights.

4.35 Develop a world university system. Obtain the correction of prejudicialcommunicative materials which cause misunderstandings or conflicts due to differences of race, religion, sex, national origin or affiliation.

4.36 Organize, coordinate and/or administer a voluntary, non-military World Service Corps, to carry out a wide variety of projects designed to serve human welfare.

4.37 Designate as may be found desirable an official world language or official world languages.

4.38 Establish and operate a system of world parks, wild life preserves, natural places, and wilderness areas.

4.39 Define and establish procedures for initiative and referendum by the Citizens of Earth on matters of supra-national legislation not prohibited by this World Constitution.

4.40 Establish such departments, bureaus, commissions, institutes, corporations, administrations, or agencies as may by needed to carry out any and all of the functions and powers of the World Government.

4.41 Serve the needs of humanity in any and all ways which are now, or may prove in the future to be, beyond the capacity of national and local governments.

Article 5   The World Parliament

Section 5.1   Functions and Powers of the World Parliament

5.1.1 To prepare and enact detailed legislation in all areas of authority and jurisdiction granted to the World Government under Article 4 of this World Constitution.

5.1.2 To amend or repeal world laws as may be found necessary or desirable.

5.1.3 To approve, amend or reject the international laws developed prior to the advent of World Government, and to codify and integrate the system of world law and world legislation under the World Government.

5.1.4 To establish such regulations and directions as may be needed, consistent with this world constitution, for the proper functioning of all organs, branches, departments, bureaus, commissions, institutes, agencies or parts of the World Government.

5.1.5 To review, amend and give final approval to each budget for the World Government, as submitted by the World Executive; to devise the specific means for directly raising funds needed to fulfill the budget, including taxes, licenses, fees, globally accounted social and public costs which must be added into the prices for goods and services, loans and credit advances, and any other appropriate means; and to appropriate and allocate funds for all operations and functions of the World Government in accordance with approved budgets, but subject to the right of the Parliament to revise any appropriation not yet spent or contractually committed.

5.1.6 To create, alter, abolish or consolidate the departments, bureaus, commissions, institutes, agencies or other parts of the World Government as may be needed for the best functioning of the several organs of the World Government, subject to the specific provisions of this World Constitution.

5.1.7 To approve the appointments of the heads of all major departments, commissions, offices, agencies and other parts of the several organs of the World Government, except those chosen by electoral or civil service procedures.

5.1.8 To remove from office for cause any member of the World Executive, and any elective or appointive head of any organ, department, office, agency or other part of the World Government, subject to the specific provisions in this World Constitution concerning specific offices.

5.1.9 To define and revise the boundaries of the World Electoral and Administrative Districts, the World Electoral and Administrative Regions and Magna Regions, and the Continental Divisions.

5.1.10 To schedule the implementation of those provisions of the World Constitution which require implementation by stages during the several stages of Provisional World Government, First Operative Stage of World Government, Second Operative Stage of World Government, and Full Operative Stage of World Government, as defined in Articles 17 and 19 of this World Constitution.

5.1.11 To plan and schedule the implementation of those provisions of the World Constitution which may require a period of years to be accomplished.

Section 5.2   Composition of the World Parliament

5.2.1 The World Parliament shall be composed of three houses, designated as follows:

- **The House of Peoples**, to represent the people of Earth directly and equally;

- **The House of Nations**, to represent the nations which are joined together in the Federation of Earth;
- **The House of Counsellors**, with particular functions to represent the highest good and best interests of humanity as a whole.

5.2.2 All members of the World Parliament, regardless of House, shall be designated as Members of the World Parliament.

Section 5.3   The House of Peoples

5.3.1 The House of Peoples shall be composed of the peoples delegates directly elected in proportion to population from the World Electoral and Administrative Districts, as defined in Article 2.4.

5.3.2 Peoples delegates shall be elected by universal adult suffrage, open to all persons of age 18 and above.

5.3.3 One peoples delegate shall be elected from each World Electoral and Administrative District to serve a five year term in the House of Peoples. Peoples delegates may be elected to serve successive terms without limit. Each peoples delegate shall have one vote.

5.3.4 A candidate for election to serve as a peoples delegate must be at least 21 years of age, a resident for at least one year of the electoral district from which the candidate is seeking election, and shall take a pledge of service to humanity.

Section 5.4   The House of Nations

5.4.1 The House of Nations shall be composed of national delegates elected or appointed by procedures to be determined by each national government on the following basis:

5.4.1.1 One national delegate from each nation of at least 100,000 population, but less than 10,000,000 population.

5.4.1.2 Two national delegates from each nation of at least 10,000,000 population, but less than 100,000,000 population.

5.4.1.3 Three national delegates from each nation of 100,000,000 population or more.

5.4.2 Nations of less than 100,000 population may join in groups with other nations for purposes of representation in the House of Nations.

5.4.3 National delegates shall be elected or appointed to serve for terms of five years, and may be elected or appointed to serve successive terms without limit. Each national delegate shall have one vote.

5.4.4 Any person to serve as a national delegate shall be a citizen for at least two years of the nation to be represented, must be at least 21 years of age, and shall take a pledge of service to humanity.

Section 5.5   The House of Counsellors

5.5.1 The House of Counsellors shall be composed of 200 counsellors chosen in equal numbers from nominations submitted from the twenty World Electoral and Administrative Regions, as defined in Article 2.5. and 2.6., ten from each Region.

5.5.2 Nominations for members of the House of Counsellors shall be made by the teachers and students of universities and colleges and of scientific academies and institutes within each world electoral and administrative region. Nominees may be persons who are off campus in any walk of life as well as on campus.

5.5.3 Nominees to the House of Counsellors from each World Electoral and Administrative Region shall, by vote taken among themselves, reduce the number of nominees to no less than two times and no more than three times the number to be elected.

5.5.4 Nominees to serve as members of the House of Counsellors must be at least 25 years of age, and shall take a pledge of service to humanity. There shall be no residence requirement, and a nominee need not be a resident of the region from which nominated or elected.

5.5.5 The members of the House of Counsellors from each region shall be elected by the members of the other two houses of the World Parliament from the particular region.

5.5.6 Counsellors shall be elected to serve terms of ten years. One-half of the members of the House of Counsellors shall be elected every five years. Counsellors may serve successive terms without limit. Each Counsellor shall have one vote.

Section 5.6   Procedures of the World Parliament

5.6.1 Each house of the World Parliament during its first session after general elections shall elect a panel of five chairpersons from among its own members, one from each of five Continental Divisions. The chairpersons shall rotate annually so that each will serve for one year as chief presiding officer, while the other four serve as vice-chairpersons.

5.6.2 The panels of Chairpersons from each House shall meet together, as needed, for the purpose of coordinating the work of the Houses of the World Parliament, both severally and jointly.

5.6.3 Any legislative measure or action may be initiated in either House of Peoples or House of Nations or both concurrently, and shall become effective when passed by a simple majority vote of both the House of Peoples and of the House of Nations, except in those cases where an absolute majority vote or other voting majority is specified in this World Constitution.

5.6.4 In case of deadlock on a measure initiated in either the House of Peoples or House of Nations, the measure shall then automatically go to the House of Counsellors for decision by simple majority vote of the House of Counsellors, except in the cases where other majority vote is required in this World Constitution. Any measure may be referred for decision to the House of Counsellors by a concurrent vote of the other two houses.

5.6.5 The House of Counsellors may initiate any legislative measure, which shall then be submitted to the other two houses and must be passed by simple majority vote of both the House of Peoples and House of Nations to become effective, unless other voting majority is required by some provision of this World Constitution.

5.6.6 The House of Counsellors may introduce an opinion or resolution on any measure pending before either of the other two houses; either of the other houses may request the opinion of the House of Counsellors before acting upon a measure.

5.6.7 Each house of the World Parliament shall adopt its own detailed rules of procedure, which shall by consistent with the procedures set forth in this World Constitution, and which shall be designed to facilitate coordinated functioning of the three houses.

5.6.8 Approval of appointments by the World Parliament or any house thereof shall require simple majority votes, while removals for cause shall require absolute majority votes.

5.6.9 After the full operative stage of World Government is declared, general elections for members of the World Parliament to the House of Peoples shall be held every five years. The first general elections shall be held within the first two years following the declaration of the full operative stage of World Government.

5.6.10 Until the full operative stage of World Government is declared, elections for members of the World Parliament to the House of Peoples may be conducted whenever feasible in relation to the campaign for ratification of this World Constitution.

5.6.11 Regular sessions of the House of Peoples and House of Nations of the World Parliament shall convene on the second Monday of January of each and every year.

5.6.12 Each nation, according to its own procedures, shall appoint or elect members of the World Parliament to the House of Nations at least thirty days prior to the date for convening the World Parliament in January.

5.6.13 The House of Peoples together with the House of Nations shall elect the members of the World Parliament to the House of Counsellors during the month of January after the general elections. For its first session after general elections, the House of Counsellors shall convene on the second Monday of March, and thereafter concurrently with the other two houses.

5.6.14 Bi-elections to fill vacancies shall be held within three months from occurrence of the vacancy or vacancies.

5.6.15 The World Parliament shall remain in session for a minimum of nine months of each year. One or two breaks may be taken during each year, at times and for durations to be decided by simple majority vote of the House of Peoples and House of Nations sitting jointly.

5.6.16 Annual salaries for members of the World Parliament of all three houses shall be the same, except for those who serve also as members of the Presidium and of the Executive Cabinet.

5.6.17 Salary schedules for members of the World Parliament and for members of the Presidium and of the Executive Cabinet shall be determined by the World Parliament.

Article 6 The World Executive

Section 6.1 Functions and Powers of the World Executive

6.1.1 To implement the basic system of world law as defined in the World Constitution and in the codified system of world law after approval by the World Parliament.

6.1.2 To implement legislation enacted by the World Parliament.

6.1.3 To propose and recommend legislation for enactment by the World Parliament.

6.1.4 To convene the World Parliament in special sessions when necessary.

6.1.5 To supervise the World Administration and the Integrative Complex and all of the departments, bureaus, offices, institutes and agencies thereof.

6.1.6 To nominate, select and remove the heads of various organs, branches, departments, bureaus, offices, commissions, institutes, agencies and other parts of the World Government, in accordance with the provisions of this World Constitution and as specified in measures enacted by the World Parliament.

6.1.7 To prepare and submit annually to the World Parliament a comprehensive budget for the operations of the World Government, and to prepare and submit periodically budget projections over periods of several years.

6.1.8 To define and propose priorities for world legislation and budgetary allocations.

6.1.9 To be held accountable to the World Parliament for the expenditures of appropriations made by the World Parliament in accordance with approved and longer term budgets, subject to revisions approved by the World Parliament.

Section 6.2   Composition of the World Executive

The World Executive shall consist of a Presidium of five members, and of an Executive Cabinet of from twenty to thirty members, all of whom shall be members of the World Parliament.

Section 6.3   The Presidium

6.3.1 The Presidium shall be composed of five members, one to be designated as President and the other four to be designated as Vice Presidents. Each member of the Presidium shall be from a different Continental Division.

6.3.2 The Presidency of the Presidium shall rotate each year, with each member in turn to serve as President, while the other four serve as Vice Presidents. The order of rotation shall be decided by the Presidium.

6.3.3 The decisions of the Presidium shall be taken collectively, on the basis of majority decisions.

6.3.4 Each member of the Presidium shall be a member of the World Parliament, either elected to the House of Peoples or to the House of Counsellors, or appointed or elected to the House of Nations.

6.3.5 Nominations for the Presidium shall be made by the House of Counsellors. The number of nominees shall be from two to three times the number to be elected. No more than one-third of the nominees shall be from the House of Counsellors or from the House of Nations, and nominees must be included from all Continental Divisions.

6.3.6 From among the nominees submitted by the House of Counsellors, the Presidium shall be elected by vote of the combined membership of all three houses of the World Parliament in joint session. A plurality vote equal to at least 40 percent of the total membership of the World Parliament shall be required for the election of each member to the Presidium, with successive elimination votes taken as necessary until the required plurality is achieved.

6.3.7 Members of the Presidium may be removed for cause, either individually or collectively, by an absolute majority vote of the combined membership of the three houses of the World Parliament in joint session.

6.3.8 The term of office for the Presidium shall be five years and shall run concurrently with the terms of office for the members as Members of the World Parliament, except that at the end of each five year period, the Presidium members in office shall continue to serve until the new Presidium for the succeeding term is elected. Membership in the Presidium shall be limited to two consecutive terms.

Section 6.4 The Executive Cabinet

6.4.1 The Executive Cabinet shall be composed of from twenty to thirty members, with at least one member from each of the ten World Electoral and Administrative Magna Regions of the world.

6.4.2 All members of the Executive Cabinet shall be Members of the World Parliament.

6.4.3 There shall be no more than two members of the Executive Cabinet from any single nation of the World Federation. There may be only one member of the Executive Cabinet from a nation from which a Member of the World Parliament is serving as a member of the Presidium.

6.4.4 Each member of the Executive Cabinet shall serve as the head of a department or agency of the World Administration or Integrative Complex, and in this capacity shall be designated as Minister of the particular department or agency.

6.4.5 Nominations for members of the Executive Cabinet shall be made by the Presidium, taking into consideration the various functions which Executive Cabinets members are to perform. The Presidium shall nominate no more than two times the number to be elected.

6.4.6 The Executive Cabinet shall be elected by simple majority vote of the combined membership of all three houses of the World Parliament in joint session.

6.4.7 Members of the Executive Cabinet either individually or collectively may be removed for cause by an absolute majority vote of the combined membership of all three houses of the World Parliament sitting in joint session.

6.4.8 The term of office in the Executive Cabinet shall be five years, and shall run concurrently with the terms of office for the members as Members of the World Parliament, except that at the end of each five year period, the Cabinet members in office shall continue to serve until the new Executive Cabinet for the succeeding term is elected. Membership in the Executive Cabinet shall be limited to three consecutive terms, regardless of change in ministerial position.

Section 6.5 Procedures of the World Executive

6.5.1 The Presidium shall assign the ministerial positions among the Cabinet members to head the several administrative departments and major agencies of the Administration and of the Integrative Complex. Each Vice President may also serve as a Minister to head an administrative department, but not the President. Ministerial positions may be changed at the discretion of the Presidium. A Cabinet member or Vice President may hold more than one ministerial post, but no more than three, providing that no Cabinet member is without a Ministerial post.

6.5.2 The Presidium, in consultation with the Executive Cabinet, shall prepare and present to the World Parliament near the beginning of each year a proposed program of world legislation. The Presidium may propose other legislation during the year.

6.5.3 The Presidium, in consultation with the Executive Cabinet, and in consultation with the World Financial Administration, (see Article 8, Sec. 7.1.9.) shall be responsible for preparing and submitting to the World Parliament the proposed annual budget, and budgetary projections over periods of years.

6.5.4 Each Cabinet Member and Vice President as Minister of a particular department or agency shall prepare an annual report for the particular department or agency, to be submitted both to the Presidium and to the World Parliament.

6.5.5 The members of the Presidium and of the Executive Cabinet at all times shall be responsible both individually and collectively to the World Parliament.

6.5.6 Vacancies occurring at any time in the World Executive shall be filled within sixty days by nomination and election in the same manner as specified for filling the offices originally.

Section 6.6 Limitations on the World Executive

6.6.1 The World Executive shall not at any time alter, suspend, abridge, infringe or otherwise violate any provision of this World Constitution or any legislation or world law enacted or approved by the World Parliament in accordance with the provisions of this World Constitution.

6.6.2 The World Executive shall not have veto power over any legislation passed by the World Parliament.

6.6.3 The World Executive may not dissolve the World Parliament or any House of the World Parliament.

6.6.4 The World Executive may not act contrary to decisions of the World Courts.

6.6.5 The World Executive shall be bound to faithfully execute all legislation passed by the World Parliament in accordance with the provisions of this World Constitution, and may not impound or refuse to spend funds appropriated by the World Parliament, nor spend more funds than are appropriated by the World Parliament.

6.6.6 The World Executive may not transcend or contradict the decisions or controls of the World Parliament, the World Judiciary or the Provisions of this World Constitution by any device of executive order or executive privilege or emergency declaration or decree.

Article 7 The World Administration

Section 7.1 Functions of the World Administration

7.1.1 The World Administration shall be organized to carry out the detailed and continuous administration and implementation of world legislation and world law.

7.1.2 The World Administration shall be under the direction of the World Executive, and shall at all times be responsible to the World Executive.

7.1.3 The World Administration shall be organized so as to give professional continuity to the work of administration and implementation.

Section 7.2 Structure and Procedures of the World Administration

7.2.1 The World Administration shall be composed of professionally organized departments and other agencies in all areas of activity requiring continuity of administration and implementation by the World Government.

7.2.2 Each Department or major agency of the World Administration shall be headed by a Minister who shall be either a member of the Executive Cabinet or a Vice President of the Presidium.

7.2.3 Each Department or major agency of the World Administration shall have as chief of staff a Senior Administrator, who shall assist the Minister and supervise the detailed work of the Department or agency.

7.2.4 Each Senior Administrator shall be nominated by the Minister of the particular Department or agency from among persons in the senior lists of the World Civil Service Administration, as soon as senior lists have been established by the World Civil Service Administration, and shall be confirmed by the Presidium. Temporary qualified appointments shall be made by the Ministers, with confirmation by the Presidium, pending establishment of the senior lists.

7.2.5 There shall be a Secretary General of the World Administration, who shall be nominated by the Presidium and confirmed by absolute majority vote of the entire Executive Cabinet.

7.2.6 The functions and responsibilities of the Secretary General of the World Administration shall be to assist in coordinating the work of the Senior Administrators of the several Departments and agencies of the World Administration. The Secretary General shall at all times be subject to the direction of the Presidium, and shall be directly responsible to the Presidium.

7.2.7 The employment of any Senior Administrator and of the Secretary General may be terminated for cause by absolute majority vote of both the Executive Cabinet and Presidium combined, but not contrary to civil service rules which protect tenure on grounds of competence.

7.2.8 Each Minister of a Department or agency of the World Administration, being also a Member of the World Parliament, shall provide continuous liaison between the particular Department or agency and the World Parliament, shall respond at any time to any questions or requests for information from the Parliament, including committees of any House of the World Parliament.

7.2.9 The Presidium, in cooperation with the particular Ministers in each case, shall be responsible for the original organization of each of the Departments and major agencies of the World Administration.

7.2.10 The assignment of legislative measures, constitutional provisions and areas of world law to particular Departments and agencies for administration and implementation shall be done by the Presidium in consultation with the Executive Cabinet and Secretary General, unless specifically provided in legislation passed by the World Parliament.

7.2.11 The Presidium, in consultation with the Executive Cabinet, may propose the creation of other departments and agencies to have ministerial status; and may propose the alteration, combination or termination of existing Departments and agencies of ministerial status as may seem necessary or desirable. Any such creation, alteration, combination or termination shall require a simple majority vote of approval of the three houses of the World Parliament in joint session.

7.2.12 The World Parliament by absolute majority vote of the three houses in joint session may specify the creation of new departments or agencies of ministerial status in the World Administration, or may direct the World Executive to alter, combine, or terminate existing departments or agencies of ministerial status.

7.2.13 The Presidium and the World Executive may not create, establish or maintain any administrative or executive department or agency for the purpose of circumventing control by the World Parliament.

Section 7.3   Departments of the World Administration

7.3.1 Disarmament & War Prevention.

7.3.2 Population.

7.3.3 Food and Agriculture.

7.3.4 Water Supplies and Waterways.

7.3.5 Health and Nutrition.

7.3.6 Education.

7.3.7 Cultural Diversity and the Arts.

7.3.8 Habitat and Settlements.

7.3.9 Environment and Ecology.

7.3.10 World Resources.

7.3.11 Oceans and Seabeds.

7.3.12 Atmosphere and Space.

7.3.13 Energy.

7.3.14 Science and Technology.

7.3.15 Genetic Research & Engineering.

7.3.16 Labor and Income.

7.3.17 Economic & Social Development.

7.3.18 Commerce & Industry

7.3.19 Transportation and Travel.

7.3.20 Multi-National Corporations.

7.3.21 Communications & Information.

7.3.22 Human Rights.

7.3.23 Distributive Justice.

7.3.24 World Service Corps.

7.3.25 World Territories, Capitals & Parks.

7.3.26 Exterior Relations.

7.3.27 Democratic Procedures.

7.3.28 Revenue.

Article 8 The Integrative Complex

Section 8.1 Definition

8.1.1 Certain administrative, research, planning and facilitative agencies of the World Government which are particularly essential for the satisfactory functioning of all or most aspects of the World Government, shall be designated as the Integrative Complex. The Integrative Complex shall include the agencies listed under this section, with the proviso that other such agencies may be added upon recommendation of the Presidium followed by decision of the World Parliament.

8.1.1.1 The World Civil Service Administration.

8.1.1.2 The World Boundaries and Elections Administration.

8.1.1.3 The Institute on Governmental Procedures and World Problems.

8.1.1.4 The Agency for Research and Planning.

8.1.1.5 The Agency for Technological and Environmental Assessment.

8.1.1.6 The World Financial Administration.

8.1.1.7 Commission for Legislative Review.

8.1.2 Each agency of the Integrative Complex shall be headed by a Cabinet Minister and a Senior Administrator, or by a Vice President and a Senior Administrator, together with a Commission as provided hereunder. The rules of procedure for each agency shall be decided by majority decision of the Commission members together with the Administrator and the Minister or Vice President.

8.1.3 The World Parliament may at any time define further the responsibilities, functioning and organization of the several agencies of the Integrative Complex, consistent with the provisions of Article 8 and other provisions of the World Constitution.

8.1.4 Each agency of the Integrative Complex shall make an annual report to the World Parliament and to the Presidium.

Section 8.2 The World Civil Service Administration

8.2.1 The functions of the World Civil Service Administration shall be the following, but not limited thereto:

8.2.1.1 To formulate and define standards, qualifications, tests, examinations and salary scales for the personnel of all organs, departments, bureaus, offices, commissions and agencies of the World Government, in conformity with the provisions of this World Constitution and requiring approval by the Presidium and Executive Cabinet, subject to review and approval by the World Parliament.

8.2.1.2 To establish rosters or lists of competent personnel for all categories of personnel to be appointed or employed in the service of the World Government.

8.2.1.3 To select and employ upon request by any government organ, department, bureau, office, institute, commission, agency or authorized official, such competent personnel as may be needed and authorized, except for those positions which are made elective or appointive under provisions of the World Constitution or by specific legislation of the World Parliament.

8.2.2 The World Civil Service Administration shall be headed by a ten member commission in addition to the Cabinet Minister or Vice President and Senior Administrator. The Commission shall be composed of one commissioner from each of ten World Electoral and Administrative Magna-Regions. The persons to serve as Commissioners shall be nominated by the House of Counsellors and then appointed by the Presidium for five year terms. Commissioners may serve consecutive terms.

Section 8.3 The World Boundaries and Elections Administration

8.3.1 The functions of the World Boundaries and Elections Administration shall include the following, but not limited thereto:

8.3.1.1 To define the boundaries for the basic World Electoral and Administrative Districts, the World Electoral and Administrative Regions and Magna-Regions, and the Continental Divisions, for submission to the World Parliament for approval by legislative action.

8.3.1.2 To make periodic adjustments every ten or five years, as needed, of the boundaries for the World Electoral and Administrative Districts, the World Electoral and Administrative Regions and Magna-Regions, and of the Continental Divisions, subject to approval by the World Parliament.

8.3.1.3 To define the detailed procedures for the nomination and election of Members of the World Parliament to the House of Peoples and to the House of Counsellors, subject to approval by the World Parliament.

8.3.1.4 To conduct the elections for Members of the World Parliament to the House of Peoples and to the House of Counsellors.

8.3.1.5 Before each World Parliamentary Election, to prepare Voters' Information Booklets which shall summarize major current public issues, and shall list each candidate for elective office together with standard information about each candidate, and give space for each candidate to state his or her views on the defined major issues as well as on any other major issue of choice; to include information on any initiatives or referendums which are to be voted upon; to distribute the Voters' Information Booklets for each World Electoral District, or suitable group of Districts; and to obtain the advice of the Institute on Governmental Procedures and World Problems, the Agency for Research and Planning, and the Agency for Technological and Environmental Assessment in preparing the booklets.

8.3.1.6 To define the rules for world political parties, subject to approval by the World Parliament, and subject to review and recommendations of the World Ombudsmus.

8.3.1.7 To define the detailed procedures for legislative initiative and referendum by the Citizens of Earth, and to conduct voting on supra- national or global initiatives and referendums in conjuction with world parliamentary elections.

8.3.1.8 To conduct plebiscites when requested by other Organs of the World Government, and to make recommendations for the settlement of boundary disputes.

8.3.1.9 To conduct a global census every five years, and to prepare and maintain complete demographic analyses for Earth.

8.3.2 The World Boundaries and Elections Administration shall be headed by a ten member commission in addition to the Senior Administrator and the Cabinet Minister or Vice President. The commission shall be composed of one commissioner each from ten World Electoral and Administrative Magna-Regions. The persons to serve as commissioners shall be nominated by the House of Counsellors and then appointed by the World Presidium for five year terms. Commissioners may serve consecutive terms.

Section 8.4 Institute on Governmental Procedures and World Problems

8.4.1 The functions of the World Boundaries and Elections Administration shall include the following, but not limited thereto:

8.4.1.1 To prepare and conduct courses of information, education and training for all personnel in the service of the World Government, including Members of the World Parliament and of all other elective, appointive and civil service personnel, so that every person in the service of the World Government may have a better understanding of the functions, structure, procedures and inter-relationships of the various organs, departments, bureaus, offices, institutes, commissions, agencies and other parts of the World Government.

8.4.1.2 To prepare and conduct courses and seminars for information, education, discussion, updating and new ideas in all areas of world problems, particularly for Members of the World Parliament and of the World Executive, and for the chief personnel of all organs, departments and agencies of the World Government, but open to all in the service of the World Government.

8.4.1.3 To bring in qualified persons from private and public universities, colleges and research and action organizations of many countries, as well as other qualified persons, to lecture and to be resource persons for the courses and seminars organized by the Institute on Governmental Procedures and World Problems.

8.4.1.4 To contract with private or public universities and colleges or other agencies to conduct courses and seminars for the Institute.

8.4.2 The Institute on Governmental Procedures and World Problems shall be supervised by a ten member commission in addition to the Senior Administrator and Cabinet Minister or Vice President. The commission shall be composed of one commissioner each to be named by the House of Peoples, the House of Nations, the House of Counsellors, the Presidium, the Collegium of World Judges, The World Ombudsmus, The World Attorneys General Office, the Agency for Research and Planning, the Agency for Technological and Environmental Assessment, and the World Financial Administration. Commissioners shall serve five year terms, and may serve consecutive terms.

Section 8.5 The Agency for Research and Planning

8.5.1 The functions of the Agency for Research and Planning shall be as follows, but not limited thereto:

8.5.1.1 To serve the World Parliament, the World Executive, the World Administration, and other organs, departments and agencies of the World Government in any matter requiring research and planning within the competence of the agency.

8.5.1.2 To prepare and maintain a comprehensive inventory of world resources.

8.5.1.3 To prepare comprehensive long-range plans for the development, conservation, recycling and equitable sharing of the resources of Earth for the benefit of all people on Earth, subject to legislative action by the World Parliament.

8.5.1.4 To prepare and maintain a comprehensive list and description of all world problems, including their interrelationships, impact time projections and proposed solutions, together with bibliographies.

8.5.1.5 To do research and help prepare legislative measures at the request of any Member of the World Parliament or of any committee of any House of the World Parliament.

8.5.1.6 To do research and help prepare proposed legislation or proposed legislative programs and schedules at the request of the Presidium or Executive Cabinet or of any Cabinet Minister.

8.5.1.7 To do research and prepare reports at the request of any other organ, department or agency of the World Government.

8.5.1.8 To enlist the help of public and private universities, colleges, research agencies, and other associations and organizations for various research and planning projects.

8.5.1.9 To contract with public and private universities, colleges, research agencies and other organizations for the preparation of specific reports, studies and proposals.

8.5.1.10 To maintain a comprehensive World Library for the use of all Members of the World Parliament, and for the use of all other officials and persons in the service of the World Government, as well as for public information.

8.5.2 The Agency for Research and Planning shall be supervised by a ten member commission in addition to the Senior Administrator and Cabinet Minister or Vice President. The commission shall be composed of one commissioner each to be named by the House of Peoples, the House of Nations, the House of Counsellors, the Presidium, the Collegium of World Judges, the Office of World Attorneys General, World Ombudsmus, the Agency for Technological and Environmental Assessment, the Institute on Governmental Procedures and World Problems, and the World Financial Administration. Commissioners shall serve five year terms, and may serve consecutive terms.

Section 8.6 The Agency for Technological and Environmental Assessment

8.6.1 The functions of the agency for Technological and Environmental Assessment shall include the following, but not limited thereto:

8.6.1.1 To establish and maintain a registration and description of all significant technological innovations, together with impact projections.

8.6.1.2 To examine, analyze and assess the impacts and consequences of technological innovations which may have either significant beneficial or significant harmful or dangerous consequences for human life or for the ecology of life on Earth, or which may require particular regulations or prohibitions to prevent or eliminate dangers or to assure benefits.

8.6.1.3 To examine, analyze and assess environmental and ecological problems, in particular the environmental and ecological problems which may result from any intrusions or changes of the environment or ecological relationships which may be caused by technological innovations, processes of resource development, patterns of human settlements, the production of energy, patterns of economic and industrial development, or other man-made intrusions and changes of the environment, or which may result from natural causes.

8.6.1.4 To maintain a global monitoring network to measure possible harmful effects of technological innovations and environmental disturbances so that corrective measures can be designed.

8.6.1.5 To prepare recommendations based on technological and environmental analyses and assessments, which can serve as guides to the World Parliament, the World Executive, the World Administration, the Agency for Research and Planning, and to the other organs, departments and agencies of the World Government, as well as to individuals in the service of the World Government and to national and local governments and legislative bodies.

8.6.1.6 To enlist the voluntary or contractual aid and participation of private and public universities, colleges, research institutions and other associations and organizations in the work of technological and environmental assessment.

8.6.1.7 To enlist the voluntary or contractual aid and participation of private and public universities and colleges, research institutions and other organizations in devising and developing alternatives to harmful or dangerous technologies and environmentally disruptive activities, and in devising controls to assure beneficial results from technological innovations or to prevent harmful results from either technological innovations or environmental changes, all subject to legislation for implementation by the World Parliament.

8.6.2 The Agency for Technological and Environmental Assessment shall be supervised by a ten member commission in addition to the Senior Administrator and Cabinet Minister or Vice President. The commission shall be composed of one commissioner from each of ten World Electoral and Administrative Magna-Regions. The persons to serve as commissioners shall be nominated by the House of Counsellors, and then appointed by the World Presidium for five year terms. Commissioners may serve consecutive terms.

Section 8.7 The World Financial Administration

8.7.1 The functions of the World Financial Administration shall include the following, but not limited thereto:

8.7.1.1 To establish and operate the procedures for the collection of revenues for the World Government, pursuant to legislation by the World Parliament, inclusive of taxes, globally accounted social and public costs, licenses, fees, revenue sharing arrangements, income derived from supra-national public enterprises or projects or resource developments, and all other sources.

8.7.1.2 To operate a Planetary Accounting Office, and thereunder to make cost/benefit studies and reports of the functioning and activities of the World Government and of its several organs, departments, branches, bureaus, offices, commissions, institutes, agencies and other parts or projects. In making such studies and reports, account shall be taken not only of direct financial costs and benefits, but also of human, social, environmental, indirect, long-term and other costs and benefits, and of actual or possible hazards and damages. Such studies and reports shall also be designed to uncover any wastes, inefficiencies, misapplications, corruptions, diversions, unnecessary costs, and other possible irregularities.

8.7.1.3 To make cost/benefit studies and reports at the request of any House or committee of the World Parliament, and of the Presidium, the Executive Cabinet, the World Ombudsmus, the Office of World Attorneys General, the World Supreme Court, or of any administrative department or any agency of the Integrative Complex, as well as upon its own initiative.

8.7.1.4 To operate a Planetary Comptrollers Office and thereunder to supervise the disbursement of the funds of the World Government for all purposes, projects and activities duly authorized by this World Constitution, the World Parliament, the World Executive, and other organs, departments and agencies of the World Government.

8.7.1.5 To establish and operate a Planetary Banking System, making the transition to a common global currency, under the terms of specific legislation passed by the World Parliament.

8.7.1.6 Pursuant to specific legislation enacted by the World Parliament, and in conjunction with the Planetary Banking System, to establish and implement the procedures of a Planetary Monetary and Credit System based upon useful productive capacity and performance, both in goods and services. Such a monetary and credit system shall be designed for use within the Planetary Banking System for the financing of the activities and projects of the World Government, and for all other financial purposes approved by the World Parliament, without requiring the payment of interest on bonds, investments or other claims of financial ownership or debt.

8.7.1.7 To establish criteria for the extension of financial credit based upon such considerations as people available to work, usefulness, cost/benefit accounting, human and social values, environmental health and esthetics, minimizing disparities, integrity, competent management, appropriate technology, potential production and performance.

8.7.1.8 To establish and operate a Planetary Insurance System in areas of world need which transcend national boundaries and in accordance with legislation passed by the World Parliament.

8.7.1.9 To assist the Presidium as may be requested in the technical preparation of budgets for the operation of the World Government.

8.7.2 The World Financial Administration shall be supervised by a commission of ten members, together with a Senior Administrator and a Cabinet Minister or Vice President. The commission shall be composed of one commissioner each to be named by the House of Peoples, the House of Nations, the House of Counsellors, the Presidium, the Collegium of World Judges, the Office of Attorneys General, the World Ombudsmus, the Agency for Research and Planning, the Agency for Technological and Environmental Assessment, and the Institute on Governmental Procedures and World Problems. Commissioners shall serve terms of five years, and may serve consecutive terms.

Section 8.8   Commission for Legistlative Review

8.8.1 The functions of the Commission for Legislative Review shall be to examine World Legislation and World Laws which the World Parliament enacts or adopts from the previous Body of International Law for the purpose of analyzing whether any particular legislation or law has become obsolete or obstructive or defective in serving the purposes intended; and to make recommendations to the World Parliament accordingly for repeal or amendment or replacement.

8.8.2 The Commission for Legislative Review shall be composed of twelve members, including two each to be elected by the House of Peoples, the House of Nations, the House of Counsellors, the Collegium of World Judges, the World Ombudsmus and the Presidium. Members of the Commission shall serve terms of ten years, and may be re-elected to serve consecutive terms. One half of the Commission members after the Commission is first formed shall be elected every five years, with the first terms for one half of the members to be only five years.

Article 9   The World Judiciary

Section 9.1   Jurisdiction of the World Supreme Court

9.1.1 A World Supreme Court shall be established, together with such regional and district World Courts as may subsequently be found necessary. The World Supreme Court shall comprise a number of benches.

9.1.2 The World Supreme Court, together with such regional and district World Courts as may be established, shall have mandatory jurisdiction in all cases, actions, disputes, conflicts, violations of law, civil suits, guarantees of civil and human rights, constitutional interpretations, and other litigations arising under the provisions of this World Constitution, world legislation, and the body of world law approved by the World Parliament.

9.1.3 Decisions of the World Supreme Court shall be binding on all parties involved in all cases, actions and litigations brought before any bench of the World Supreme Court for settlement. Each bench of the World Supreme Court shall constitute a court of highest appeal, except when matters of extra-ordinary public importance are assigned or transferred to the Superior Tribunal of the World Supreme Court, as provided in Section 5 of Article 9.

Section 9.2 Benches of the World Supreme Court

The benches of the World Supreme Court and their respective jurisdictions shall be as follows:

9.2.1 Bench for Human Rights: To deal with issues of human rights arising under the guarantee of civil and human rights provided by Article 12 of this World Constitution, and arising in pursuance of the provisions of Article 13 of this World Constitution, and arising otherwise under world legislation and the body of world law approved by the World Parliament.

9.2.2 Bench for Criminal Cases: To deal with issues arising from the violation of world laws and world legislation by individuals, corporations, groups and associations, but not issues primarily concerned with human rights.

9.2.3 Bench for Civil Cases: To deal with issues involving civil law suits and disputes between individuals, corporations, groups and associations arising under world legislation and world law and the administration thereof.

9.2.4 Bench for Constitutional Cases: To deal with the interpretation of the World Constitution and with issues and actions arising in connection with the interpretation of the World Constitution.

9.2.5 Bench for International Conflicts: To deal with disputes, conflicts and legal contest arising between or among the nations which have joined in the Federation of Earth.

9.2.6 Bench for Public Cases: To deal with issues not under the jurisdiction of another bench arising from conflicts, disputes, civil suits or other legal contests between the World Government and corporations, groups or individuals, or between national governments and corporations, groups or individuals in cases involving world legislation and world law.

9.2.7 Appellate Bench: To deal with issues involving world legislation and world law which may be appealed from national courts; and to decide which bench to assign a case or action or litigation when a question or disagreement arises over the proper jurisdiction.

9.2.8 Advisory Bench: To give opinions upon request on any legal question arising under world law or world legislation, exclusive of contests or actions involving interpretation of the World Constitution. Advisory opinions may be requested by any House or committee of the World Parliament, by the Presidium, any Administrative Department, the Office of World Attorneys General, the World Ombudsmus, or by any agency of the Integrative Complex.

9.2.9 Other benches may be established, combined or terminated upon recommendation of the Collegium of World Judges with approval by the World Parliament; but benches number one through eight may not be combined nor terminated except by amendment of this World Constitution.

Section 9.3   Seats of the World Supreme Court

9.3.1 The primary seat of the World Supreme Court and all benches shall be the same as for the location of the Primary World Capital and for the location of the World Parliament and the World Executive.

9.3.2 Continental seats of the World Supreme Court shall be established in the four secondary capitals of the World Government located in four different Continental Divisions of Earth, as provided in Article 15.

9.3.3 The following permanent benches of the World Supreme Court shall be established both at the primary seat and at each of the continental seats: Human Rights, Criminal Cases, Civil Cases, and Public Cases.

9.3.4 The following permanent benches of the World Supreme Court shall be located only at the primary seat of the World Supreme Court: Constitutional Cases, International Conflicts, Appellate Bench, and Advisory Bench.

9.3.5 Benches which are located permanently only at the primary seat of the World Supreme Court may hold special sessions at the other continental seats of the World Supreme Court when necessary, or may establish continental circuits if needed.

9.3.6 Benches of the World Supreme Court which have permanent continental locations may hold special sessions at other locations when needed, or may establish regional circuits if needed.

Section 9.4 The Collegium of World Judges

9.4.1 A Collegium of World Judges shall be established by the World Parliament. The Collegium shall consist of a minimum of twenty member judges, and may be expanded as needed but not to exceed sixty members.

9.4.2 The World Judges to compose the Collegium of World Judges shall be nominated by the House of Counsellors and shall be elected by plurality vote of the three Houses of the World Parliament in joint session. The House of Counsellors shall nominate between two and three times the number of world judges to be elected at any one time. An equal number of World Judges shall be elected from each of ten World Electoral and Administrative Magna-Regions, if not immediately then by rotation.

9.4.3 The term of office for a World Judge shall be ten years. Successive terms may be served without limit.

9.4.4 The Collegium of World Judges shall elect a Presiding Council of World Judges, consisting of a Chief Justice and four Associate Chief Justices. One member of the Presiding Council of World Judges shall be elected from each of five Continental Divisions of Earth. Members of the Presiding Council of World Judges shall serve five year terms on the Presiding Council, and may serve two successive terms, but not two successive terms as Chief Justice.

9.4.5 The Presiding Council of World Judges shall assign all World Judges, including themselves, to the several benches of the World Supreme Court. Each bench for a sitting at each location shall have a minimum of three World Judges, except that the number of World Judges for benches on Continental Cases and International Conflicts, and the Appellate Bench, shall be no less than five.

9.4.6 The member judges of each bench at each location shall choose annually a Presiding Judge, who may serve two successive terms.

9.4.7 The members of the several benches may be reconstituted from time to time as may seem desirable or necessary upon the decision of the Presiding Council of World Judges. Any decision to re-constitute a bench shall be referred to a vote of the entire Collegium of World Judges by request of any World Judge.

9.4.8 Any World Judge may be removed from office for cause by an absolute two thirds majority vote of the three Houses of the World Parliament in joint session.

9.4.9 Qualifications for Judges of the World Supreme Court shall be at least ten years of legal or juristic experience, minimum age of thirty years, and evident competence in world law and the humanities.

9.4.10 The salaries, expenses, remunerations and prerogatives of the World Judges shall be determined by the World Parliament, and shall be reviewed every five years, but shall not be changed to the disadvantage of any World Judge during a term of office. All members of the Collegium of World Judges shall receive the same salaries, except that additional compensation may be given to the Presiding Council of World Judges.

9.4.11 Upon recommendation by the Collegium of World Judges, the World Parliament shall have the authority to establish regional and district world courts below the World Supreme Court, and to establish the jurisdictions thereof, and the procedures for appeal to the World Supreme Court or to the several benches thereof.

9.4.12 The detailed rules of procedure for the functioning of the World Supreme Court, the Collegium of World Judges, and for each bench of the World Supreme Court, shall be decided and amended by absolute majority vote of the Collegium of World Judges.

Section 9.5 The Superior Tribunal of World Supreme Court

9.5.1 A Superior Tribunal of the World Supreme Court shall be established to take cases which are considered to be of extra-ordinary public importance. The Superior Tribunal for any calendar year shall consist of the Presiding Council of World Judges together with one World Judge named by the Presiding Judge of each bench of the World Court sitting at the primary seat of the World Supreme Court. The composition of the Superior Tribunal may be continued unchanged for a second year by decision of the Presiding Council of World Judges.

9.5.2 Any party to any dispute, issue, case or litigation coming under the jurisdiction of the World Supreme Court, may apply to any particular bench of the World Supreme Court or to the Presiding Council of World Judges for the assignment or transfer of the case to the Superior Tribunal on the grounds of extra-ordinary public importance. If the application is granted, the case shall be heard and disposed of by the Superior Tribunal. Also, any bench taking any particular case, if satisfied that the case is of extra-ordinary public importance, may of its own discretion transfer the case to the Superior Tribunal.

Article 10   The Enforcement System

Section 10.1   Basic Principles

10.1.1 The enforcement of world law and world legislation shall apply directly to individual, and individuals shall be held responsible for compliance with world law and world legislation regardless of whether the individuals are acting in their own capacity or as agents or officials of governments at any level or of the institutions of governments, or as agents or officials of corporations, organizations, associations or groups of any kind.

10.1.2 When world law or world legislation or decisions of the world courts are violated, the Enforcement System shall operate to identify and apprehend the individuals responsible for violations.

10.1.3 Any enforcement action shall not violate the civil and human rights guaranteed under this World Constitution.

10.1.4 The enforcement of world law and world legislation shall be carried out in the context of a non-military world federation wherein all member nations shall disarm as a condition for joining and benefiting from the world federation, subject to Article 17, Sec. 3.8 and 4.6 The Federation of Earth and World Government under this World Constitution shall neither keep nor use weapons of mass destruction.

10.1.5 Those agents of the enforcement system whose function shall be to apprehend and bring to court violators of world law and world legislation shall be equipped only with such weapons as are appropriate for the apprehension of the individuals responsible for violations.

10.1.6 The enforcement of world law and world legislation under this World Constitution shall be conceived and developed primarily as the processes of effective design and administration of world law and world legislation to serve the welfare of all people on Earth, with equity and justice for all, in which the resources of Earth and the funds and the credits of the World Government are used only to serve peaceful human needs, and none used for weapons of mass destruction or for war making capabilities.

Section 10.2 The Structure for Enforcement: World Attorneys General

10.2.1 The Enforcement System shall be headed by an Office of World Attorneys General and a Commission of Regional World Attorneys.

10.2.2 The Office of World Attorneys General shall be comprised of five members, one of whom shall be designated as the World Attorney General and the other four shall each be designated an Associate World Attorney General.

10.2.3 The Commission of Regional World Attorneys shall consist of twenty Regional World Attorneys.

10.2.4 The members to compse the Office of World Attorneys General shall be nominated by the House of Counsellors, with three nominees from each Continental Division of Earth. One member of the Office shall be elected from each of five Continental Divisions by plurality vote of the three houses of the World Parliament in joint session.

10.2.5 The term of office for a member of the Office of World Attorneys General shall be ten years. A member may serve two consecutive terms. The position of World Attorney General shall rotate every two years among the five members of the Office. The order of rotation shall be decided among the five members of the Office.

10.2.6 The Office of World Attorneys General shall nominate members for the Commission of twenty Regional World Attorneys from the twenty World Electoral and Administrative Regions, with between two and three nominees submitted for each Region. From these nominations, the three Houses of the World Parliament in joint session shall elect one Regional World Attorney from each of the twenty Regions. Regional World Attorneys shall serve terms of five years, and may serve three consecutive terms.

10.2.7 Each Regional World Attorney shall organize and be in charge of an Office of Regional World Attorney. Each Associate World Attorney General shall supervise five Offices of Regional World Attorneys.

10.2.8 The staff to carry out the work of enforcement, in addition to the five members of the Office of World Attorneys General and the twenty Regional World Attorneys, shall be selected from civil service lists, and shall be organized for the following functions:

10.2.8.1 Investigation.

10.2.8.2 Apprehension and arrest.

10.2.8.3 Prosecution.

10.2.8.4 Remedies and correction.

10.2.8.5 Conflict resolution.

10.2.9 Qualifications for a member of the Office of World Attorneys General and for the Regional World Attorneys shall be at least thirty years of age, at least seven years legal experience, and education in law and the humanities.

10.2.10 The World Attorney General, the Associate World Attorneys General, and the Regional World Attorneys shall at all times be responsible to the World Parliament. Any member of the Office of World Attorneys General and any Regional World Attorney can be removed from office for cause by a simple majority vote of the three Houses of the World Parliament in joint session.

Section 10.3   The World Police

10.3.1 That section of the staff of the Office of World Attorneys General and of the Offices of Regional World Attorneys responsible for the apprehension and arrest of violators of world law and world legislation, shall be designated as World Police.

10.3.2 Each regional staff of the World Police shall be headed by a Regional World Police Captain, who shall be appointed by the Regional World Attorney.

10.3.3 The Office of World Attorneys General shall appoint a World Police Supervisor, to be in charge of those activities which transcend regional boundaries. The World Police Supervisor shall direct the Regional World Police Captains in any actions which require coordinated or joint action transcending regional boundaries, and shall direct any action which requires initiation or direction from the Office of World Attorneys General.

10.3.4 Searches and arrests to be made by World Police shall be made only upon warrants issued by the Office of World Attorneys General or by a Regional World Attorney.

10.3.5 World Police shall be armed only with weapons appropriate for the apprehension of the individuals responsible for violation of world law.

10.3.6 Employment in the capacity of World Police Captain and World Police Supervisor shall be limited to ten years.

10.3.7 The World Police Supervisor and any Regional World Police Captain may be removed from office for cause by decision of the

Office of World Attorneys General or by absolute majority vote of the three Houses of the World Parliament in joint session.

Section 10.4 The Means of Enforcement

10.4.1 Non-military means of enforcement of world law and world legislation shall be developed by the World Parliament and by the Office of World Attorneys General in consultation with the Commission of Regional World Attorneys, the Collegium of World Judges, the World Presidium, and the World Ombudsmus. The actual means of enforcement shall require legislation by the World Parliament.

10.4.2 Non-military means of enforcement which can be developed may include: Denial of financial credit; denial of material resources and personnel; revocation of licenses, charters, or corporate rights; impounding of equipment; fines and damage payments; performance of work to rectify damages; imprisonment or isolation; and other means appropriate to the specific situations.

10.4.3 To cope with situations of potential or actual riots, insurrection and resort to armed violence, particular strategies and methods shall be developed by the World Parliament and by the Office of World Attorneys General in consultation with the Commission of Regional World Attorneys, the collegium of World Judges, the Presidium and the World Ombudsmus. Such strategies and methods shall require enabling legislation by the World Parliament where required in addition to the specific provisions of this World Constitution.

10.4.4 A basic condition for preventing outbreaks of violence which the Enforcement System shall facilitate in every way possible, shall be to assure a fair hearing under non-violent circumstances for any person or group having a grievance, and likewise to assure a fair opportunity for a just settlement of any grievance with due regard for the rights and welfare of all concerned.

Article 11 The World Ombudsmus

Section 11.1 Functions and Powers of the World Ombudsmus

The functions and powers of the World Ombudsmus, as public defender, shall include the following:

11.1.1 To protect the People of Earth and all individuals against violations or neglect of universal human and civil rights which are stipulated in Article 12 and other sections of this World Constitution.

11.1.2 To protect the People of Earth against violations of this World Constitution by any official or agency of the World Government, including both elected and appointed officials or public employees regardless of organ, department, office, agency or rank.

11.1.3 To press for the implementation of the Directive Principles for the World Government as defined in Article 13 of this World Constitution.

11.1.4 To promote the welfare of the people of Earth by seeking to assure that conditions of social justice and of minimizing disparities are achieved in the implementation and administration of world legislation and world law.

11.1.5 To keep on the alert for perils to humanity arising from technological innovations, environmental disruptions and other diverse sources, and to launch initiatives for correction or prevention of such perils.

11.1.6 To ascertain that the administration of otherwise proper laws, ordinances and procedures of the World Government do not result in unforseen injustices or inequities, or become stultified in bureaucracy or the details of administration.

11.1.7 To receive and hear complaints, grievances or requests for aid from any person, group, organization, association, body politic or agency concerning any matter which comes within the purview of the World Ombudsmus.

11.1.8 To request the Office of World Attorneys General or any Regional World Attorney to initiate legal actions or court proceedings whenever and wherever considered necessary or desirable in the view of the World Ombudsmus.

11.1.9 To directly initiate legal actions and court proceedings whenever the World Ombudsmus deems necessary.

11.1.10 To review the functioning of the departments, bureaus, offices, commissions, institutes, organs and agencies of the World Government to ascertain whether the procedures of the World government are adequately fulfilling their purposes and serving the welfare of humanity in optimum fashion, and to make recommendations for improvements.

11.1.11 To present an annual report to the World Parliament and to the Presidium on the activities of the World Ombudsmus, together with any recommendations for legislative measures to improve the functioning of the World Government for the purpose of better serving the welfare of the People of Earth.

Section 11.2 Composition of the World Ombudsmus

11.2.1 The World Ombudsmus shall be headed by a Council of World Ombudsen of five members, one of whom shall be designated as Principal World Ombudsan, while the other four shall each be designated as an Associate World Ombudsan.

11.2.2 Members to compose the Council of World Ombudsen shall be nominated by the House of Counsellors, with three nominees from each Continental Division of Earth. One member of the Council shall be elected from each of five Continental Divisions by plurality vote of the three Houses of the World Parliament in joint session.

11.2.3 The term of office for a World Ombudsan shall be ten years. A World Ombudsan may serve two successive terms. The position of Principal World Ombudsan shall be rotated every two years. The order of rotation shall be determined by the Council of World Ombudsen.

11.2.4 The Council of World Ombudsen shall be assisted by a Commission of World Advocates of twenty members. Members for the Commission of World Advocates shall be nominated by the Council of World Ombudsen from twenty World Electoral and Administrative Regions, with between two and three nominees submitted for each Region. One World Advocate shall be elected from each of the twenty World Electoral and Administrative Regions by the three Houses of the World Parliament in joint session. World Advocates shall serve terms of five years, and may serve a maximum of four successive terms.

11.2.5 The Council of World Ombudsen shall establish twenty regional offices, in addition to the principal world office at the primary seat of the World Government. The twenty regional offices of the World Ombudsmus shall parallel the organization of the twenty Offices of Regional World Attorney.

11.2.6 Each regional office of the World Ombudsmus shall be headed by a World Advocate. Each five regional offices of the World Ombudmus shall be supervised by an Associate World Ombudsan.

11.2.7 Any World Ombudsan and any World Advocate may be removed from office for cause by an absolute majority vote of the three Houses of the World Parliament in joint session.

11.2.8 Staff members for the World Ombudsmus and for each regional office of the World Ombudsmus shall be selected and employed from civil service lists.

11.2.9 Qualifications for World Ombudsan and for World Advocate shall be at least thirty years of age, at least five years legal experience, and education in law and other relevant education.

Article 12 Bill of Rights for the Citizens of Earth

12.1 Equal rights for all citizens of the Federation of Earth, with no discrimination on grounds of race, color, caste, nationality, sex, religion, political affiliation, property, or social status.

12.2 Equal protection and application of world legislation and world laws for all citizens of the Federation of Earth.

12.3 Freedom of thought and conscience, speech, press, writing, communication, expression, publication, broadcasting, telecasting, and cinema, except as an overt part of or incitement to violence, armed riot or insurrection.

12.4 Freedom of assembly, association, organization, petition and peaceful demonstration.

12.5 Freedom to vote without duress, and freedom for political organization and campaigning without censorship or recrimination.

12.6 Freedom to profess, practice and promote religion or religious beliefs or no religion or religious belief.

12.7 Freedom to profess and promote political beliefs or no political beliefs.

12.8 Freedom for investigation, research and reporting.

12.9 Freedom to travel without passport or visas or other forms of registration used to limit travel between, among or within nations.

12.10 Prohibition against slavery, peonage, involuntary servitude, and conscription of labor.

12.11 Prohibition against military conscription.

12.12 Safety of person from arbitrary or unreasonable arrest, detention, exile, search or seizure; requirement of warrants for searches and arrests.

12.13 Prohibition against physical or psychological duress or torture during any period of investigation, arrest, detention or imprisonment, and against cruel or unusual punishment.

12.14 Right of habeous corpus; no ex-post-facto laws; no double jeopardy; right to refuse self-incrimination or the incrimination of another.

12.15 Prohibition against private armies and paramilitary organizations as being threats to the common peace and safety.

12.16 Safety of property from arbitrary seizure; protection against exercise of the power of eminent domain without reasonable compensation.

12.17 Right to family planning and free public assistance to achieve family planning objectives.

12.18 Right of privacy of person, family and association; prohibition against surveillance as a means of political control.

Article 13 Directive Principles for the Earth Federation

It shall be the aim of the World Government to secure certain other rights for all inhabitants within the Federation of Earth, but without immediate guarantee of universal achievement and enforcement. These rights are defined as Directive Principles, obligating the World Government to pursue every reasonable means for universal realization and implementation, and shall include the following:

13.1 Equal opportunity for useful employment for everyone, with wages or remuneration sufficient to assure human dignity.

13.2 Freedom of choice in work, occupation, employment or profession.

13.3 Full access to information and to the accumulated knowledge of the human race.

13.4 Free and adequate public education available to everyone, extending to the pre-university level; Equal opportunities for elementary and higher education for all persons; equal opportunity for continued education for all persons throughout life; the right of any person or parent to choose a private educational institution at any time.

13.5 Free and adequate public health services and medical care available to everyone throughout life under conditions of free choice.

13.6 Equal opportunity for leisure time for everyone; better distribution of the work load of society so that every person may have equitable leisure time opportunities.

13.7 Equal opportunity for everyone to enjoy the benefits of scientific and technological discoveries and developments.

13.8 Protection for everyone against the hazards and perils of technological innovations and developments.

13.9 Protection of the natural environment which is the common heritage of humanity against pollution, ecological disruption or damage which could imperil life or lower the quality of life.

13.10 Conservation of those natural resources of Earth which are limited so that present and future generations may continue to enjoy life on the planet Earth.

13.11 Assurance for everyone of adequate housing, of adequate and nutritious food supplies, of safe and adequate water supplies, of pure air with protection of oxygen supplies and the ozone layer, and in general for the continuance of an environment which can sustain healthy living for all.

13.12 Assure to each child the right to the full realization of his or her potential.

13.13 Social Security for everyone to relieve the hazards of unemployment, sickness, old age, family circumstances, disability, catastrophies of nature, and technological change, and to allow retirement with sufficient lifetime income for living under conditions of human dignity during older age.

13.14 Rapid elimination of and prohibitions against technological hazards and manmade environmental disturbances which are found to create dangers to life on Earth.

13.15 Implementation of intensive programs to discover, develop and institute safe alternatives and practical substitutions for technologies which must be eliminated and prohibited because of hazards and dangers to life.

13.16 Encouragement for cultural diversity; encouragement for decentralized administration.

13.17 Freedom for peaceful self-determination for minorities, refugees and dissenters.

13.18 Freedom for change of residence to anywhere on Earth conditioned by provisions for temporary sanctuaries in events of large numbers of refugees, stateless persons, or mass migrations.

13.19 Prohibition against the death penalty.

Article 14   Safeguards and Reservations

Section 14.1   Certain Safeguards

The World Government shall operate to secure for all nations and peoples within the Federation of Earth the safeguards which are defined hereunder:

14.1.1 Guarantee that full faith and credit shall be given to the public acts, records, legislation and judicial proceedings of the member nations within the Federation of Earth, consistent with the several provisions of this World Constitution.

14.1.2 Assure freedom of choice within the member nations and countries of the Federation of Earth to determine their internal political, economic and social systems consistent with the guarantees and protections given under this World Constitution to assure civil liberties and human rights and a safe environment for life, and otherwise consistent with the several provisions of this World Constitution.

14.1.3 Grant the right of asylum within the Federation of Earth for persons who may seek refuge from countries or nations which are not yet included within the Federation of Earth.

14.1.4 Grant the right of individuals and groups, after the Federation of Earth includes 90 percent of the territory of Earth, to peacefully leave the hegemony of the Federation of Earth and to live in suitable territory set aside by the Federation neither restricted nor protected by the World Government, provided that such territory does not extend beyond five percent of Earth's habitable territory, is kept completely disarmed and not used as a base for inciting violence or insurrection within or against the Federation of Earth or any member nation, and is kept free of acts of environmental or technological damage which seriously affect Earth outside such territory.

Section 14.2   Reservation of Powers

The powers not delegated to the World Government by this World Constitution shall be reserved to the nations of the Federation of Earth and to the people of Earth.

Article 15 World Federal Zones and the World Capitals

Section 15.1 Word Federal Zones

15.1.1 Twenty World Federal Zones shall be established within the twenty World Electoral and Administrative Regions, for the purposes of the location of the several organs of the World Government and of the administrative departments, the world courts, the offices of the Regional World Attorneys, the offices of the World Advocates, and for the location of other branches, departments, institutes, offices, bureaus, commissions, agencies and parts of the World Government.

15.1.2 The World Federal Zones shall be established as the needs and resources of the World Government develop and expand. World Federal Zones shall be established first within each of five Continental Divisions.

15.1.3 The location and administration of the World Federal Zones, including the first five, shall be determined by the World Parliament.

Section 15.2 The World Capitals

15.2.1 Five World Capitals shall be established in each of five Continental Divisions of Earth, to be located in each of the five World Federal Zones which are established first as provided in Article 15 of this World Constitution.

15.2.2 One of the World Capitals shall be designated by the World Parliament as the Primary World Capital, and the other four shall be designated as Secondary World Capitals.

15.2.3 The primary seats of all organs of the World Government shall be located in the Primary World Capital, and other major seats of the several organs of the World Government shall be located in the Secondary World Capitals.

Section 15.3   Locational Procedures

15.3.1 Choices for location of the twenty World Federal Zones and for the five World Capitals shall be proposed by the Presidium, and then shall be decided by a simple majority vote of the three Houses of the World Parliament in joint session. The Presidium shall offer choices of two or three locations in each of the twenty World Electoral and Administrative Regions to be World Federal Zones, and shall offer two alternative choices for each of the five World Capitals.

15.3.2 The Presidium in consultation with the Executive Cabinet shall then propose which of the five World Capitals shall be the Primary World Capital, to be decided by a simply majority vote of the three Houses of the World Parliament in joint session.

15.3.3 Each organ of the World Government shall decide how best to apportion and organize its functions and activities among the five World Capitals, and among the twenty World Federal Zones, subject to specific directions from the World Parliament.

15.3.4 The World Parliament may decide to rotate its sessions among the five World Capitals, and if so, to decide the procedure for rotation.

15.3.5 For the first two operative stages of World Government as defined in Article 17, and for the Provisional World Government as defined in Article 19, a provisional location may be selected for the Primary World Capital. The provisional location need not be continued as a permanent location.

15.3.6 Any World Capital or World Federal Zone may be relocated by an absolute two-thirds majority vote of the three Houses of the World Parliament in joint session.

15.3.7 Additional World Federal Zones may be designated if found necessary by proposal of the Presidium and approval by an absolute majority vote of the three Houses of the World Parliament in joint session.

Article 16   World Territories and Exterior Relations

Section 16.1   World Territory

16.1.1 Those areas of the Earth and Earth's moon which are not under the jurisdiction of existing nations at the time of forming the Federation of Earth, or which are not reasonably within the province of national ownership and administration, or which are declared to be World Territory subsequent to establishment of the Federation of Earth, shall be designated as World Territory and shall belong to all of the people of Earth.

16.1.2 The administration of World Territory shall be determined by the World Parliament and implemented by the World Executive, and shall apply to the following areas:

16.1.2.1 All oceans and seas having an international or supranational character, together with the seabeds and resources thereof, beginning at a distance of twenty kilometers offshore, excluding inland seas of traditional national ownership.

16.1.2.2 Vital straits, channels, and canals.

16.1.2.3 The atmosphere enveloping Earth, beginning at an elevation of one kilometer above the general surface of the land, excluding the depressions in areas of much variation in elevation.

16.1.2.4 Man-made satellites and Earth's moon.

16.1.2.5 Colonies which may choose the status of World Territory; non-independent territories under the trust administration of nations or of the United Nations; any islands or atolls which are unclaimed by any nation; independent lands or countries which choose the status of World Territory; and disputed lands which choose the status of World Territory.

16.1.3 The residents of any World Territory, except designated World Federal Zones, shall have the right within reason to decide by plebiscite to become a self-governing nation within the Federation of Earth, either singly or in combination with other World Territories, or to unite with an existing nation with the Federation of Earth.

Section 16.2   Exterior Relations

16.2.1 The World Government shall maintain exterior relations with those nations of Earth which have not joined the Federation of Earth. Exterior relations shall be under the administration of the Presidium, subject at all times to specific instructions and approval by the World Parliament.

16.2.2 All treaties and agreements with nations remaining outside the Federation of Earth shall be negotiated by the Presidium and must be ratified by a simple majority vote of the three Houses of the World Parliament.

16.2.3 The World Government for the Federation of Earth shall establish and maintain peaceful relations with other planets and celestial bodies where and when it may become possible to establish communications with the possible inhabitants thereof.

16.2.4 All explorations into outer space, both within and beyond the solar system in which Planet Earth is located, shall be under the exclusive direction and control of the World Government, and shall be conducted in such manner as shall be determined by the World Parliament.

Article 17   Ratification and Implementation

Section 17.1   Ratification of the World Constitution

17.1.1 The World Constitution shall be transmitted to the General Assembly of the United Nations Organization and to each national government on Earth, with the request that the World Constitution be submitted to the national legislature of each nation for preliminary ratification and to the people of each nation for final ratification by popular referendum.

17.1.2 Preliminary ratification by a national legislature shall be accomplished by simple majority vote of the national legislature.

17.1.3 Final ratification by the people shall be accomplished by a simple majority of votes cast in a popular referendum, provided that a minimum of twenty-five percent of eligible voters of age eighteen years and over have cast ballots within the nation or country or within World Electoral and Administrative Districts.

17.1.4 In the case of a nation without a national legislature, the head of the national government shall be requested to give preliminary ratification and to submit the World Constitution for final ratification by popular referendum.

17.1.5 In the event that a national government, after six months, fails to submit the World Constitution for ratification as requested, then the global agency assuming responsibility for the worldwide ratification campaign may proceed to conduct a direct referendum for ratification of the World Constitution by the people. Direct referendums may be organized on the basis of entire nations or countries, or on the basis of existing defined communities within nations.

17.1.6 In the event of a direct ratification referendum, final ratification shall be accomplished by a majority of the votes cast whether for an entire nation or for a World Electoral and Administrative District, provided that ballots are cast by a minimum of twenty-five percent of eligible voters of the area who are over eighteen years of age.

17.1.7 For ratification by existing communities within a nation, the procedure shall be to request local communities, cities, counties, states, provinces, cantons, prefectures, tribal jurisdictions, or other defined political units within a nation to ratify the World Constitution, and to submit the World Constitution for a referendum vote by the citizens of the community or political unit. Ratification may be accomplished by proceeding in this way until all eligible voters of age eighteen and above within the nation or World Electoral and Administrative District have had the opportunity to vote, provided that ballots are cast by a minimum of twenty-five percent of those eligible to vote.

17.1.8 Prior to the Full Operative Stage of World Government, as defined under Section 5 of Article 17, the universities, colleges and scientific academies and institutes in any country may ratify the World Constitution, thus qualifying them for participation in the nomination of Members of the World Parliament to the House of Counsellors.

17.1.9 In the case of those nations currently involved in serious international disputes or where traditional enmities and chronic disputes may exist among two or more nations, a procedure for concurrent paired ratification shall be instituted whereby the nations which are parties to a current or chronic international dispute or conflict may simultaneously ratify the World Constitution. In such cases, the paired nations shall be admitted into the Federation of Earth simultaneously, with the obligation for each such nation to immediately turn over all weapons of mass destruction to the World Government, and to turn over the conflict or dispute for mandatory peaceful settlement by the World Government.

17.1.10 Each nation or political unit which ratifies this World Constitution, either by preliminary ratification or final ratification, shall be bound never to use any armed forces or weapons of mass destruction against another member or unit of the Federation of Earth, regardless of how long it may take to achieve full disarmament of all the nations and political units which ratify this World Constitution.

17.1.11 When ratified, the Constitution for the Federation of Earth becomes the supreme law of Earth. By the act of ratifying this Earth Constitution, any provision in the Constitution or Legislation of any country so ratifying, which is contrary to this Earth Constitution, is either repealed or amended to conform with the Constitution for the Federation of Earth, effective as soon as 25 countries have so ratified. The amendment of National or State Constitutions to allow entry into World Federation is not necessary prior to ratification of the Constitution for the Federation of Earth.

Section 17.2   Stages of Implementation

17.2.1 Implementation of this World Constitution and the establishment of World Government pursuant to the terms of this World Constitution, may be accomplished in three stages, as follows, in addition to the stage of a Provisional World Government as provided under Article 19:

17.2.1.1 First Operative Stage of World Government.

17.2.1.2 Second Operative Stage of World Government.

17.2.1.3 Full Operative Stage of World Government.

17.2.2 At the beginning and during each stage, the World Parliament and the World Executive together shall establish goals and develop means for the progressive implementation of the World

Constitution, and for the implementation of legislation enacted by the World Parliament.

Section 17.3 First Operative Stage of World Government

17.3.1 The first operative stage of World Government under this World Constitution shall be implemented when the World Constitution is ratified by a sufficient number of nations and/or people to meet one or the other of the following conditions or equivalent:

17.3.1.1 Preliminary or final ratification by a minimum of twenty-five nations, each having a population of more than 100,000.

17.3.1.2 Preliminary or final ratification by a minimum of ten nations above 100,000 population, together with ratification by direct referendum within a minimum of fifty additional World Electoral and Administrative Districts.

17.3.1.3 Ratification by direct referendum within a minimum of 100 World Electoral and Administrative Districts, even though no nation as such has ratified.

17.3.2 The election of Members of the World Parliament to the House of Peoples shall be conducted in all World Electoral and Administrative Districts where ratification has been accomplished by popular referendum.

17.3.3 The election of Members of the World Parliament to the House of Peoples may proceed concurrently with direct popular referendums both prior to and after the First Operative Stage of World Government is reached.

17.3.4 The appointment or election of Members of the World Parliament to the House of Nations shall proceed in all nations where preliminary ratification has been accomplished.

17.3.5 One-fourth of the Members of the World Parliament to the House of Counsellors may be elected from nominees submitted by universities and colleges which have ratified the World Constitution.

17.3.6 The World Presidium and the Executive Cabinet shall be elected according to the provisions in Article 6, except that in the absence of a House of Counsellors, the nominations shall be made by the members of the House of Peoples and of the House of Nations in joint session. Until this is accomplished, the Presidium and Executive Cabinet of the Provisional World Government as provided in Article 19, shall continue to serve.

17.3.7 When composed, the Presidium for the first operative stage of World Government shall assign or re-assign Ministerial posts among Cabinet and Presidium members, and shall immediately establish or confirm a World Disarmament Agency and a World Economic and Development Organization.

17.3.8 Those nations which ratify this World Constitution and thereby join the Federation of Earth, shall immediately transfer all weapons of mass destruction as defined and designated by the World Disarmament Agency to that Agency. (See Article 19, Sections A-2-d, B-6 and E-5). The World Disarmament Agency shall immediately immobilize all such weapons and shall proceed with dispatch to dismantle, convert to peacetime use, re-cycle the materials thereof or otherwise destroy all such weapons. During the first operative stage of World Government, the ratifying nations may retain armed forces equipped with weapons other than weapons of mass destruction as defined and designated by the World Disarmament Agency.

17.3.9 Concurrently with the reduction or elimination of such weapons of mass destruction and other military expenditures as can be accomplished during the first operative stage of World Government, the member nations of the Federation of Earth shall pay annually to the Treasury of the World Government amounts equal to one-half the amounts saved from their respective national military budgets during the last year before joining the Federation, and shall continue such payments until the full operative stage of World Government is reached. The World Government shall use fifty percent of the funds thus received to finance the work and projects of the World Economic Development Organization.

17.3.10 The World Parliament and the World Executive shall continue to develop the organs, departments, agencies and activities originated under the Provisional World Government, with such amendments as deemed necessary; and shall proceed to establish and beg in the following organs, departments and agencies of the

World Government, if not already underway, together with such other departments, and agencies as are considered desirable and feasible during the first operative stage of World Government:

17.3.10.1 The World Supreme Court;

17.3.10.2 The Enforcement System;

17.3.10.3 The World Ombudsmus;

17.3.10.4 The World Civil Service Administration;

17.3.10.5 The World Financial Administration;

17.3.10.6 The Agency for Research and Planning;

17.3.10.7 The Agency for Technological and Environmental Assessment;

17.3.10.8 An Emergency Earth Rescue Administration, concerned with all aspects of climate change and related factors;

17.3.10.9 An Integrated Global Energy System, based on environmentally safe sources;

17.3.10.10 A World University System, under the Department of Education;

17.3.10.11 A World Corporations Office, under the Department of Commerce and Industry;

17.3.10.12 The World Service Corps;

17.3.10.13 A World Oceans and Seabeds Administration.

17.3.11 At the beginning of the first operative stage, the Presidium in consultation with the Executive Cabinet shall formulate and put forward a proposed program for solving the most urgent world problems currently confronting humanity.

17.3.12 The World Parliament shall proceed to work upon solutions to world problems. The World Parliament and the World Executive working together shall institute through the several organs, departments and agencies of the World Government whatever means shall seem appropriate and feasible to accomplish the implementation and enforcement of world legislation, world law and the World Constitution; and in particular shall take certain decisive actions for the welfare of all people on Earth, applicable throughout the world, including but not limited to the following:

17.3.12.1 Expedite the organization and work of an Emergency Earth Rescue Administration, concerned with all aspects of climate change and climate crises;

17.3.12.2 Expedite the new finance, credit and monetary system, to serve human needs;

17.3.12.3 Expedite an integrated global energy system, utilizing solar energy, hydrogen energy, and other safe and sustainable sources of energy;

17.3.12.4 Push forward a global program for agricultural production to achieve maximum sustained yield under conditions which are ecologically sound;

17.3.12.5 Establish conditions for free trade within the Federation of Earth;

17.3.12.6 Call for and find ways to implement a moratorium on nuclear energy projects until all problems are solved concerning safety, disposal of toxic wastes and the dangers of use or diversion of materials for the production of nuclear weapons;

17.3.12.7 Outlaw and find ways to completely terminate the production of nuclear weapons and all weapons of mass destruction;

17.3.12.8 Push forward programs to assure adequate and non-polluted water supplies and clean air supplies for everybody on Earth;

17.3.12.9 Push forward a global program to conserve and re-cycle the resources of Earth.

17.3.12.10 Develop an acceptable program to bring population growth under control, especially by raising standards of living.

Section 17.4 Second Operative Stage of World Government

17.4.1 The second operative stage of World Government shall be implemented when fifty percent or more of the nations of Earth have given either preliminary or final ratification to this World Constitution, provided that fifty percent of the total population of Earth is included either within the ratifying nations or within the ratifying nations together with additional World Electoral and Administrative Districts where people have ratified the World Constitution by direct referendum.

17.4.2 The election and appointment of Members of the World Parliament to the several Houses of the World Parliament shall proceed in the same manner as specified for the first operative stage in Section 3.2, 3.3, 3.4 and 3.5 of Article 17.

17.4.3 The terms of office of the Members of the World Parliament elected or appointed for the first operative stage of World Government, shall be extended into the second operative stage unless they have already served five year terms, in which case new elections or appointments shall be arranged. The terms of holdover Members of the World Parliament into the second operative stage shall be adjusted to run concurrently with the terms of those who are newly elected at the beginning of the second operative stage.

17.4.4 The World Presidium and the Executive Cabinet shall be reconstituted or reconfirmed, as needed, at the beginning of the second operative stage of World Government.

17.4.5 The World Parliament and the World Executive shall continue to develop the organs, departments, agencies and activities which are already underway from the first operative stage of World Government, with such amendments as deemed necessary; and shall proceed to establish and develop all other organs and major departments and agencies of the World Government to the extent deemed feasible during the second operative stage.

17.4.6 All nations joining the Federation of Earth to compose the second operative stage of World Government, shall immediately transfer all weapons of mass destruction and all other military weapons and equipment to the World Disarmament Agency, which shall immediately immobilize such weapons and equipment and shall proceed forthwith to dismantle, convert to peacetime uses, recycle the materials thereof, or otherwise destroy such weapons and equipment. During the second operative stage, all armed forces and para-military forces of the nations which have joined the Federation of Earth shall be completely disarmed and either disbanded or converted on a voluntary basis into elements of the non-military World Service Corps.

17.4.7 Concurrently with the reduction or elimination of such weapons, equipment and other military expenditures as can be accomplished during the second operative stage of World Government, the member nations of the Federation of Earth shall pay annually to the Treasury of the World Government amounts equal to one-half of the amounts saved from their national military budgets during the last year before joining the Federation and shall continue such payments until the full operative stage of World Government is reached. The World Government shall use fifty percent of the funds thus received to finance the work and projects of the World Economic Development Organization.

17.4.8 Upon formation of the Executive Cabinet for the second operative stage, the Presidium shall issue an invitation to the General Assembly of the United Nations Organization and to each of the specialized agencies of the United Nations, as well as to other useful international agencies, to transfer personnel, facilities, equipment, resources and allegiance to the Federation of Earth and to the World Government thereof. The agencies and functions of the United Nations Organization and of its specialized agencies and of other international agencies which may be thus transferred, shall be reconstituted as needed and integrated into the several organs, departments, offices and agencies of the World Government.

17.4.9 Near the beginning of the second operative stage, the Presidium in consultation with the Executive cabinet, shall formulate and put forward a proposed program for solving the most urgent world problems currently confronting the people of Earth.

17.4.10 The World Parliament shall proceed with legislation necessary for implementing a complete program for solving the current urgent world problems.

17.4.11 The World Parliament and the World Executive working together shall develop through the several organs, departments and agencies of the World Government whatever means shall seem appropriate and feasible to implement legislation for solving world problems; and in particular shall take certain decisive actions for the welfare of all people on Earth, including but not limited to the following:

17.4.11.1 Declaring all oceans, seas and canals having supra-national character (but not including inland seas traditionally belonging to particular nations) from twenty kilometers offshore, and all the seabeds thereof, to be under the ownership of the Federation of Earth as the common heritage of humanity, and subject to the control and management of the World Government.

17.4.11.2 Declare the polar caps and surrounding polar areas, including the continent of Antartica but not areas which are traditionally a part of particular nations, to be world territory owned by the Federation of Earth as the common heritage of humanity, and subject to control and management by the World Government.

17.4.11.3 Outlaw the possession, stockpiling, sale and use of all nuclear weapons, all weapons of mass destruction, and all other military weapons and equipment.

17.4.11.4 Establish an ever-normal grainery and food supply system for the people of Earth.

17.4.11.5 Develop and carry forward insofar as feasible all actions defined under Sec. 3.10, and 3.12 of the First Operative Stage.

Section 17.5 Full Operative Stage of World Government

17.5.1 The full operative stage of World Government shall be implemented when this World Constitution is given either preliminary or final ratification by meeting either condition (17.5.1.1) or (17.5.1.2):

17.5.1.1 Ratification by eighty percent or more of the nations of Earth comprising at least ninety percent of the population of Earth; or

17.5.1.2 Ratification which includes ninety percent of Earth's total population, either within ratifying nations or within ratifying nations together with additional World Electoral and Administrative Districts where ratification by direct referendum has been accomplished, as provided in Article 17, Section 1.

17.5.2 When the full operative stage of World Government is reached, the following conditions shall be implemented:

17.5.2.1 Elections for Members of the House of Peoples shall be conducted in all World Electoral and Administrative Districts where elections have not already taken place; and Members of the House of Nations shall be elected or appointed by the national legislatures or national governments in all nations where this has not already been accomplished.

17.5.2.2 The terms of office for Members of the House of Peoples and of the House of Nations serving during the second operative stage, shall be continued into the full operative stage, except for those who have already served five years, in which case elections shall be held or appointments made as required.

17.5.2.3 The terms of office for all holdover Members of the House of Peoples and of the House of Nations who have served less than five years, shall be adjusted to run concurrently with those Members of the World Parliament whose terms are beginning with the full operative stage.

17.5.2.4 The second 100 Members of the House of Counsellors shall be elected according to the procedure specified in Section 5 of Article 5. The terms of office for holdover Members of the House of Counsellors shall run five more years after the beginning of the full operative stage, while those beginning their terms with the full operative stage shall serve ten years.

17.5.2.5 The Presidium and the Executive Cabinet shall be reconstituted in accordance with the provisions of Article 6.

17.5.2.6 All organs of the World Government shall be made fully operative, and shall be fully developed for the effective administration and implementation of world legislation, world law and the provisions of this World Constitution.

17.5.2.7 All nations which have not already done so shall immediately transfer all military weapons and equipment to the World Disarmament Agency, which shall immediately immobilize all such weapons and shall proceed forthwith to dismantle, convert to peaceful usage, recycle the materials thereof, or otherwise to destroy such weapons and equipment.

17.5.2.8 All armies and military forces of every kind shall be completely disarmed, and either disbanded or converted and integrated on a voluntary basis into the nonmilitary World Service Corps.

17.5.2.9 All viable agencies of the United Nations Organization and other viable international agencies established among national governments, together with their personnel, facilities and resources, shall be transferred to the World Government and reconstituted and integrated as may be useful into the organs, departments, offices, institutes, commissions, bureaus and agencies of the World Government.

17.5.2.10 The World Parliament and the World Executive shall continue to develop the activities and projects which are already underway from the second operative stage of World Government, with such amendments as deemed necessary; and shall proceed with a complete and full scale program to solve world problems and serve the welfare of all people on Earth, in accordance with the provisions of this World Constitution.

Section 17.6   Costs of Ratification

The work and costs of private Citizens of Earth for the achievement of a ratified Constitution for the Federation of Earth, are recognized as legitimate costs for the establishment of constitutional world government by which present and future generations will benefit, and shall be repaid double the original amount by the World Financial Administration of the World Government when it becomes operational after 25 countries have ratified this Constitution for the Federation of Earth. Repayment specifically includes contributions to the World Government Funding Corporation and other costs and expenses recognized by standards and procedures to be established by the World Financial Administration.

Article 18   Amendments

Section 18.1

Following completion of the first operative stage of World Government, amendments to this World Constitution may be proposed for consideration in two ways:

18.1.1 By a simple majority vote of any House of the World Parliament.

18.1.2 By petitions signed by a total of 200,000 persons eligible to vote in world elections from a total of at least twenty World Electoral and Administrative Districts where the World Constitution has received final ratification.

Section 18.2

Passage of any amendment proposed by a House of the World Parliament shall require an absolute two-thirds majority vote of each of the three Houses of the World Parliament voting separately.

Section 18.3

An amendment proposed by popular petition shall first require a simple majority vote of the House of Peoples, which shall be obliged to take a vote upon the proposed amendment. Passage of the amendment shall then require an absolute two-thirds majority vote of each of the three Houses of the World Parliament voting separately.

Section 18.4

Periodically, but no later than ten years after first convening the World Parliament for the First Operative Stage of World Government, and every 20 years thereafter, the Members of the World Parliament shall meet in special session comprising a Constitutional Convention to conduct a review of this World Constitution to consider and propose possible amendments, which shall then require action as specified in Clause 2 of Article 18 for passage.

Section 18.5

If the First Operative Stage of World Government is not reached by the year 1995, then the Provisional World Parliament, as provided under Article 19, may convene another session of the World Constituent Assembly to review the Constitution for the Federation of Earth and consider possible amendments according to procedure established by the Provisional World Parliament.

Section 18.6

Except by following the amendment procedures specified herein, no part of this World Constitution may be set aside, suspended or subverted, neither for emergencies nor caprice nor convenience.

Article 19 Provisional World Government

Section 19.1 Actions to be Taken by the World Constituent Assembly

Upon adoption of the World Constitution by the World Constituent Assembly, the Assembly and such continuing agency or agencies as it shall designate shall do the following, without being limited thereto:

19.1.1 Issue a Call to all Nations, communities and people of Earth to ratify this World Constitution for World Government.

19.1.2 Establish the following preparatory commissions:

19.1.2.1 Ratification Commission.

19.1.2.2 World Elections Commission.

19.1.2.3 World Development Commission.

19.1.2.4 World Disarmament Commission.

19.1.2.5 World Problems Commission.

19.1.2.6 Nominating Commission.

19.1.2.7 Finance Commission.

19.1.2.8 Peace Research and Education Commission.

19.1.2.9 Special commissions on each of several of the most urgent world problems.

19.1.2.10 Such other commissions as may be deemed desirable in order to proceed with the Provisional World Government.

19.1.3 Convene Sessions of a Provisional World Parliament when feasible under the following conditions:

19.1.3.1 Seek the commitment of 500 or more delegates to attend, representing people in 20 countries from five continents, and having credentials defined by Article 19, Section 3;

19.1.3.2 The minimum funds necessary to organize the sessions of the Provisional World Parliament are either on hand or firmly pledged.

19.1.3.3 Suitable locations are confirmed at least nine months in advance, unless emergency conditions justify shorter advance notice.

Section 19.2   Work of the Preparatory Commissions

19.2.1 The Ratification Commission shall carry out a worldwide campaign for the ratification of the World Constitution, both to obtain preliminary ratification by national governments, including national legislatures, and to obtain final ratification by people, including communities. The ratification commission shall continue its work until the full operative stage of World Government is reached.

19.2.2 The World Elections Commission shall prepare a provisional global map of World Electoral and Administrative Districts and Regions which may be revised during the first or second operative stage of World Government, and shall prepare and proceed with plans to obtain the election of Members of the World Parliament to the House of Emerging World Law 225 Peoples and to the House of Counsellors. The World Elections Commission shall in due course be converted into the World Boundaries and Elections Administration.

19.2.3 After six months, in those countries where national governments have not responded favorable to the ratification call, the Ratification Commission and the World Elections Commission may proceed jointly to accomplish both the ratification of the World Constitution by direct popular referendum and concurrently the election of Members of the World Parliament.

19.2.4 The Ratification Commission may also submit the World Constitution for ratification by universities and colleges throughout the world.

19.2.5 The World Development Commission shall prepare plans for the creation of a World Economic Development Organization to serve all nations and people ratifying the World Constitution, and in particular less developed countries, to begin functioning when the Provisional World Government is established.

19.2.6 The World Disarmament Commission shall prepare plans for the organization of a World Disarmament Agency, to begin functioning when the Provisional World Government is established.

19.2.7 The World Problems Commission shall prepare an agenda of urgent world problems, with documentation, for possible action by the Provisional World Parliament and Provisional World Government.

19.2.8 The Nominating Commission shall prepare, in advance of convening the Provisional World Parliament, a list of nominees to compose the Presidium and the Executive Cabinet for the Provisional World Government.

19.2.9 The Finance Commission shall work on ways and means for financing the Provisional World Government.

19.2.10 The several commissions on particular world problems shall work on the preparation of proposed world legislation and action on each problem, to present to the Provisional World Parliament when it convenes.

Section 19.3 Composition of the Provisional World Parliament

19.3.1 The Provisional World Parliament shall be composed of the following members:

19.3.1.1 All those who were accredited as delegates to the 1977 and 1991 Sessions of the World Constituent Assembly, as well as to any previous Session of the Provisional World Parliament, and who re-confirm their support for the Constitution for the Federation of Earth, as amended.

19.3.1.2 Persons who obtain the required number of signatures on election petitions, or who are designated by Non-Governmental Organizations which adopt approved resolutions for this purpose, or who are otherwise accredited according to terms specified in Calls which may be issued to convene particular sessions of the Provisional World Parliament.

19.3.1.3 Members of the World Parliament to the House of Peoples who are elected from World Electoral and Administrative Districts up to the time of convening the Provisional World Parliament. Members of the World Parliament elected to the House of Peoples may continue to be added to the Provisional World Parliament until the first operative stage of World Government is reached.

19.3.1.4 Members of the World Parliament to the House of Nations who are elected by national legislatures or appointed by national governments up to the time of convening the Provisional World Parliament. Members of the World Parliament to the House of Nations may continue to be added to the Provisional World Parliament until the first operative stage of World Government is reached.

19.3.1.5 Those universities and colleges which have ratified the World Constitution may nominate persons to serve as Members of the World Parliament to the House of Counsellors. The House of Peoples and House of Nations together may then elect from such nominees up to fifty Members of the World Parliament to serve in the House of Counsellors of the Provisional World Government.

19.3.2 Members of the Provisional World Parliament in categories (1) and (2) as defined above, shall serve only until the first operative stage of World Government is declared, but may be duly elected to continue as Members of the World Parliament during the first operative stage.

Section 19.4   Formation of the Provisional World Executive

19.4.1 As soon as the Provisional World Parliament next convenes, it will elect a new Presidium for the Provisional World Parliament and Provisional World Government from among the nominees submitted by the Nominating Commission.

19.4.2 Members of the Provisional World Presidium shall serve terms of three years, and may be re-elected by the Provisional World Parliament, but in any case shall serve only until the Presidium is elected under the First Operative Stage of World Government.

19.4.3 The Presidium may make additional nominations for the Executive Cabinet.

19.4.4 The Provisional World Parliament shall then elect the members of the Executive Cabinet.

19.4.5 The Presidium shall then assign ministerial posts among the members of the Executive Cabinet and of the Presidium.

19.4.6 When steps (1) through (4) of section 19.4. are completed, the Provisional World Government shall be declared in operation to serve the welfare of humanity.

Section 19.5   First Actions of the Provisional World Government

19.5.1 The Presidium, in consultation with the Executive Cabinet, the commissions on particular world problems and the World Parliament, shall define a program for action on urgent world problems.

19.5.2 The Provisional World Parliament shall go to work on the agenda of world problems, and shall take any and all actions it considers appropriate and feasible, in accordance with the provisions of this World Constitution.

19.5.3 Implementation of and compliance with the legislation enacted by the Provisional World Parliament shall be sought on a voluntary basis in return for the benefits to be realized, while strength of the Provisional World Government is being increased by the progressive ratification of the World Constitution.

19.5.4 Insofar as considered appropriate and feasible, the Provisional World Parliament and Provisional World Executive may undertake some of the actions specified under Section 3.12.of Article 17 for the first operative stage of World Government.

19.5.5 The World Economic Development Organization and the World Disarmament Agency shall be established, for correlated actions.

19.5.6 The World Parliament and the Executive Cabinet of the Provisional World Government shall proceed with the organization of other organs and agencies of the World Government on a provisional basis, insofar as considered desirable and feasible, in particular those specified under Section 3.10. of Article 17.

19.5.7 The several preparatory commissions on urgent world problems may be reconstituted as Administrative Departments of the Provisional World Government.

19.5.8 In all of its work and activities, the Provisional World Government shall function in accordance with the provisions of this Constitution for the Federation of Earth.

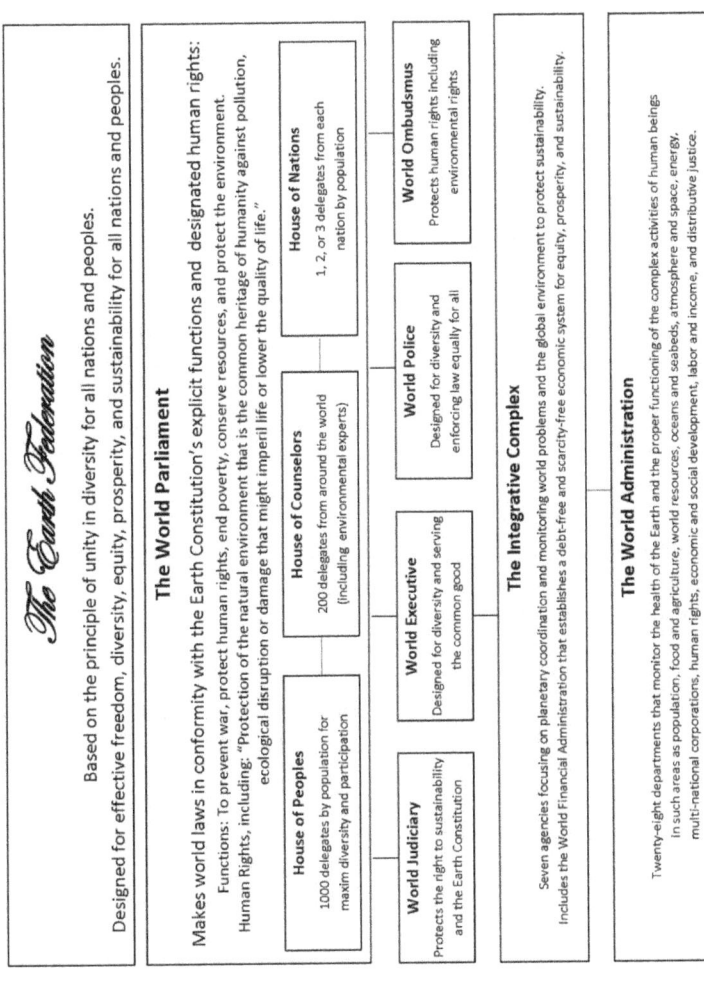

The Earth Federation

Based on the principle of unity in diversity for all nations and peoples.

Designed for effective freedom, diversity, equity, prosperity, and sustainability for all nations and peoples.

The World Parliament

Makes world laws in conformity with the Earth Constitution's explicit functions and designated human rights:

Functions: To prevent war, protect human rights, end poverty, conserve resources, and protect the environment.

Human Rights, including: "Protection of the natural environment that is the common heritage of humanity against pollution, ecological disruption or damage that might imperil life or lower the quality of life."

House of Peoples

1000 delegates by population for maxim diversity and participation

House of Counselors

200 delegates from around the world (including environmental experts)

House of Nations

1, 2, or 3 delegates from each nation by population

World Judiciary

Protects the right to sustainability and the Earth Constitution

World Executive

Designed for diversity and serving the common good

World Police

Designed for diversity and enforcing law equally for all

World Ombudsmus

Protects human rights including environmental rights

The Integrative Complex

Seven agencies focusing on planetary coordination and monitoring world problems and the global environment to protect sustainability.

Includes the World Financial Administration that establishes a debt-free and scarcity-free economic system for equity, prosperity, and sustainability.

The World Administration

Twenty-eight departments that monitor the health of the Earth and the proper functioning of the complex activities of human beings in such areas as population, food and agriculture, world resources, oceans and seabeds, atmosphere and space, energy, multi-national corporations, human rights, economic and social development, labor and income, and distributive justice.

WE strongly believe that the Earth Constitution is entirely adequate for the global legal renaissance of emerging world law. We citizens of the world who have encountered this marvelous document urge the rest of the citizens of our world to seriously consider the value of the Constitutions rapid adoption, so that there is the elevation of democratic self-government to the planetary level. Ratification and implementation of this Constitution will forever put an end to the war system, the poverty system, the exploitation system, and the system of environmental destruction now in place.

On the following pages are the signatures of persons from every walk of life who attended the second and fourth sessions of the World Constituent Assembly, where there were official signing ceremonies, together with a list of persons on the last page who had wanted to attend and who agreed to support the Earth Constitution. Since the time of the official ceremonies, hundreds of thousands more people have signed their support for the document.

Our immediate goal is to get both the joint ratification of a large number of national governments (about 25, perhaps) and also the measured direct ratification by the people of the world adequate to initiate the first operative stage as defined in the Earth Constitution.

Participants in the World Constituent Assembly, 16 to 29 of June, 1977, have affixed their signatures to the draft of the CONSTITUTION FOR THE FEDERATION OF EARTH herewith:

[page of handwritten signatures with country/organization labels, including:]

India

MEXICO

EARTH, USA

Lucile W. Green — Earth, USA

Hon. Legal Advisor

Canada

T.P. Amerasinghe — Sri Lanka.

Korea

Archie Casely-Hayford — Ghana.

K. Koma — Botswana

Helen Tucker (Canada) Women's Universal Movement

Fed. Rep. of Germany

Thane Read — U.S.A.

Spencer — India.

Prachoomsuk A. Ammujing — Thailand.

Rose J. Chesney — Australia.

Netherlands

JAPAN

[signatures]

Note: This list of initial signers of the CONSTITUTION FOR THE FEDERATION OF EARTH would include several hundred more persons from fifty countries, prevented only by the cost of travel to attend the Assembly at Innsbruck, Austria.

HELD AT TROIA, PORTUGAL, 29th APRIL, to 9th MAY, 1991

Prof. Dr. Kaiman Abraham, Hungary

Atiku Abubakar, Nigeria

Dr. Ebenezer Ade. Adenekan, Nigeria

Malcolm S. Adiseshiah, India

Abdur Rahim Ahamed, Bangladesh

Shahzada/Kabir Ahmed

Mohsin A. Alaini, Yemen

MD. Nural Alam, U.S.A.

MD. Maser Ali, Bangladesh

Dr. Terence P. Amerasinghe, Sri Lanka

Samir Amin, Senegal

Benjamin K. Amonoo, Ghana

George Anca, Romania

Mauricio Andres-Ribeiro, Brazil

Dr. Munawar A. Anees, U.S.A.

Rev. Ebenezer Annan, Ivory Coast

Jose Ayala-Lasso, Ecuador

Ir. Hasan Basri, Indonesia

Samar Basu, India

Tony Benn, United Kingdom

Prof. Mrs. Edvige Bestazzi, Italy

Petter Jakob Bjerve, Norway

Goran von Bonsdorff, Finland

Selma Brackman, U.S.A.

Jean-Marie Breton, Int. Regis. World Citizens

Tomas Bruckman, Germany (East)

Dennis Brutus, South Africa (U.S.A.)

Dr. Mihai Titus Carapancea, Romania

Prof. Henri Cartan, France

Amb. Khub Chand, India

Dr. Sripati Chandrasekhar, India

Most Rev. French Chang-Him, Seychelles

Munyaradzi Chiwashira, Zimbabwe

Dr. Pratap Chandra Chunder, India

Prof. Dr. Rodney Daniel, France

Daniel G. De Culla, Spain

Dr. Dimitrios J. Delivanis, Greece

Prof. Dr. Francis Dessert, Belgium

Raymond F. Douw, Germany

Prof. Hans-Peter Duerr, Germany

Kennedy Emekan, Nigeria

M. Necati Munir Ertekun, Cyprus

Douglas Nixon Everingham, Australia

John R. Ewbank, U.S.A.

Marjorie Ewbank, U.S.A.

Miss Lianmangi Fanai, India

Dr. Mark Farber, U.S.A.

Feng Ping-Chung, China

Prof. Dr. Mihnea Georghiu, Romania

Lucile W. Green, U.S.A.

Dr. Dauji Gupta, India

Kisholoy Gupta, India

Takeshi Haruki, Japan

Dr. Gerhard Herzberg, Canada

Jozsef Hotp, Hungary

A. K. Fazlul Hogue, Bangladesh

Chowdhury Anwar Husain, Bangladesh

Margaret Isely, U.S.A. (Earth)

Philip Isely, U.S.A. (Earth)

Ram K. Jiwanmitra, Nepal

Roy E. Johnstone, Jamaica

Mohammed Kamaluddin, Bangladesh

Mohammad Rezaul Karim, Bangladesh

Rev. George Karunakaran, India

Dr. Inamullah Khan, Pakistan

Johnson S. Khan, Pakistan

Roger Kotila, Ph.D., U.S.A.

David M. Krieger, U.S.A.

Diemuth Kuebart, Germany

Jul Lag, Norway

Ben M. Leito, Netherlands Antilles

Thomas Lim, East Malaysia

Adam Lopatka, Poland

Anwarul Majid, Bangladesh

Dr. M. Sadiq Malik, Pakistan

Guy Marchand, France

Alvin M. Marks, U.S.A.

Bernardshaw Mezi, Nigeria

Dr. Zhores A. Medvedev, U. K. (USSR)

Anna Medvegey, Hungary

R. C. Mehrotra, India

Charles Mercieca, U.S.A.

Lt. Col. Pedro B. Merida, Philippines

Yerucham Meshel, Israel

Sheta Mikayele, Zaire

Mohamed Ezzedine Mili, Switzerland

Rev. Toshio Miyake, Japan

Shettima Ali Monguno, Nigeria

Swapan Mukherjee, India

Hanna Newcombe, Canada

Brij P. Nigam, India

Josephine Okafor, Nigeria

Johnson Olatunde, Sierra Leone

Rev. Nelson Onono-Onweng, Uganda

Umit Ozturk, Turkey

Yasar Ozturk, Turkey

Linus Pauling, U.S.A.

Fernando Perez Tella, Spain

Emil Otto Peter, Austria

Dr. Alex Quaison-Sackey, Ghana

Soili Raikkonen, Finland

Sudhir Kumar Rangh, India

Thane Read, U.S.A.

Dr. Sayed Qassem Reshtia, Switzerland

Erzsebet Rethy, Hungary

Miguel B. Ricardo, Portugal

G. Rivas Mijares, Venezuela

Reinhart Ruge, Mexico

Prof. Sir A. M. Sadek, South Africa

Abdus Salam, Italy

Akber Ali Saleh, Comoros Islands

Blagovest Sendov, Bulgaria

Indira Shrestha, Nepal

Rabi Charan Shrestha, Nepal

Jon Silkin, United Kingdom

Jozef Simuth, Slovak Republic

Dr. Kewal Singh, India

Blaine Sloan, U.S.A.

Ross Smyth, Canada

Lord Donald Soper, United Kingdom

Scott Jefferson Starquester, U.S.A.

Homi J. H. Taleyarkhan, India

Rev. Yoshiaki Toeda, Japan

Dr. Duja K. Torki, Tunisia

Helen Tucker, Canada

Evelyn Utulu, Nigeria

Mrs. Justina N. Uwechue, Nigeria

Ogieva O. Uwuigbe, Nigeria

Ann Valentin, U.S.A.

P. Najat Vezirogu., U.S.A.

Jorger Laursen Vig, Denmark

George Wald, U.S.A.

Prof. P. A. Walker, United Kingdom

Kenneth A. Clark, U.S.A.

David Daube, U.S.A.

Niro Fleerwakt, Cameroon

Richard W. Wilbur, U.S.A.

Dr. Sylwester Zawadzki, Poland

Prof. Chief J.O. Agboye, Nigeria
Dr. Francis Alexis, Grenada
Sir Abdul W.M. Ameer, Sri Lanka
Hanan Awwad, Palestine
Hon. Lukasz Baleer, Poland
Chief Dr. Kolawole Balogun, Nigeria
Dr. Sabnzi O. Biobaku, Nigeria
Dr. Jur. Jan Carnogursky, Slovakia
Dr. Glouin Gedieu, Cote D'Ivorie
Amarsinh Chaudhary, India
Mdm. Justice L. P. Chibesakunda, Zambia
Ashis Kumar De, India
Dr. Mostafa El Desouky, Kuwait
Dr. Rolf Edberg, Sweden
Dr. Benjamin B. Ferencz, U.S.A.
Prof. Vitalii I.Goldansksi, Russia
Prof. Dr. Zbigniew Gorrych, Poland
Prof. Errol E. Harris, U.S.A./U.K.
LIC Juan Horacio S., Argentina
Sir Dr. Akanu Ibiam, Nigeria
K. Jeevagathas, Sri Lanka
R. B. Junoo, India
Dr. Jan Kleinert, Slovakia
Dr. Yuri A. Kosygin, Russia
Adv. Ranjan Lakhanpal, India
Adv. Aqil Lodhi, Pakistan
Dr. Nikolai A. Logulchev, Russia
Mochtar Lubis, Indonesia
Perry Maison, Ghana
Kapuka Makasa, Zambia
Dr. Ignacy Malecki, Poland
Prof. Ivan Malek, Czechoslovakia
Dr. Mrs. Alla G. Massevitch, Russia
Mbliagano S. Maasschela, Switzerland

Dr. Mihailo Mihajlov, Yugoslavia
Hon. Rani Niwas Mirdha, India
Dr. Robert Muller, Costa Rica
Justice M. A. Muttalib, Bangladesh
Dr. Sileke G Mwale, Zambia
Dr. Rashmi Mayur, India
Dr. Jayan. V. Narikar, India
Paul Nkadi, Nigeria
Osman N. Orek, Turkish Rep. N. Cyprus
Prof. Lenard Pal, Poland
Prof. Jean-Claude Pecker, France
Prof. Gamini L. Peiris, Sri Lanka
Gerard Piel, U.S.A.
Rev. Daniel O. Peprah, Cote D'Ivoire
Prof. M. S. Rajan, India
Prof. C. N. R. Rao, India
Sri N. S. Rao, India
Michal Rusinek, Poland
Dr. Frederick Sanger, U.K.
Sir Ainsworth D. Scott, Jamaica
David Shahar, Israel
Tema Sik, Israel
Chandan Som, India
Hon. Robert D. G. Stanbury, Canada
Dr. Bogdan Suchodolski, Poland
Abdul Lathy Suliman, Sri Lanka
Dr. Sol Tax, U.S.A.
Millicent Obenewaa Terry, Ghana
Dr. Walter B. Thirring, Austria
Most Rev. Desmond M. Tutu, South Africa
Kenji Urata, Japan
Dr. Pieter Van Dyk, Netherlands
Carlos Warter, M.D., U.S.A.
Rod Welford, M.L.A., Australia

A Pledge of Allegiance to the Earth Constitution

I pledge allegiance to the Constitution for the Federation of Earth, and to the Republic of free world citizens for which it stands,

One Earth Federation, protecting by law the rich diversity of the Earths citizens, One Earth Federation, protecting the precious ecology of our planet.

I pledge allegiance to the World Parliament representing all nations and peoples, and to the democratic processes by which it proceeds,

One law for the Earth, with freedom and equality for all, One standard of justice, with a bill of rights protecting each.

I pledge allegiance to the future generations protected by the Earth Constitution, And to the unity, integrity, and beauty of humankind, living in harmony on the Earth,

One Earth Federation, conceived in love, truth, and hope, with peace and prosperity for all.

Bibliography

Agar, H, Aydelotte, F., Broch, H., Brooks, van W., Comstock, A. L., Elliott, W. Y., Fisher, D. C., Gauss, C., Jaszi, O.,Johnson, A., Kohn, H., Mann, T., Mumford, L., Neilson W. A., Niebuhr, R., Barker, E., *Principles of Social and Political Theory*, Oxford, Clarendon Press, 1951.

Bassett, Noble, P., *Constitution ofthe United Nations of the World*, Boston, MA., Christopher Publishing House, 1944.

—. *Federation of the World*, San Francisco, CA, Murdock Press, 1906.

Borgese, G. A., *Foundations of the World Republic*, Chicago, IL., Chicago University Press, 1953.

Breitner, T. C., *World Constitution; a Study on the Legal Framework of a World Federation*, Berkeley, CA., 1963.

Brown, L. A., *The State of the World*, Annual Worldwatch Report, New York, W. W. Norton and Co.

Clark and Sohn, *Peace through Law*, University of North Carolina Press, Chapel Hill, NC, 1944.

Collingwood, R. G., *The New Leviathan*, Oxford, Clarendon Press, 1942.

Crozier, A. 0., *Nation of Nations: The Way to Permanent Peace: A Supreme Constitution for the Government of Governments*, Cincinatti, Stewart and Kidd Co., 1915.

Curry, W. B., *The Case for Federal Union*, Harmondsworth, England, Penguin Books, 1939.

Curtis, L., *The Way to Peace*, London, Oxford University Press, 1944.

—. *Civitas Dei*, London, G. Allen and Unwin, 1938.

—. *World War, Its Cause and Cure*, London, Oxford University Press, 1945.

Duguit, L. *Traite du droit constitutionnel*, Paris, Boccard, 1921.

Falk, R., *Explorations at the Edge of Time: The Prospects for World Order*, Philadelphia, Temple University Press, 1992.

Ferencz, B. B., and Keyes, K., *Planethood*, Coos Bay, OR., Vision Books, 1988.

Gore, A., *Earth in the Balance: Ecology and the Human Spirit*, Boston, MA., Houghton Mifflin, 1992.

Green, T. H., *Lectures on Political Obligation*, London, Longmans, 1924.

Hamilton, A., Jay, J., and Madison, J., *The Federalist*, Washington DC, National Home Library; New York, House Random House, 1938.

Hammond, A., (Ed.) *EnvironmentalAlmanac*, Compiled by World Resources Institute, Boston, MA, Houghton Mifflin Company.

Harris, E. E., *The Survival of Political Man*, Johannesburg, Witwatersrand University Press, 1950.

—. *Annihilation and Utopia*, London, G. Allen and Unwin, 1966

—. *Cosmos andAnthropos*, Atlantic HigWands NJ, Humanities Press, 1991.

—. *Cosmos and Theos*, Atlantic HigWands, NJ, Humanities Press, 1992.

—. *Apocalypse and Paradigm*, Westport CT, London, Praeger, 2000.

Harris, E. E. and Junker,J. A. (Eds.) *Toward Genuine Global Governance*, Westport CT, London, Praeger, 1999.

Harris J. M., *Environmental and Natural Resource Economics: A Contemporary Approach*. Boston, New York, Houghton Mifflin Company, 2002.

—. *World Agriculture and the Environment*, New York, Garland, 1990.

Harris,J. M. and Anne-Marie Codur, *Macro-Economics and the Environment*, Medford, Tufts University Press, 1998.

Harris. J. M. (Ed.) *Rethinking Sustainability: Power, Knowledge and Institutions*. Ann Arbor, The University of Michigan Press, 2000.

Hegel, G. W. F., *Grundlinien der Philosophie des Rechts*, translated by T. M. Knox as *Hegel's Philosophy of Right*, Oxford, Clarendon Press, 1942-1953.

Hobbes, T., *Leviathan*, Reprinted from the Edition of 1651, Oxford, Clarendon Press, 1909, 1929-1943.

Hoyland,J. S., *The World in Union*, London, Peace Book Co., 1940.

Hutchins, R. M., *Preliminary Draft of a World Constitution*, Chicago, University of Chicago Press, 1948.

Jessup, P. C. *A Modern Law of Nations*, New York, the Macmillan Co., 1952.

Johnson, J. E., *Federal World Government*, New York, Wilson and Co., 1948.

Junger, E., Der Weltstaat, *Organismus und Organisation*, Juett, Stuttgart, 1960.

Kelsen, H., *General Theory of Law and the State*, Cambridge, MA, Harvard. University Press, 1945, 1949, New York, Russell and Russell, 1961.

—. *Law and Peace in International Relations*, Cambridge, MA, Harvard

University Press, 1942.

Krabbe, H., *The Modern Theory of the State*, New York, London, D. Appleton and Co., 1922.

Keeton, G. W., *National Sovereignty and International Order*, London, 1939.

Keeton, G. W. and Schwartzenberger, G., *Making International Law Work*, London, Peace Book Co., 1939.

Laski, H. J., *A Grammar of Politics*, London, G. Allen and Unwin, 1926-1941

Lauterpacht, H., *The Function of Law in the International Community*, Oxford, Clarendon Press, 1933.

Lilienthal, A. M., *Which Way to World Government?* New York, Foreign Policy Association, 1950.

Lipsky, M., *Never Again War: The Case for World Government*, South Brunswick, AS Barnes, 1971.

Lothian, P. H. K., Lord, *The Ending of Armageddon*, Aldon Press, Oxford, England, 1939.

Millard, E. L., *Freedom in a Federal World*, Dobbs Ferry, NY., Oceania Publications, 1959, 1964.

Newfang, 0., *World Federation*, New York, Barnes and Noble, 1939.

—. *The Road to Peace; a Federation of the Nations*, New York, London, G. P. Putnam, 1924.

—. *World Government*, New York, Barnes and Noble, 1942.

Perry R. B., *One World in the Making*, New York, Current Books, 1945.

Pinheiro, de V. H., *The World State, or The New Order of Common Sense*, Rio de Janeiro, Grafica Olimpia, 1944.

Robbins, L., *Economic Aspects of Federation*, London, Macmillan, 1941.

Salvimini, G., *The City of Man*, New York, The Viking Press, 1940.

Scelle, G., *Precis de Droit des Gens*, Librarie du Recueil, Paris, Sirey, 1932-34.

Schiffer, W., *The Legal Community of Mankind; a Critical Analysis of the Concept of World Organization*, New York, Columbia University Press, 1954.

Selander,]. B., *World Union Now*, Berkeley, CA., Gazette Press, 1944.

Spinoza, B. de, *Political Works*, translated by A. G. Wernham, Oxford, Clarendon Press, 1958-1965.

Streit, C., *Union Now, a Proposal for an Atlantic Federal Union of the Free*, New York, Harper, 1949.

—. *World Government or Anarchy? Our Urgent Need for World Order*, Chicago, IL, World CitKens Association, . 1939.

Wagar, W., *The City of Man*, Boston, MA, Houghton Mifflin, 1963.

Wheare,K. C., *Federal Government*, London, Oxford University Press, 1946.

Wofford, H., *It's Up to Us; Federal World Government in Our Time*, New York, Harcourt Brace, 1946.

Wootton, B., *Socialism and Federation*, London, Macmillan, 1941.

Wynner, E., *World Federal Government: Why? What? How?*, Afton, NY, Fedonat Press, 1954.

Index

CPSIA information can be obtained
at www.ICGtesting.com
Printed in the USA
LVHW031719021220
673226LV00002B/318

9 781933 567495